D1879731

Taking the Stock of: NATIONALISM IN SOUTH ASIA

Taking the Stock of: NATIONALISM IN SOUTH ASIA

Edited by

R. Sreekantan Nair,

Shashikant Pandey & Moushumi Mahato

GenNext Publication

Published by

GenNext Publication
5, Ansari Road
Daryaganj, New Delhi-110002
Phone: 011-47034999, 9811692060
E-mail: gennextpublication@hotmail.com

Distribution Network
gyanbooks.com
India, USA, Canada, UK, Australia, France

© Author

All rights reserved. No part of this work may be reproduced, stored, adapted, or transmitted in any form or by any means, electronic, mechanical, photocopying, micro-filming recording or otherwise, or translated in any language, without the prior written permission of the copyright owner and the publisher. The book is sold subject to the condition that it shall not, by way of trade or otherwise, be lent, resold, hired out, or otherwise circulated without the prior publisher's written consent in any form of binding or cover other than that in which it is published.

ISBN: 978-93-5663-580-7 (PB)
First Published, 2025

Printed at: Gyan Press, Delhi.

The views and opinions expressed in this book are author(s) own and the facts reported by them have been verified to the extent possible, and the publishers are not in any way liable for the same.

Taking the Stock of: NATIONALISM IN SOUTH ASIA
Edited By: R. Sreekantan Nair, Shashikant Pandey & Moushumi Mahato

Dedicated to:

The Fond memory of my Friend, Dr Jamini Kant Mahato, a great visionary, Educationalist and the Founder of JKM Group of Educational Institutions.

Contents

Acknowledgement

Living in the era of post-globalisation and information technology one is gifted to have the rare experiences of the marvel of democracy. However, this new possibility of democracy is not uniform all parts of the world. Two objective paradigms mark gap in the social reality of this uneven reflection of the democratic process in the world. The mature democratic systems reflected more social and political experiences and the same turned out to be more inclusive and open towards the citizens. Whereas, in the case of developing societies, particularly in Asia and Africa State-systems become mere spectators. In these areas the new political leaderships go hand in hand with the superstate entities and corporates resulting in a shift in the value system itself. This new alliance try to rule the roof of the respective societies where there is a specific go back from its liberal democratic values. Some of such societies turned out to be sectarian in nature and new icons and symbols of fundamentalism and exclusiveness make open entry and try to influence the socio-political domains in a bigger way. The process tend to derail the democratic track such societies were experimenting to and the civil societies are put to trial, whereby the minorities and the marginalised sections are further put to suffer. All these find its natural reflections in the domains of nationalism whereby more sectarian and toxic forms of nationalism are being advocated and experimented. The trend is very much manifested in South Asia where the political process in the region, including in the Indian Subcontinent, find a 'U' turn where by the liberal democratic values, secularism and constitutional ethos are put to suffer. It is the general socio-political backdrop by which we organised an International seminar in the JKM College, Salboni, Jharkhand. A good number of scholars from different parts of India and elsewhere participated in the seminar proceedings and this volume is the outcome of the proceedings.

I am extremely happy to compile all the papers presented in the seminar proceedings in the form of a book. In this mission I was assisted by many of my friends and students at different stages of this compilation. I am happy to express my gratitude to Dr Chinna Rao, Chaiman, Center for the Study of Social Exclusion and Inclusive Policy, School of Social Sciences, JNU, New Delhi, Dr Srisha, JNU, New Delhi, Shashikant Pandey, Agra College, Agra, Nadeeka Damayanti, Srilanka, Moushumi Mahato, JKM College, Salboni, Jharkhand for their timely assistance. I also record my gratitude to Narayan Prasad Mahato, Secretary, JKM Group of Educational Institutions, for being good enough to organise such a programme which facilitated to interact with a good number of scholars across the nation and others from South Asia, and for his further assistance and cooperation made available towards this publication. Equally, I am thankful to Binita Bhakat, my student and Sayan, the technical staff for their timely assistance and help extended to me at different stages of the completion of this work. Finally, I thank Mr Amit Garg, my friend and the proprietor of the Gyan Books, New Delhi for acceptance of the manuscript and timely processing the same for making this publication possible on the time scheduled.

15/01/2025

R. Sreekantan Nair,
Academic Director,
JKM Group of Educational Institutions,
Salboni, Jharkhand

Introduction

Ever since the formation of nation-states, discussion on nationalism has been in the forefront both in the academic as well as in the political domains. Nationalism is a complex phenomenon. It reveals the common underlying structure of self-other relations in distinct contexts of time. Serious attempts were made to conceptualise the same from different notions and rationale by earlier scholars. The phenomenon continue to influence and shape political process and economic developments even in the post globalised era in different ways. The process is subject to the degrees of democratic paces and levels of maturity attained by different state systems. In the European and other Asian contexts, Nationalism manifested a cultural synthesis of secular, developmental and inclusive expressions. However, the enthusiasm on the concept has been increasing eversince most of the colonised states came out of their foreign rule and became free and independent states through their own struggles for self-determination.

In most of the states in Asia and Africa, they had come out with their own liberation struggles and set to motion the process of nation building. Such a new comity of nations drew much of their inspirations from the European nationalist movements and took their own nationalist spirit from the struggles and defence against the colonial masters. In this way Nationalism added new flame to the newly independent states for the task of the nation-building process. In most of such societies, it was impossible to separate between Nationalism and their indigenous struggles for freedom. In this way, in such societies freedom and nationalism were interdependent and inter-related components. However, Gunnar Myrdal looked at things from a distinct stand point. Myrdal attributed a separate vision of development that accounted for institutions. In this regard, he looked at the European nationalism very much favourably, helping the developmental process. This he declared that 'in Europe, nationalism despite its association with romanticism, remained secular and rationale in its core' [Myrdal 1968; 2112].

However, he was critical about the developing countries, particularly in Asia where he believed that nationalism is fueled by ignorant and superstitious religiosity, which build block to development process there. It seems the prediction and analysis of Myrdal suits well to South Asia even after six decades of his observation and that most of these states, even today, tryst with the democratic destiny and nation building struggles and process.

South Asia

New narratives are being scripted in most of the South Asian states where new types of Nationalism found a come back with distinct colours and forms. One of the dominant themes is nothing but the Majoritarian nationalism, which is none other than there turn of religious-fundamentalist rise in the region. The new move is part of a specific drive to destabilise the democratic, secular and other progressive forces and raises serious questions about the free existence and democratic survival of minority communities. It goes with out saying that almost all states in South Asia became independent, in more or less, in the same periods of time and equally they share almost uniform pattern of socio-economic and political challenges. Despite these, they had endorsed with the European notions of liberal democracy and secular and progressive ideas along with their task of nation-building and developmental process. Except the case of some of the Islamic states like Pakistan, Bangladesh etc, others had come to the line of such a political position. The task ahead of all these states were to sort out the heterogenous socio-cultural character of the respective societies in to more practical ways by endorsing different sections of societies, through more of an inclusive and accommodative approaches, to the process of development and nation building.

The Indian context

However, even after decades of experiments with democracy, most of these states, including India, seemed shifted to a parochial position on nationalism with its narrow connotations, spreading hate and exclusive policies, which was fully rejected by the great freedom fighters of the nationalist movements. In the case of India, while the nationalist freedom movements were taking full momentum there were three ideological positions. The liberal democrats, the leftists and the right wing stream [who kept away from the freedom movement and tried to organise people only in the name of Hindu religious identity] While the liberal democrats were headed by Gandhi and Nehru, the Leftists, though had differences with them, tried to accept their positions on the question of freedom and independence. However the right wing idealogues were very much critical of the liberal democratic leadership of the nation and kept themselves cut apart from the freedom struggle itself. In a way the progressive content of liberal democracy and secularist positions nationalist leaders had taken was well endorsed by the people at large and the Indian masses stood with Gandhi and Nehru. Otherwise, the parochial position of the right wing ideologues did not find their roots in the Indian society which was well ploughed by the leaders of the freedom movement with a dominant input of secular and democratic values. The Indian society as a whole, even today, is fully emerged in to such a social and cultural reality of secular and democratic ethos. However things find a new turn when over the last two decades a total transformation of socio-cultural texture of life began to change due to advent of the process of globalisation and its negative implications of market economic culture inculcated by increasing corporatism.

The paradigm shifts

Thanks to the neo-liberal economic reforms introduced by the Narasimha Rao Government and his finance Minister Dr Manmohan Singh. When such reforms did open new avenues for India, it stabilised Indian economy consistently even after their periods, including Dr Singh's, consecutive two terms as the Prime Minister. Subsequently, when recession affected almost all states including the dominant powers at different times, India stood unique with a stable growth rate.[2] At a time while countries like USA and those across Europe were affected by inflation and structural problems damaging much on their economies, the Indian economy remained insulated. The same thing repeated during the 2020s as well. Again, thanks to the farsightedness of Narasimha Rao and Dr Singh. Equally, the Prime Minister Modi did consolidate the Indian stand by his 'Making in India' projects when he stepped in as the Prime Minister in 2014. However, when the power was shifted from Dr Manmohan Singh to Prime Minister Narendra Modi, there was sea changes that took place in the domestic economic contexts. When Dr Singh controlled the domestic market forces with restricted entries and all, Prime Minister Modi did its reverse. The NDA government has established a more economic understanding with a section of dominant market forces in India, which was at the cost of major public sector institutions.

Thus what was apprehensive of the negative implications of globalisation took blatant manifestations in India in the name of Market

Culture and crony capitalism. Such forces also brought up market and market based cultures in to the fore front of every Indian. Interestingly, new market giants emerged in to the social sphere and they became the dispensers of common man's life in the village as well as in their cultural domains. This conditioned the life style of ordinary people, their dress, food, taste and what not, every thing took an upside down, where by some of the Individuals became the super rich in the world on a specific time frame. The ambiance of market they created opened new shelters for the political leaderships and there developed new unhealthy nexus between such market giants and the new political leaderships in India. The programme and policies of the government got a special consideration for these forces and they in turn promoted all types of parochial and fundamentalist ideas. It is the general background of the resurgence of majoritarian nationalism in India and the same thing repeated elsewhere in the region with the changes in the political leaderships.

Democracy matters

This discussion doesn't oppose the globalisation process as and when the same promotes development, transparency and democracy. This has been the story of most of the regions in the mature democracies including the Europe. On the other hand, where democratic advancements were in its infancy, like many of the developing societies including the South Asia, the spell of the Market forces created cultural mischief whereby they stood with opportunistic political leaderships and favoured the religiosity and fundamentalism whereby democratic drive began to take a back seat and a right wing cultural revival took its appearance. This was facilitated by questioning the intellectuals, curtailing the freedom of the press, murdering the authors, imposing ifs and buts 'on the life of minorities, conditioning their taste and dress, creating fear psychosisamong the minority communities and other ethnic groups, destabilising prestigious educational institutions with idiotic academics, and morally degrading the constitutional bodies and institutions. These are not the case with India alone but equally applicable to almost all states in the South Asian region. In the case of India, the last one decade of NDA rule testifies this cultural shift. Nationalism in the region assumed toxic character and features. It is in the specific backdrop that that new debate and narratives on majoritarian Nationalism appears in in the public and intellectual domains. In a way, such narratives did away with the values of democracy and all other progressive substances the societies carried forwarded so far.

Nationalism Defined

Among the western scholars, right from Anderson to Antony Giddens and in India, Partha Chatterjee to Irfan Habib and Rajive Bharghava, had specified their detailed narratives and positions on nationalism and its secular implications in more realistic ways of analysis. However, more authentic version of the same had come from the leftists circles right from the Marxian school of thought particularly from Lenin to Rosa Luxumberg. None of these version could catch up the new rightist perspective of nationalism discoursed by the right wing camps, particularly their version of majority nationalism. In the case of India, it is Hindu nationalism, in Sri Lanka, it is Sinhala nationalism and in the case of Islamic states it is Islamic in character. Whatever be the content or theme of Majoritarian nationalism, it seems all such claims are against religious minorities, secular ethos and basic democratic principles. As such the apostles of majoritarian nationalism try to go back to history and reclaim their ethnic or religious purity and want to implement a rule for the majority community alone. This is an alarming situation not only for the prospects of democracy and secularism but against the identity and culture of the microscopic minorities whose liberty and rights are well defined and assured in the respective constitutions.

It is the backdrop in which the JKM College, Salboni, Jharkhand organised an international seminar in 2023 for taking stock of the position and situations of Nationalism in South Asia. Scholars and researchers from different part of India and elsewhere from South Asia took part in this programme. Being the coordinator of the seminar, I felt it very much prudent to compile the papers presented in the programme in the form of an edited volume in to four parts for the convenience of the readers.

Part – I

Discourse, Debate and Dissent

If renaissance and reformations were capable of redefining the empires built on ethnic, religious and other sectarian backdrops, nationalism did the same in breaking down the erstwhile state systems formed in the names of homogenous unity based on ethnic, linguistic and other cultural parameters. Yagati Chinna Rao of JNU, New Delhi, in his paper "**Indian Nationalism and Marginalised: Investigating the Question of Inclusivity**" catches up with this dynamic aspect of nation-building process and argues that rise of nationalism led to the breakdown of many political entities formed in the name of sectarian and regional identities. In this process he argues that nationalism played a historical and significant role in the liquidation of great empires and further for the formation of new state-systems in Europe. However, in his view the situation of the developing societies, particularly of the South Asian region are distinct from that of the Europe. Nationalism did mark its spell in the region which was often equated with the struggle against the colonial rule and quest for self-determination. However, the region in contemporary times give way for sectarian and narrow forms and versions of nationalism.

Taking a right sketch on the socio-cultural reflections on the life of people in the region, the author makes the observation that most of the states in South Asia, to a large extent, have multi-ethnic, racial, lingual and religious societies. As such these countries are destined with the problemsof horizontal and vertical disparities. These complexities and divisions have made the question of nationality and nationalism very tedious and it is true that South Asian states lacked that ethno-cultural homogeneity which affected a process of fusion to unify people into a political community. The paper identifies that Nationalism is a complex process in the region which he tries to dissect in its historical and socio-cultural contexts. According to him, the challenges facing nationalism in South Asia include the tension between secular and inclusive nationalism and the reality of ethnic and religious diversity, the rise of identity politics, and the instrumentalisation of nationalist sentiment by political elites. To address these challenges, it is essential to promote a more inclusive and pluralistic nationalism that recognizes and respects the diversity of South Asia's cultures, religions, and languages. At the same time, South Asia faces the very pertinent contradictions in terms if its nationalist and secular discourses which could only be sorted out by resorting to more inclusive and democratic accom-modation of all sections of society and that too by addressing the basic issues like inequality, poverty and discriminations. However, Turning to the Indian experiences the paper takes a very significant political position that, inspite of the initiative of Marxian frame work of analysis of History, the deprived sections, particularly the Dalits, were not properly endorsed in making either the history of the nation nor in the nationalist discourses. This gap was strategically filled by Dr Ambedkar when he said in the nationalist discourse that he is "an Indian First and last". This implies that other sectarian identities are secondary to the nationalist feelings. This simple logic should be an eye-opener to the sections trying to impose new nationalist [hyper and toxic] versions not only in India, but to the entire region.

R. Sreekantan Nair, takes a critical view on the rise of toxic modes of nationalism in India. In his paper **Nationalism in India; shifting paradigms of Narratives, Notions and Nonsenses,** he sketches out how nationalism flourished in the subcontinent along with the struggles for self determination and freedom struggle. Equally, he draws the main ideological streams flourished during the freedom movement like the liberal democratic stream, the left wing and the right wing of sectarian majoritarian claim. He take the position that in the body politik of the nation the liberal democratic stream rooted much in to the notions and believe system of the masses just because two stalwarts of the freedom movements Gandhi and Nehru propagated the liberal and secular values and themes. As such the other ideological offspring could not catch up with the national mainstream. However, in the free India, the set back of the INC and the negative implications of Globalisation brought up a situation of crony capitalism where by the system indirectly promoted the right wing and fundamentalist camps which indirectly set a new wave majoritarian nationalist claims, supported by the Modi administration over the last decades time frame.

The Modi administration did every thing reverse to the liberal, secular and progressive contents of mainstream thinking of the nation by repeatedly questioning the contributions of Gandhi and Nehru in lieu of whom they preferred to place the right wing idealogues of their choice. This is nothing but de-ideologising a nation and its great tradition. According to the author, in this mission the NDA government had resorted to various strategies in injecting narrow and sectarian nationalism, which really do not fit in to the basic thinking of the plural, diversified and a heterogenous socio-political reality of India. In short, the author concludes that the paper with that the prophetic caution of Dr Ambedkar according to whom the brilliant constitution of the nation drafted with much enthusiasm and caution will become meaningless if the people of the nation selects a bad leader to work on it. Prime Minister Modi and his men at the helm of affairs repeatedly prove that the prophesy of Dr Ambedkar becomes true when they insist for a one nation, one party and one language theory to a secular, democratic and diverse society like India.

Nadeeka Damayanti, from Sri Lanka looks at the dynamics of the nation building process in Sri Lanka right from the formation of the Sate in 1948. In her paper **State Building in Sri Lanka: Is a Hazy Dream or Lofty Goal?** she looks in to how the Srilankan Nationalism plays its vital role in the mission. According to her Srilanka after independence, resorted to various steps to build a state, including establishing the Decentralised Budget and District Political Authority systems in 1973, District Minister System in 1978, Development Councils in1981, Provincial Councils in 1987, and Divisional Secretariat systems in 1992. Furthermore, in order to facilitate providing efficient, effective, and customer-oriented public service the government of Sri Lanka has enacted several acts. However though these state initiatives were successively carried forwarded by successive governments over a pretty long time it failed to fetch the desired results. According to Nadeeka, most of the state-building activities in Sri Lanka faced numerous obstacles in the pursuit of their objectives. These variables included political, administrative, and governance elements.

She takes a position that unless and until these complex issues are addressed in its totality the mission of the state building process will not be completed. In between Sri Lanka also witness to the rise of the Majoritarian nationalism in the form of Sinhala community which no doubt poses direct threat both to the nation building process aswell as to the democratic survival of the minority communities in Sri Lanka. In short, nation building process in the Sri Lanka is long due. It has to evolve its own indigenous strategies by upholding the democratic and secular tradition of the nation.

Apart from the contours of liberal narratives, ideas and notions of nationalism experienced and experimented by the liberal democratic tradition of India, a shift to the neoliberal economy put the Indian society to have the rare experience of the claims of majoritarian and sectarian modes of nationalism advocated by the right wing sections of the nation. The process reached its zenith when the NDA government came to the helm of affairs with their Hindutva agenda who were, in turn, supported by the corporate giants. Shashikant Pandey, catches up the dynamics of this trajectory of Modi Governments inclination with crony capitalism which further fomented to germinate a neo-cultural and sectarian corridor whereby religious fundamentalist ideas and notions began to manifest its ugliest face the nation had never been earlier confronted to. In his paper, **Accumulation and Dispossession: Neo-liberal Hindutva Nationalism in Contemporary India**, he argues that the process has resulted in the acquisition of public wealth by the Corporates at the cost of dispossession in the name of Bourgeois nationalism. Ironically, the saga of anti-colonial struggles and political movements for self-determination had conditioned a secular Indian nationalism, which is now being questioned and attacked by the right wing sections, who were never either in the freedom struggle or anywhere in the anti-colonial protests. This being a political fix to the nation, the author tries to pin point how the sectarian models of nationalism supported by the corporate finances tend to hijack the liberal nationalist ethos and spirit and inflict damages to the democratic process by bringing out communal and sectarian divisions within the nation.

Though the author takes a rigid stand on the process of globalisation and privatisation, he acknowledges rightly the facts that the process started in 1980s and the same had many negative implications on the socio-cultural domains. At the same time he suggests that a balanced approach to serve the public interest without compromising social equity, harmony, and accountability, is crucial for sustainable development. Thus, he concludes the paper with an optimistic note that India, being at the crossroads needs a comprehensive check on the corporate Hindutva's agenda of accumulation and dispossession with the strong collusion of political party in power at the centre. Bourgeois nationalism, as a political strategy of corporate finance capital, reflects a complex interplay of economic interests and nationalist ideologies. By leveraging nationalist sentiments, corporate finance capital secures favourable conditions for capital accumulation and expansion, often at the expense of economic equality, democratic integrity, and social cohesion. In short, the religious fundamentalist mode of nationalism is nothing but reciprocal engagement between the power center in New Delhi and the Corporates, a process which destabilises the democratic and secular fabrics of the nation at large.

Dr Hamid Rasool in his paper **'Supremacy of Religious Majoritarian Nationalism in South Asia** tries to analyze the dynamics of Majoritarian nationalism getting predominance in the South Asian region. According to the author, religion becomes the determining factor which attempt to determine the national identity of the nation. As such the Majoritarian nationalism prefers to promote the preservation and promotion of dominant religious customs, traditions and practices as a major part of national identity. The process often produces counter reflection of marginalisation and discrimination of the religious and other cultural minorities to a larger extent. As far as South Asia is concerned, this phenomenon gets higher momentum in almost all states. The author tries to make a sketch on the democratic Asian States including India take a general observation that it is the historical, cultural and political factors which predominantly work out for the formation of dominant nationalism in the region. According to the Author some of these states like India, Pakistan, Bangladesh, Sri Lanka, Nepal etc. religious identity has often been used as a tool to mobilise political support and to justify discriminatory policies against minority communities.

This new trend also counter produces tension and political violences in these states.

However, against these contemporary trends and indicators the author conclude the paper with an optimistic hope that given the historical backdrop of secular and progressive and plural ideological backups the civil society groups and organisations can do much for the revival of the reverse trends in these societies. According to him the Governments and civil society in the region need to work towards promoting a more inclusive and tolerant society, where diversity is celebrated and minority rights are promoted and preserved.

Dr Raju Ojha takes a historical perspective of looking at the entire phenomenon of nationalism in South Asia. In his paper, Nationalism in South Asia: A Historical Perspective, he identifies the historical dynamics which went in to condition and shape the political process which led most of the South Asian states to assume the varying modes of nationalism in the region. According to the author, South Asia has been a true laboratory for nation-building and nationalism. No other region has experienced two partitions of the magnitude of those of 1947 and 1971. The rise and growth of nationalism in South Asia was a reaction against colonial exploitation and subjugation.

The new form of nationalism that became the basis of the new states in South Asia derived much of its ideology and political theory from the West but was adapted to particular circumstances and experiences of self determination struggles. The basis of this new nationalism was an instinctive and xenophobic hatred for imperialism and symbols of imperialism. It was a simple hatred against those who had occupied their land by force, exploited their riches by force, crushed their government, and enslaved their people. Thus, historical attempt to identify the nationalist sentiments starts from the political struggles against the colonial and imperialist powers.

However, he argues that Nationalism also became a creative force which aimed at building a nation based upon the principles of liberty, independence, economic justice and nationality. It not only united the people, but also inspired them to contribute their share in the national reconstruction. The lead in this regard was given by India whereby she manifested to the world how a nation could be developed using progressive ideas and secular ethos. The author tries to identify the roots of Indian nationalism through the activities of Indian national congress and their related political developments which took place over a period of a century in the process of the freedom struggle. Equally he identifies the struggles and developments which took place in Bangladesh and Nepal for the liberation process and pin point how such societies emerged with their own nationalist slogans and sentiments. The author argues that apart from the historical imperatives which determine the contours of nationalism in South Asia, the character of the same under goes a political shift where the right wing forces use the nationalist sentiments and nationalism itself for objective sectarian ends.

Part-II

Globalisation, Development and Identity Questions

Dr. Veeragoni Shirisha, in her paper **Globalisation Vs Nationalism; The striking balance in a connected world**, attempts to catch up with the dynamism of interconnectedness the process of globalisation and nationalism and examines how the mutual cooperation and interactions contribute to shape new cultures thereby conditioning the nationalism and development itself. According to her globalisation acts as a catalyst in connecting nations and this interconnected and interdependence is directly and indirectly benefiting the entrepreneurs in terms of greater economic transactions. Globalisation and nationalism thus represent two inter-connected yet opposing concepts. Globalisation pertains to the growing interconnectedness and mutual reliance of economies, societies, and cultures on a global scale, whereas nationalism signifies a profound allegiance to one's nation, coupled with the aspiration for self-governance and autonomy. Critics of globalisation within the framework of nationalism contend that it weakens the sovereignty and self-reliance of nations. The increased movement of capital, goods, and services across international borders has eroded national boundaries and diminished control over economic policies. Consequently, wealth has become concentrated in the hands of a select few multinational corporations, leaving ordinary citizens and smaller enterprises at a disadvantage. As for as the cultural dimensions are concerned, the increase in economic activities do make its own cultural reflections as well. The process of globalisation do interfere with the aesthetical aspects of life as well.

While examining the different dimensions political, cultural and economic dimensions of Globalisation on Nationalism she concludes that the divides the globalisation spills over to different sections of marginalised sections and communities be bridged with a view to integrating them with the rest of the main stream and policy formulations will have to be made by the respective political leaderships so that the fragmented benefits of the process of globalisation be brought home to and all which will indirectly help and promote the nationalist feelings. Thus, she prefers to conclude the paper with the specific position that the future of nationalism in a globalised world is contingent on our individual and societal choices. Therefore, embracing an inclusive, collaborative, and forward-looking form of nationalism could help construct a more equitable and sustainable world whereby the whole sections of the society would be at the beneficiary end.

If nationalism is having the substantial potential for economic growth and integrating itself in to the international economic domain, what shall be the nature of such nationalism? Prity Kumari attempts to look at this intrinsic question in the context the Modi regime. In her paper **Nationalism and International Integration; The Case of India's economic performance and its marked presence,** She prefers to take a rightist position that the sort of nationalism during the two terms of Prime Minister Modi has reflected in terms of economic growth and international fame and nationalist vibrancy. The question here come for consideration is the sort of nationalism being propagated is having the substantiation of the majority community and no doubt it carried some negative connotations on the minority sections and progressive forces of the nation. According to her, Globalisation stands for interconnectedness of different nations in terms of economy, society, culture etc. and that while nationalism is a belief of nationalist sentiments. India makes a crucial juncture in economic trajectory because of the dual forces of globalisation and nationalism.

In her paper she tries to identify the impact of globalisation on economic growth of India and challenges posed by minorities due to the sectarian and the new versions and discourses nationalism of recent times. Due to globalisation many new opportunities has opened for Indian economy but simultaneously concerns about protecting national identity has also increased. Initiatives for protectionist measures like "Make in India" reflect the light on self reliance. In this way she prefers to argue that India should make balance between globalisation and emerging nationalism for safe-guarding its national sovereignty and suggest that the important policies and strategies are to be worked out to Navigating Nationalism and International Integration of the Indian economy for which she strikes a balance between the importance of inclusive and sustainable economic growth.

Equally, when nationalism is something attributed to the historical and cultural dynamics of a society and nation, what about the developmental paradigms whereby a particular pattern of growth at a given time could be sanctified as the reflection of nationalism? Shivangi Singh, M. Meena and V. Patel raise this question in the specific context of the Modi administration in India. In their joint paper "**Nationalism and Development in India; The case of Modi Administration** they take a position that the development and nationalism are inter connected and contributory factors which happened to be a reality in the specific context of India. Referring to the Modi era they claim that there was a high growth rate. The objective growth rate was the by product of an effective inflow of nationalism, which indirectly shaped the pattern of development and growth. According to them the Modi government has emphasized the importance of a strong, united, and self-reliant India, while also pushing for economic growth and development. On the nationalist front, the Modi government has taken several steps to promote a sense of pride in Indian culture and heritage. For instance, there has been a push to revive traditional practices and promote the use of Indian languages. Additionally, the government has implemented policies aimed at promoting Hindu nationalism, which has led to some controversy and criticism. The thesis put forward by the authors is a bit challenging when it comes in to the context of the concept of development. No doubt during the Modi regime there was development in certain sectors and such pattern of developments were in tune to some of the policies followed by the NDA administration. The programme like MAKE IN INDIA and Athma Nirbhar had a tremendous effect on our economy. Equally these policies had kindled the sense of nationalism as well.

However, as a result of the same administration there was sectarianism, hate and exclusion of certain sections of the society which pull back the democratic and developmental track of the nation. More over the track of growth attained in 2014 and 2020s was nothing but the continuation of the policies followed by the UPA Government under Dr Man Mohan Singh. In short the claim of nationalism itself stands criticized on the reason that its only the majoritarian nationalism which was propagated and forcibly injected. At the same time, India had the rare rhythm of nationalism chanted and flowed from the hearts of all sections of peoples in the nation, which prompted them to attain freedom in their struggle for self-determination, where the right wing version of nationalism was totally absent due to conspicuous reasons.

Vinay Chandra Pathak in his paper **Nationalism and Development in South Asia,** attempts to look at the contradictions in the developmental process of the nations in South Asia while identifying themselves with the changing faces of nationalism in modern times. The auther identifies that

South Asian states are undergoing a fundamental transformation with ethno-political conflict. At the core of ethno-political conflict are issues about state power and the distribution of economic and other material resources. The settlement of these conflict has entailed a political process of negotiating how to alter radically the way in which state power is organised and distributed which, in turn, is resulting in democratisation of the political community, pluralisation of the state and sharing of state sovereignty.

According to him, Nehru's ideas were implemented during the first decades of the Republic through the Five Year Plans of the Planning Commission. Other South Asian countries also copied the same pattern and developed national plans that stressed self-sufficiency, national markets, growth, and reduction of poverty and inequality. To be sure, these plans were not anti-market, but rather pro-national market. The Nehruvian model of a mixed economy and a secular, democratic political system remained a powerful imaginary of the nation that also became deeply entrenched as different interests and path dependencies became fixed into it. Finally, the author cautions and concludes that Nationalism is simultaneously a way of constructing groups and anormative claim. The two sides come together in ideas about who properly belongs together in a society and in arguments that members have moral obligations to the nation as a whole—perhaps even to kill on its behalf or die for it in a war. On the other side, Hyper nationalism can be highly disruptive, it advancing the interests of one group above all else—even at the expense of others.

Nationalism and Nation-state systems are natural sources of power of modern states. This being a very biological combination of power structure, how the phenomenon of political violence takes place in the political process of states? Dr Deo Krishna Choudhary in his paper **"Nationalism and Political violence"** attempts to have a closer look on the theme and related questions. According to him nationalism took its intellectual origin from distinct sources and regions. All these had contributed to the development and strengthening of nationalism India. However, there are various ways by which intolerance and exclusiveness emerged in the body politic of the nation which directly and indirectly contribute to the phenomenon of what is termed political violence. Often political violence take place as a result of overaction or inaction on the part of the state. According to him the imbalances of power which exist between state and non-state actors is the primary reason for political violence. Political violence often takes the form of asymmetric warfare where neither side is able to directly assault the other, instead relying on tactics such as guerrilla warfare and terrorism. It can often include attacks on civilian or otherwise non-combatant targets. People may be targeted collectively based on perception of being part of a social, ethnic, religious, or political group; or selectively, targeting specific individuals.

Further the author goes in details to dissect different types of political violence taking place in the contemporary world. It includes terrorism, rioting, genocide, civil war, torture, famine, capital punishment and even wars. As a consequence of this there takes place changes in both on the social, economic and political imbalances which farther destabilises the democratic fabric of the societies concerned. According to the author, all these negative impacts coming out of political violence are nothing but the attacks and efforts to infringe the democratic process of a nation. No doubt, the kind of political violence erupting in and around the world testifies his assumption and its true that no democracy goes far a war and it dare not to persecute its own people.

In their paper, **The Interrelationships of Nationalism, Political Violence, Environmental Issues and Public Policy,** Bir Abhimanyu Kumar and Rajiv Kumar try to analyze the dynamics of interplay among nationalism, political violence environmental issues by exploring the possibility and potentials of public policy making. According to the authors understanding the intersections of nationalism, political violence, and environmental issues is essential for developing holistic public policies. They do acknowledge that the interplay between nationalism, political violence and any other related issues become the complex and multifaceted landscape that largely influence global and local social dynamics and realities. As such it is imperative on the policy-makers to adopt integrated approaches that address the root causes of conflict and foster social and political stability. Therefore effective public policy can act as a preventative measure, curbing the potential for environmental degradation to incite conflict and ensuring that nationalist agendas do not undermine environmental and social stability. The discussion that proceeds explores the relationships between nationalism, political violence, environmental issues, and public policy. It highlights the importance of integrated approaches and underscores the need for policies that consider these interdependencies to effectively address the complex challenges facing contemporary societies.

Its from this theoretical proposition and frame work that the authors attempt to look at various issues confronted by the contemporary societies and bring home the message that the proper policy formulation will enable to counter such issues in future. The paper also try to highlights the necessity of integrated approaches in policy-making to effectively address the multifaceted challenges posed by the intersection of nationalism, political violence, and environmental issues. Holistic policy-making that considers these interconnections can lead to more comprehensive and effective solutions. Strategies such as conflict-sensitive environmental management, inclusive governance, and environmental peace building demonstrate the benefits of integrated approaches. Such policies not only mitigate the immediate impacts of conflicts but also contribute to long-term sustainability and stability by addressing root causes and promoting social cohesion.

Its true that the freedom struggle was fought by different segments of Indian society under the spell of unending quest for nationalism. In this mission all categories, groups and even religious divisions had played bigger role. Kuswant Kaur looks at the contribution made by the **Kuka movement** towards the building of national consciousness which had cemented the resistance of Sikh community in India under the leadership of Sadjuru ji. According to her the Indian masses who were under the yoke of colonial oppression were in fetters and the sense of national consciousness aroused peoples awareness of the geographical, religious, political, economic, historical, cultural and social unity of their country. Countless patriots happily sacrificed their lives to realise the dream of an independent India and the dawn of freedom came in the lives of Indians after a long night of slavery. In this saga of independence the role made by the kuka movement and its leaders form a separate golden chapter in the national freedom movement and history. Sadguru was the originator of the 'Kuka Movement'. According to her, Sadguruji inspired people to awaken their spiritual consciousness and exhorted them to abandon the frustrated ideologies of the society. He continuously strove towards the upliftment of the country and society. Satguru Ram Singh Ji had said that when a community becomes subjugated or enslaved, the spiritual progress of the people of that community cannot take place.

Satguru Ram Singh Ji started 'Sant Khalsa' or Kuka which initiated the non-cooperation movement under which they announced complete boycott of the British rule and raised the cry of freedom. Adopting (reliance of self, on indigenous products), the Kukas took the lead in fighting the war of independence by following the path of truth and non-violence. To make the Non-Cooperation Movement successful, the Kukas boycotted the English administrative and judicial system, the English postal system, the railway system for transportation, the English education system, the English medical system. They even boycotted the roads built by the British. Thus, the Non co-operation movements, based on non-violence was virtually taking strong inroads in to the Sikh community which further fomented the nationalist sentiments to aggregate the fight for freedom. Thus Kuswant Kaur concludes her paper with the proud legacy of the role played by the Sikh community In India. She make it further clear that, the spirit of the Kuka Movement breathed life into our collective pursuit of liberty. It was not just dry impersonal historical facts and figures, but the emotions, sacrifices, and unwavering determination, that define the soul of India's quest for independence.

Ashita. R in her paper 'Indian Nationalism' attempt to reflect the historical and political aspects which form itself in to the mojor components of Indian nationalism. According to her, nationalism is a cultural reflection of the people of the land. With reference to the French Revolution and its possible reflection in terms of peoples government, she argues that the concept of equality principle was first echoed through the revolution and all the subsequent governments formed carried, the positive impact of the spirit of the values of revolution and thus the general will of the people in building a nation got its natural manifestations. As such, the struggle between the popular will and the religious/racial identities confronted each other and the world wars weeded out the narrow senses of nationalism to a larger extent in both in Germany and the rest of the Europe. No doubt, the rise of nationalism in Europe did way to the nationalist movements in Asia and Africa where new forms of struggles appeared with the popular participation of the masses, irrespective of sectarian and parochial differences. The case was true in the case of Indian nationalism.

Ashita's analysis of Indian nationalism transcends through nineteenth and twentieth century realities and rests with the liberal progressive ideologies put forward by Mahatma Gandhi and Jawahar Lal Nehru. According to her, the post-Independent era witnessed to the continuation of such a liberal democratic tradition till the Hindu right wing camps found a come back strongly in the Indian politics. The emergence of Prime Minister Modi made things upside down and the right wing discourse of nationalism found reversal of the liberal democratic appeal of the nation. The programme and policies implemented by the NDA government for appeasing the majority community in India are looked at by the progressive forces of the nation with a pinch of salt and she concludes the paper with full hope that the liberal democratic tradition of the nation and its values will be the litmus test for the Indian democracy and to the Indian nationalism as such.

Part-III

Science and Objective Reality

Setting India's scientific path for growth, then Prime Minister Jawaharlal Nehru said that 'we can not change man by law but can only create a circumstance of scientific temper' whereby he may be influenced to become a new man with greater scientific spirit. Really, Nehru was laying the foundation for the national institute of science in 1948 with the intention of creating a new nation with full scientific vision and outlook. It goes with out saying that the domains of science and development go hand in hand and thanks to the social changes and developmental process followed in Europe following renaissance and reformation brought in by the unending spirit of scientific temper and spirit. If science and development are intrinsically related what about its relationship with nationalism? Really it is a very significant question which could be addressed by checking the inputs and components of nationalism, particularly of the contemporary times in South Aisa. This significant discourse is undertaken by Dr Prasahant Kumar Kain in his paper, **'Science and nationalism: Discursive shift in political discourses in India'.** Actually, the discourse put forward by the author is very much timely, for some sort of irrational and unscientific discourses were taking roots in the nationalism domains in the general context of South Asia and very much particular to India.

The author from the very outset itself takes a political position on science and its misuse. Quoting from the misdeeds of Hiroshima and Nagasaki, he emphasizes that the immense power of science, if used for destructive causes could be fatal when the same is at the hands of sectarian interests. He testifies by historic experiences that the sectarian interests can go to any extent to use science for self glory and self-fulfillment at the cost of others. The false notion of superiority, self pride and arrogance are well imbedded in the notion of nationalism. From a scientific perspective these are not a natural state of mind for human beings but nothing lesser than ubnormality. It is a cultivated belief that is based on the notions of superiority and exclusiveness of one's given self. It requires constant promotion through consistent propaganda. Such propagations easier today when the advances in information technology resulted in transfer of information with greater speed and volumes. This means that propaganda and myths can travel faster and with immense volumes, crossing the physical and cultural boundaries of nations. Human beings are becoming the repository and depository of 'information'. With the emergence of sectarian and toxic nature of nationalism the pace of this mad race assumes more propensities. This is the way how the author tries to locate the frantic sectarian nationalist discourse taking place in India and elsewhere. Further the author rightly observe that rationality is the soul of science which transcends to modernity, where it naturally contradicts with Nationalism and its false claims and beliefs. Therefore he argues that science and modernity are opposed to tradition and false cultural claims.

The author succinctly quotes the propagation and spreading of irrational myths and false notions by responsible political leaderships of India in connection with the substantiation of sectarian nationalism where by the mission was to glorify India's past. The idiotic and irrational application of such false notions come in the ways of cows products such as cow dung, Indian cows milk, divine and spiritual claims of ashes of cow dung as a anti-venom to Covid. Further the claims go to further heights with some of the 'Avatars' performing dharma in ancient social order of Hindu society. All these are done with the intention of propagating a narrow political culture, which in turn suspends the sublime gains of humanity and science-liberty, equality, freedom and justice.

Gitashri Kalindi in her paper 'Science and Indian Nationalism' takes a distinct look at the phenomenon of Nationalism in India. Her basic observation rests on the premises of Indias Scientific achievements and technological developments and she prefers to argue that rationale and tradition of Indias scientific advancements and achievements, right from the ancient times to the present helps the nation to hold its head high among the comity of nation-states and as such an average Indian is put at the liberty of taking his national self-esteem which is more or less attributed to the series of scientific and technological inventions made by the native scientists. Equally she attributes the developments in other domains of wisdom and knowledge to the frequency of development of science and technology in the nation. She makes the basic assumption that in India, most of the developments have taken place through the spreading and spirit of science and technology. This she attributes with respect to the developments of rural areas India where she argues technical factors have had a major role to play. This implies that there have been various sectors such as the agriculture, small-scale industries, dwellings, medical facilities, education system etc. It is only through the developments of science and technology that major improvements in all these sectors were made.

The rationale and significance of her paper is fully based on a hypothetical assumption which she try to manifest by way of a nationalism calculus. Very objectively she lists out the major achievements the Indian scientists have made so far which ranges from ancient times to the land mark of successful launching of **Chandrayan** which according to her held Indian prestige high among the International community. This in turn raises the nationalism levels of average Indian to a higher frequency in its own ways and proportions.

Part-IV

Art, Culture, Literary Reflections

The most brilliant manifestations of nationalism is often found in the domains of art, culture and literature where different art forms try to reflect the national sentiments of different segments of people in distinct times. Among the diversified art forms, literature is the live and creative expressions of society at all times. From time immemorial various writers had expressed their views surpassing the social order and statuesque of the contemporary societies. In the case of concept of nation, nationality and nationalism did happen the same thing both in India and elsewhere. The feeling of nation and nationality was thus emerged with Indian social psych from the very colonial periods itself. A peep back to such expressions takes one to the world of Hindi literature, particularly one that of Premchand. Dr Ritambhara Pandey try to analyze how the literary expressions of Premchand had surpassed time and space and took an advanced social view on most of the ills of the society and proves himself to be a revolutionary. She takes the dynamics of Premchand views on Nationalism through his various write ups and other works and argues that Premchand was a great visionary who took specific posions based on the Marxian and Gandhian ideas. According to the her, in Premchand's literary expressions, there is a sharp criticism of the concept of the elite nation, which, in its nature, was a supporter of casteist, feudal, and classist elite values. The system of declining power balance and dominance of the nation, which was created by feudal capitalist alliances by establishing harmony with the interests of the initial capitalist elite, has found its literary expression in novels like Godaan, Sevasadan, and many of his stories.

Further, Premchand takes the concept of an Indian nation out of elite abstraction and establishes it among the major components of society: deprived castes, women, Dalits, tribes, workers, and farmers. In these very meanings, on the one hand, Premchand rejects the discourse of nationalism; on the other hand, while giving a realistic depiction of many layers of dominance and examining the emerging classes, he also expresses his commitment towards the concept of a progressive society and nation. As such the paper takes a critical position, through the write ups of Premchand, against the contemporary discourse on majoritarian nationalism. Thus, Premchand was taking a critical position against colonialism and was writing for freedom from communalism and narrow-mindedness, freedom from economic and class discrimination, freedom from patriarchy and exploitation of women, freedom from casteism.

Asha. S Nair catches up this sensitive dynamics of Hindi literature in India. Her relative narrations of nationalism in the context of the leading literary figures in Hindi literature worth mentioning. According to her the development of literature from ancient to modern times and from there to post-modern and technological era is amazing and thrilling. She argues that in ancient times the seeds of cultural and national consciousness which were sown in the hearts of the people, started flourishing in the time of Bhakti period. The Bhakti movement started spreading all over India. The lamp lit by Kabir, Soor and Tulsi and its flame is still burning in literature and in public mind without being extinguished. Poets like Maithilisharan Gupt a Makhanlal Chaturvedi, Dinakar, Pant, Nirala, Subhadra Kumari Chauhan etc. tried to maintain it through their writings which directly and indirectly helped promote nationalism in India.

Equally, the writings of Kabir Das, Soordas, Meera, Maithili Sharan Gupta of the ancient times and Makhanlal Chaturvedi, Jayasankar Prasad and Ramdhari Singh Dinkar of modern times did the marvels of their writings in liberating the people from sectarian and traditional myths to rational and modern thinking where by cultural revival was made to suit to laying the foundation for a modern national identity and culture. Further, even after independence there was continuous write ups in the literary expressions of modern Hindi literature whereby the desperation, disappointment hope etc of the people were reflected according to the cultural and social imperatives of the people at large. In short, ancient, through me dival and modern Hindi literature tried to induce, inculcate and influence the national sentiments of the people in different socio-political situations and contexts.

If this is the general reflection of the a cross section of Hindi literature in India, Tagore occupy a distinct position and stand with respect to nationalism. Sushama Archana Topno in her paper, **RABIDRANATH TAGORE'S CONCEPT ON NATIONALISM; A critical reflection on the majoritarian nationalism in India and Beyond** try to ventilate the ideas of Rabindranath Tagore on nationalism and explain how his concept of Nationalism stand distinct with the right wing narratives on nationalism and his idea stands in par with sublime universalism and beyond. She takes an unconventional approach in bringing home the political idea of Tagore which had no parallel both in his times as well as in the contemporary political discourses in India. The Authoress takes note of the theoretical issues with nationalism in its global contexts and try to reflect basic ideas of Tagore his characters. In this mission she quotes the anger, anguish and desperations of the leading characters of Tagore starting from his novel Gora. The arguments of these characters do take specific political positions against colonial and feudal interests of the then society. No doubt those questions are bit more relevant even today.

Finally, she concludes that the basic assumption of Tagore either on nation or nationalism find a permanent and respectable position of all times, since all those notions are resting on the rostrums of the basic ideals of humanity and human welfare rooted in love, compassion and harmony. More interestingly the paper put forward a specific political question with respect to the right wing discourse taking place in contemporary India. According to her, if Tagore represent the sublime cultural and civilisational voice of ancient India and her traditions, how the right wing majoritarian nationalist claims could be endorsed with India's past traditions? A question worth breaking the right wing campsit self, for love, compassion, sublime humanism and internationalism can not be questioned with out rejecting Tagore and his thoughts on Nationalism.

Notes and References

1. See for details, CSDS-Lokniti pre–poll survey /Redefining social justice as secularism. [The hindu. com] April 12, 2024.
2. The UPA Government Under Dr Singh, from 2004 to 2013 produced a massive boom with a growth rate of 7.74 percent per year. The performance was against the odds of global financial crisis in 2008-09.

Part-I

Discourse, Debate and Dissent

Chapter - 1

Indian Nationalism and Marginalised: Investigating the Question of Inclusivity

— Yagati Chinna Rao

Nationalism has been a strong force of political expression in the Western World. The impulses of nationalism gave way to the formation and reformation of states in Europe in the late eighteenth and early nineteenth centuries. The rise of nationalism led to the breakdown of many political entities, which derived their homogeneity and unity based on ethnicity, language, culture, etc. These homogenous cultural groups consequently emerged as independent nation-states. Thus, nationalism played a significant role in the liquidation of great empires and the formation of new states. In the third world, the idea of nationalism was borrowed from the West in the context of the rise of indigenous movements to fight against colonial rule. However, it is believed by many, that the third-world countries lacked conditions in which nationalism took root in Europe and consequently played a vital role in the emergence of nation-states. In what respect nationalism in South Asia has been different from the West has also been an important issue. In the context of Indian nationalism particularly, different explanations have been put forward. In recent decades there have been deviations in the form and contents of nationalism in South Asia, leading to the trends of sub-nationalism and secessionism.

Several scholars have defined nationalism. However, these conceptual frameworks are different in terms of the contents and the characteristics of nationalism. In the context of the world, nationalism was seen as a consciousness among a community leading to its self-assertion and the consequent emergence of a state. The Marxist on the other hand linked nationalism struggle. On the other hand, many scholars have opined that both their theoretical constructs of nationalism do not apply to third-world countries, where nationalism has been broadly a nationalist movement against colonial rule. It is difficult to trace out any clear-cut framework regarding the third-world explanations of nationalism. Secondly, they are liberal Western and Marxian theoretical constructs. One may also add here that in these countries nationalism has acquired a different form and there have been varied interpretations of nationalism.

Nationalism has been looked upon as a political doctrine of self-determination. In this nationalism may be viewed as a particularistic phenomenon that intends to distinguish between people based on various sociocultural categories. Based on distinct cultures they claim the right to self-determination and claim their right over a territory as a distinct political identity. Gellner states that nationalism is a political principle, in which the political and national unit should be congruent. Smith, on the other hand, has viewed sentiment that he believes is as old as history. Karl Deutsch dealing with the issues of nationalism quite at length viewed it as a positive historical frame that channeled race in an era of rapid urbanisation and stimulated cultural mobilisation in an era of social alienation. Many other scholars have viewed nationalism in terms of a process leading various ethnicities towards the right to self-determination.

The Marxist theoreticians viewed nationalism and national movements as a struggle for feudal or imperialist power. Several scholars have viewed nationalism in the context of developing countries and have tried to define it accordingly. Many consider it a struggle against the colonial rule. The indigenous elite in these countries are nationalist forces. Michael Hechter has defined nationalism as a popular protest against oppression. Paul Brass has associated nationalism with ethnicity and believes that both are connected with the working modern centralised states. Ethnic mobilisation and national formation are associated phenomena. These definitions explain particular situations of the rise of nationalism. It is difficult to generalise these situations. For example, ethnic mobilisation may arouse nationalism but not all kinds of ethnic mobilisation need to have nationalistic aspirations.

The South Asian countries except Maldives to a large extent have multi-ethnic, multiracial, multi-lingual and multi-religious societies. All these countries are faced with the problems of horizontal and vertical disparities. These complexities and divisions have made the question of nationality and nationalism very tedious. The South Asian states lacked that ethno-cultural homogeneity which affected a process of fusion to unify people into a political community. It was for this reason that in the wake of the nationalist movement the indigenous leadership had to discover threads of homogeneity.

Nationalism took root in South Asia in the form of a struggle for independence. The basic objective of this struggle was to overthrow colonial rule and establish self-rule. Their nationalistethos was represented by the indigenous elite which tried to mobilise the people against the rule and due to the discriminatory policies of the colonial rulers regional and ethno-cultural questions also emerged. But they did not come in conflict with the nationalist aspirations. These two streams have been defined ás great nationalism and little nationalism. The ethnic-regional identities that emerged as lesser ethno-religious nationalism during the colonial rule have continued after independence. Many of them have become more assertive in the post independent era. Faience, there is the problem of nationalism in most of the South Asian countries. Many of these smaller identities questioned the legitimacy of the post-colonial states and sought to form a new political community. It posed a serious challenge to the state. Nationalism in South Asia has played a crucial role in shaping the political, social, and cultural landscape of the region. It emerged as a response to colonialism and the struggle for independence from European powers. However, the idea of nationalism in South Asia is complex and multifaceted, reflecting the region's diverse cultural, religious, and linguistic identities. This presentation aims to explore the various dimensions of nationalism in South Asia and the challenges it faces in the region.

Historical Context

Nationalism in South Asia emerged in the late nineteenth and early twentieth century as a response to colonialism. The Indian National Congress was founded in 1885 and played a pivotal role in the country's struggle for independence from British colonial rule. The Congress advocated for a secular and inclusive nationalism that encompassed all communities, religions, and linguistic groups within India. However, the partition of India in 1947 along religious lines resulted in the creation of Pakistan as a separate Muslim-majority state and further complicated the idea of Indian nationalism. In Pakistan, nationalism is deeply tied to the country's Islamic identity, and the idea of a separate Muslim homeland was a key driving force behind the creation of the country. However, the country's religious and ethnic diversity has also led to tensions and conflicts between different groups. In Bangladesh, nationalism emerged as a response to the perceived neglect of the Bengali-speaking population by the ruling elite in Pakistan. The language movement of 1952, which sought official recognition for the Bengali language, played a significant role in the country's struggle for independence from Pakistan in 1971. In Sri Lanka, nationalism has been shaped by the Sinhala-Tamil ethnic conflict, which has been ongoing since the country's independence in 1948. The conflict is rooted in competing claims to territory, resources, and political power between the Sinhala and Tamil communities. In Nepal, nationalism has been shaped by the country's struggle for democracy and the abolition of the monarchy. The country's ethnic and linguistic diversity has also been a key factor in shaping its nationalist discourse.

Nationalism, Pluralism, and Identity

Nationalism, pluralism, and identity are complex and intertwined issues in South Asia. This region is home to diverse cultures, religions, and languages, which have shaped its history, politics, and society. Nationalism has been a unifying force in South Asia, but it has also been a source of conflict and tension due to the region's ethnic and religious diversity. The challenges facing nationalism in South Asia include the tension between secular and inclusive nationalism and the reality of ethnic and religious diversity, the rise of identity politics, and the instrumentalisation of nationalist sentiment by political elites. To address these challenges, it is essential to promote a more inclusive and pluralistic nationalism that recognizes and respects the diversity of South Asia's cultures, religions, and languages. The tension between secular and inclusive nationalism and the reality of ethnic and religious diversity is a major challenge facing nationalism in South Asia. Secular and inclusivenationalism seeks to create a unified national identity that transcends ethnic and religious differences. However, the reality is that South Asia is home to a diverse array of cultures, religions, and languages. This diversity has led to the rise of identity politics, where different groups seek to promote their interests and identities. This has further fueled tensions between different groups and undermined the idea of a unified national identity. The rise of identity politics is another challenge facing nationalism in South Asia.

Identity politics is based on the idea that different groups have distinct identities and interests that must be protected and promoted. This has led to the fragmentation of society along ethnic and religious lines and has undermined the idea of a unified national identity. In many cases, identity politics has been used to promote the interests of dominant groups at the expense of marginalised groups, which has further fueled tensions and conflicts. The instrumentalisation of nationalist sentiment by political elites is a major challenge facing nationalism in South Asia. In many cases, nationalist rhetoric has been used to promote narrow political interests or to justify discriminatory policies against minority groups. This has further fueled identity politics and exacerbated tensions between different groups. The instrumentalisation of nationalism has also been used to justify authoritarianism and to undermine democratic institutions, which has further eroded the legitimacy of nationalist movements.

To address the challenges facing nationalism in South Asia, it is essential to promote a more inclusive and pluralistic nationalism that recognizes and respects the diversity of the region's cultures, religions, and languages. This can be achieved through the promotion of inter-cultural dialogue, the strengthening of democratic institutions, and the protection of minority rights. Additionally, it is essential to address the underlying causes of conflict and tension in the region, such as inequality, poverty, and discrimination. By addressing these issues, it may be possible to create a more equitable and just society that is better able to accommodate the diversities, identities and aspirations of its citizens. Despite its importance in shaping the region's history and politics, nationalism in South Asia faces several challenges. One of the key challenges is the tension between the idea of a secular and inclusive nationalism and the reality of religious and ethnic diversity in the region. This tension has often led to conflicts between different religious and ethnic groups, as seen in the case of the Sinhala-Tamil conflict in Sri Lanka and the ongoing conflicts in Kashmir.

Another challenge to nationalism in South Asia is the rise of identity politics based on linguistic, ethnic, and religious identities. This has led to a fragmentation of the nationalist discourse and has made it difficult to create a unified sense of national identity. Furthermore, nationalism in South Asia has often been used as a tool for political mobilisation and manipulation by political elites. This has led to the instrumentalisation of nationalist sentiment and has often resulted in the exclusion of certain groups from the nationalist discourse. For example, in Pakistan, the country's Islamic identity has been used to justify the marginalisation of minority groups such as Ahmadis and Shias.

While delivering a Foundation Day Lecture, Prof K. N. Panikkar in 2010, at Assam Central University, Silchar, entitled 'Was Indian nationalism inclusive?' mentioned that One of the weaknesses of the national movement was that it did not have an effective programme to ensure the inclusion of the depressed and socially excluded classes into the nation. Whatever was attempted in this field was very superficial in as much as it did not frontally contest the power of the 'upper' castes and classes, the legacy of which continues even today. That anti-colonial Indian nationalism was not sufficiently inclusive is possibly one of the reasons why a substantial section of the population is still not a part of the nation.[1] The concept of nationalism, in the Indian colonial context, becomes meaningful only when looked at beyond the overarching relationship between colonialism and the people, and the mutual relationship among different segments of society is taken into account. Overcoming these differences was integral to nationalism.

Inclusiveness, therefore, is a necessary strategy of nationalism, even with contradictory interests finding a place in it. The attempts to resolve the secondary contradiction within the umbrella of nationalism do not overlook the primary contradiction with colonialism. In this sense, the aim of nationalism was not limited to the attainment of freedom but, as Gandhi envisaged, had to lead to the creation of a qualitatively different society, devoid of caste and religious antagonism. To a deputation of students in 1934, Gandhi said: "The two things — the social reordering and the fight for political swaraj — must go hand in hand. There can be no question of precedence or division into watertight compartments here." Nationalism was thus conceived as a combination of political freedom and social emancipation. What nationalism sought to achieve was togetherness. The very first session of the Indian National Congress recognised it by identifying its purpose as providing a platform for people to come together. What brought people together were political struggles and public agitations.

Various streams within the movement with different strategies and modes of struggle were efforts to ensure their rightful inclusion in the nation. People, however, consisted of diverse groups, castes, classes and religions with widely differing interests. What was conceived as nationalism, therefore, was bringing the people together, regardless of the differentiations.

Although the anti-colonial sentiment ironed out some of these differences and interests, they were so diverse and sharp that the national movement, functioning within a liberal framework, was not able to find an effective solution. Therefore, India emerged not only impoverished due to colonial exploitation but also socially divided. During the 1980s, a spate of historical writings appeared ardently appealing to historians towards 'history from below'[2] and 'social history',[3] the disquiet over the persisting elitism in overarching historical narratives of colonial state and nationalism. With the impetus coming from the British Marxist school of 'History from below' attention was directed towards focusing on ordinary people; the oppressed people without history-to 'humanize history' and to critically reconceptualise the superficial application of Marxian as well as the nationalist frameworks. It was evident that the oppressed, especially the Dalits constituted a thorny, a ‘deviant’ category amenable to neither historiographical models. While a perfunctory reference is made in eventual historiography about social reform or anti-colonial politics– the Dalits and Tribes rarely made appearances as historical subjects or agents. However, some of the rare and best works have come in from the ancient period and paradoxically haven’t been able to rectify the many essentialist and flawed historical understandings of Dalits in the historiography of modern or colonial Dalit histories.[4] Importantly, the critical recognition in historical analysis that there was no singular, response to colonialism to the anti-colonial movement has gained wider currency in historiography and is a productive moment for reconstructions of histories of the marginalised.

The various contradictions, alignments and tensions from diverse loci yet continue to have deeper resonance with the historical imaginations, trajectories and visions in post-colonial conditions. The intellectual commitment to exploring subaltern non-elitist history, even before it could explore concrete histories, the turn it took to discourse analysis, meant an abandoning of earlier preoccupations. Dalits could not be effectively ‘mobilized’ as historical subjects of subaltern history. Babasaheb Dr B. R. Ambedkar, in his undelivered address of 1936, later published as Annihilation of Caste, while speaking on ‘Why social reform is necessary for political reform’ said that:

> “The path of social reform, like the path to heaven (at any rate, in India), is strewn with many difficulties. Social reform in India has few friends and many critics. The critics fall into two distinct classes. One class consists of political reformers and the other of the Socialists… But soon the two wings developed into two parties, a ‘political reform party’ and a ‘social reform party’, between whom there raged a fierce controversy. The ‘political reform party’ supported the National Congress, and the ‘social reform party’ supported the Social Conference. The two bodies thus became two hostile camps. The point at issue was whether social reform should precede political reform. For a decade the forces were evenly balanced, and the battle was fought without victory for either side.”[5]

As Ambedkar Asked:

“Are you fit for political power even though you do not allow a large class of your countrymen like the untouchables to use public schools?… the use of public wells? … the use of public streets? … to eat any food they like?”[6] Dr Ambedkar’s nationalism was based on the concept of liberty, equality and fraternity of all citizens was against nationalism based on any kind of racial and religious discrimination. He had said, "Some people say that they are Hindus, Muslims or Sikhs first and Indians second, But I am an Indian from beginning to end".[7]

To summarise, Nationalism in South Asia is a complex and multi-faceted phenomenon that reflects the region's diverse cultural, religious, and linguistic identities. While it has played a crucial role in the region's struggle for independence and self-determination, it has also been a source of conflict and tension, particularly concerning issues of identity and belonging. The challenges facing nationalism in South Asia are many, including the tension between secular and inclusive nationalism and the reality of religious and ethnic diversity, the rise of identity politics, and the instrumentalisation of nationalist sentiment by political elites. To overcome thesechallenges, it is essential to promote a more inclusive and pluralistic nationalism that recognizes and respects the diversity of South Asia's cultures, religions, and languages. This can be achieved through the promotion of intercultural dialogue, the strengthening of democratic institutions, and the protection of minority rights.

Additionally, it is essential to address the underlying causes of conflict and tension in the region, such as inequality, poverty, and discrimination. By addressing these issues, it may be possible to create a more equitable and just society that is better able to accommodate the diverse identities and aspirations of its citizens. In conclusion, nationalism in South Asia is a complex and dynamic phenomenon that has shaped the region's history and politics. While it has been a source of inspiration and unity, it has also been a source of conflict and tension. To overcome the challenges facing nationalism in South Asia, it is essential to promote a more inclusive and pluralistic nationalism that recognizes and respects the diversity of the region's cultures, religions, and languages.

Notes and References

1. K. N. Panikkar, "Was Indian Nationalism Inclusive?", The Hindu, 23 February, 2010; also see hisHistory as a Site of Struggle: Essays on History, Culture and Politics, New Delhi, Three Essayscollective, 2013.
2. Sabyasachi Bhattacharya, "History from Below", Social Scientist, Vol. 11, No. 4, (April 1983), pp. 3-20.
3. Sumit Sarkar, "Presidential Address: Social History, Predicaments and Possibilities", Proceedings of the Indian History Congress, (1984), Vol. 45, pp. 479-502.

4. Suvira Jaiswal, Caste: Origin, Function and Dimensions of Change, (New Delhi: Manohar, 1981); Vivekananda Jha, Candala: Untouchability and Caste in Early India, (New Delhi: Primus Books, 2018).
5. B. R. Ambedkar, "Annihilation of caste", Dr Babasaheb Ambedkar Writings And Speeches, Vol. 1, New Delhi, Dr Ambedkar Foundation, (2014), pp. 23-98.
6. *Ibid.*
7. *Ibid.*

References

Aloysius, G., Nationalism without a Nation, Oxford University Press, 1998.

Chatterjee, Partha, The Nation and Its Fragments: Colonial and Postcolonial Histories, Princeton University Press, 1993.

Gellner, Ernest, Nations and Nationalism, Cornell University Press, 1983.

Guha, Ranajit, Elementary Aspects of Peasant Insurgency in Colonial India, Delhi, Oxford University Press, 1983.

Jaffrelot, Christophe, The Hindu Nationalist Movement and Indian Politics: 1925 to the 1990s, Penguin Books, 1996.

Jalal, Ayesha, Democracy and Authoritarianism in South Asia: A Comparative and Historical Perspective, Cambridge University Press, 1995.

Malik, H. (1996). Islam and Modernity: Muslims in South Asia. Oxford: Oxford University Press.

Menon, R. (2016). Islam, Nationalism, and the West: Issues of Identity in Pakistan. Palgrave, Macmillan.

Pandey, G. (1999). The Construction of Communalism in Colonial North India. Delhi: Oxford University Press.

Chapter - 2

Nationalism in India; Shifting Paradigms of Narratives, Notions and Nonsenses

— R. Sreekantan Nair

1. Introduction

Nationalism is a complex phenomenon and also a powerful political tool. Its emergence, potential and out-reach is situational and varying in tune to the specific terrain and contexts. In the specific background of Europe, the peculiar socio-cultural and political backdrops did its marvel in shaping the magnitude of nationalism whereby it embraced secular, developmental, civic and inclusive forms of nationalism. Whereas in the Asian contexts, though some of the states attempted to keep parity along with the European track of nationalism and state building process, there are invariable and uneven ways of fomenting nationalism in some other states in the region. In this regard, the case of South Asia stood distinct by its ethnic and religious and superstitious metaphor. Having common geographical, religious, demographic, economic and cultural features the states in the region manifest same sort of nationalist moorings too. The case of Indian nationalism does not seem different from these general perspectives and reflections. However, in the case of India there has been various notions and narratives which often served to cater and kindle the flames of nationalism in different situations and contexts. This shifting pattern perhaps determines the contours of Indian nationalism driven by distinct ideological postures. As such this paper attempts to [i] identify and sketch out the patterns of such notions and theoretical narratives on nationalism both in the context of Europe as well as in India and explain [ii] Why such notions and narratives bore fruits in the European contexts where as in India why it turned out to be failure for promoting a civic/ pluralistic nationalism from which I further argue that [iii] this failure led to the emergence of majoritarian nationalism in India and finally the paper would prefers to suggest that [iv] the majoritarian nationalism in India will have its own dialectical challenges in its due course and secular and progressive forces will determine the shape and course of Indian nationalism in the near future.

2. The backdrop

Though academic enthusiasm on nationalism have taken place during the twentieth century, as an ideology and a social and political movement, the concept has been very much in discourse since the end of the sixteenth century. However, nationalism took its first manifestations in Europe in the nineteenth century when most of the states there were benefited by the phenomenon of Enlightenment. Prior to this, there were many socio-political movements which led to the out break of British, American and French revolutions. No doubt these progressive political developments took place just because there were honest and serious debates and discourses initiated by great scholars of all times. Among them the names of Kant, J. J Rousseau, Herder, Fichte, J. S Mill, Marx, Engels, Lenin, Rosa Luxemburg etc are of greater significance.

Even with in Europe, nationalism emerged first in Western Europe through the amalgamation of several divided feudal territories into smaller kingdoms. But it remained localised and ruler-based. The French Revolution and the wars of Nepolean altered that: the latter rendered nationalism into various people-based movements. Further the creation of new nation-states in Central Europe and the Balkans, and the unification of Germany and Italy were remarkable achievements of the nineteenth-century nationalist movements. As a political and social movement, nationalism was associated with the task of promoting solidarity and a sense of belonging and oneness among the people of a territorial homogeneity.[1] Since World War II, nationalism has domesticated many such movements and created a sense of patriotism rooted in nationalism. As a result of this, the European concept fired up millions of colonised peoples in Asia, Africa and Latin America in their emergence into the process of demanding self-determination and independence. Since then, national self-determination has been closely associated with the concept of liberal nationalism, particularly among the Third World countries.

Equally, the pioneering political developments like Bill of Rights, American Declaration of Independence, and the French Declaration of the Rights etc did ground work for the subsequent political movements which led to the nationalist struggles and the other progressive movements in the rest of the world. Thus the revolutionary ideas of such movements of nineteenth and twentieth century did influence the imagination of the world and no doubt these movements inspired the people all over the world and it was natural that many states in Asia and Africa were influenced by such developments.

However, unlike the European experience, the people of the third world countries were experiencing the tyranny of colonialism and exploitation and it was quiet natural that the political movements sprouting in these regions had the underpinning of such experiences and expressions. As such, the nationalist notions of such people had more sharp edge of anti-imperial and anti-colonial slogans which also contributed to their vigorous nationalist political struggles in the twentieth century. Thus, nationalism being a significant catalyst in determining the contours of Nation-states, the concept needs further emphasis and clarification.

3. The Conceptual frame and the Discourses

Being an abstract concept and a concrete reality Nationalism attempted to foster a positive consciousness of unity, homogeneity and national aspiration among peoples at large. In this regard, the positive and negative aspects of nationalism have been very much recorded by different scholars. As such the concept could be looked at from different stand points. Often it is viewed as an aspiration for various social groups to defend, create or maintain nations. Equally, it is ascertained that Nationalism maintains autonomy, identity and unity of nations. Smith defines nationalism as an ideological movement which helps to attain and maintain identity, unity and autonomy of a social group (Smith, 2005: 23-31). Again it is viewed as political doctrine of self-determination and so is linked with sovereignty. Thus, even with in a territorial and geographical location, nationalism can be different for the different social groups in multi-cultural countries because of different culture, identity and political status. (Nanda, 2006: 24-25). In such societies Religion, culture, language, ethnicity etc. form the main parameters which make and shape nationalism. Even then there were serious attempts made by scholars to define and dissect the very phenomenon of Nationalism from distinct theoretical standpoints.

Often there are identical and diverse perspectives with respect to the way the scholars did try to define them. Hans Kohn considered nationalism as the "first and foremost a state of mind, an act of consciousness...". Heimsath defined nationalism as:... an attitude of mind, or set of beliefs, that is shared by a group of people large enough to be influential, and that embodies ideas of the nation and the nation's goals, elevates those ideas to a prime position over other public values, and compels the assertion of the identity and the aims of the nation.[2] However, Hayes moves on to have a deeper understanding of the same and included four different meanings to the idea of nationalism.[3]

These were: (1) the name of a historic process; (2) the ideas embodied in that process; (3) the activities of a particular party, and (4) a condition of mind among members of a nation. He is of the view that genuine movements of nationalism must include all of these different dimensions. Defined as the fight for nationhood, nationalism was the ideal which dominated most of Europe in the nineteenth century. It was the phenomenon which helped to merge various groups, say in Germany and Italy, having different forms of government to unite into a single nation-state.

It is rightly noted at the outset that the eighteenth century does not figure prominently in recent classifications of the theoratical debate on nationalism. However, their contributions, in a way provided sense and directions to the magnitude of enlightenment. It is from this point of realisation that Lawrence (2005) starts his overview in 1848, making it quite explicit that his aim is to produce a historiography of theories of nationalism. Day and Thompson (2004), on the other hand, begin with roughly the same period, focusing on the Marxist tradition and its legacy.

But Even then as it is pointed out, this discussion will not be total unless the earlier century's thinkers like Kant, Rousseau, Herder and Fichte etc are focussed and taken in to account. Since the subject matter of this paper is Indian nationalism and its related dynamics in contemporary times, a detailed discussion is not done towards the entire theoretical narratives, rather it is confined to the classical thinkers who had contributed the concept of nationalism at large. It is also interesting to note that the often raised the question whether nationalism produced its own 'grand thinkers'? Anderson's answer to this question is unequivocal: 'unlike most other isms, nationalism has never produced its own grand thinkers anyway: 'If one of them had fallen, others would have stepped into his place. No one was indispensable.' He concludes: 'we shall not learn too much about nationalism from the study of its own prophets' since they all suffered from a pervasive false consciousness.[4]

However, others, notably O'Leary, disagree: 'It is strange not to classify Weber as a nationalist grand thinker, stranger still that Rousseau, Burke,

John Stuart Mill and Friedrich List are not seen as nationalist grand thinkers' (1998: 87; cf. Minogue 1996). The problem here lies in determining who can be considered as a 'thinker of nationalism', not in deciding whether those who have intellectually contributed to the nationalist doctrine are 'grand' or not. This is made exceedingly clear by the following statement by Yack: 'there are no great theoretical texts outlining and defending nationalism. No Marx, no Mill, no Macchiavelli. Only minor texts by first rate thinkers, like Fichte, or major texts by second rate thinkers, like Mazzini' (cited in Beiner, 1999: 2).

According to Gellner, the existing thinkers did not make much difference and have not treated the problem in a systematic way or made it the central focus of their analyses. Most studies of nationalism trace the origins of the nationalist doctrine generally back to German Romantic thought – roughly to the end of the eighteenth and the beginning of the nineteenth centuries. But the thinkers of this period were heavily influenced by the philosophical foundations laid down by their predecessors, in particular to the writings of Immanuel Kant and Jean Jacques Rousseau, two influential figures of the Enlightenment tradition. In fact, according to Kedourie (1994), who explains nationalism in terms of seismic changes in European philosophy, it all started with Kant.

Immanuel Kant (1724–1804) Moral Universalism

Kant was the philosopher of moral universalism par excellence (see Kitromilides, 2001, among others. The political consequences of the ethical and epistemological dualism he developed were far-reaching (Smith, 1983:31–2). At the heart of this dualism lies a separation between the external, that is phenomenal world and man's inner world. For Kant, the source of knowledge was the phenomenal world; our knowledge was based on sensations emanating from things-in-themselves. But the phenomenal world was a world of 'inexplicable contingencies' and 'iron necessities', and if our morality were also derived from this kind of knowledge, 'then we could never be free but always the slave either of contingency or of blind personal laws'. Morality, then, had to be separated from knowledge, hence the phenomenal world, the world of appearances: instead, it should be 'the outcome of obedience to a universal law which is to be found within ourselves' (Kedourie, 1994: 14). Kant held that human beings can only be free when they obey the laws of morality which they find within themselves, and not in the external world.

This was, according to Kedourie, a revolutionary definition of freedom. Kant equated 'virtue' with 'free will'. On the other hand, neither freedom nor virtue depended on God's commands. Hence the new formula: 'the good will, which is the free will, is also the autonomous will'. This was revolutionary because the formula made the individual, the centre and the sovereign of the universe, 'in a way never envisaged by the French revolutionaries or their intellectual precursors'; 'self-determination thus becomes the supreme political good'. Equally, the concept of self determination was well founded by The French Philosopher JJ Rousseau, as a continuation of the Kantian narratives.

Jean-Jacques Rousseau [1712-1778]-General Will

Rousseau put forward his idea of 'General will' where the seeds of self determination was well placed. For Rousseau, the greatest danger man faces when living in society, as opposed to the state of nature, is 'the possible tyranny of will by his fellowmen'. To guard against this danger, men need to exchange their selfish will for the 'general will'. This can only be achieved if they cease to be natural men and become citizens instead. Natural men live for themselves, whereas citizens depend on the community of which they are a part: 'Each of us puts his person and all his power in common under the supreme direction of the general will, and, in our corporate capacity, we receive each member as an indivisible part of the whole' (Rousseau, 2001 [1762]: 75). A political association makes sense, Rousseau believed, only if it can protect men from the capriciousness of others: 'this it can solely bring about if it substitutes law for the individual, if it can generate a public will and arm it with a strength that is beyond the power of any individual will' (Barnard, 1984: 246).

Yet Rousseau was fully aware that citizenship, which entailed submission the general will, could not take place spontaneously. 'In order to achieve this degree of unity, a national esprit de corps had to be created in which every citizen saw in citizenship a supreme moral good' (Barnard, 1983: 239). The spirit of the consciousness of belonging together, can only be created through patriotism, that 'fine and lively feeling which gives the force of self-love all the beauty of virtue, and lends it an energy which, without disfiguring it, makes it the most heroic of all passions' (cited in Barnard, 1984: 250). The most efficient way to instil patriotism, on the other hand, is education: it is education that you must count on to shape the souls of the citizens in a national pattern. The link between the Enlightenment and German Romanticism was provide by the German thinker Herder.

Johann Gottfried Herder (1744–1803). Language and culture

Herder proposes his position on Language, Education and Culture whereby individuals contribute themselves to the national whole. He believed in the uniqueness and incommensurability of national cultures. This was particularly the case with language which 'bears the stamp of the mind and character of a national group'. According to Herder:

> Has a nationality anything more precious than the language of its fathers? In this language dwell its whole world of tradition, history, religion and principles of life, its whole heart and soul. To rob a nationality of its language or to degrade it, is to deprive it of its most precious possession. (Cited in Heater 1998: 68–9)

Language is something internal, expressing man's innermost thoughts and feelings, just like the other cultural bonds which linked members of a nation; these bonds were not 'things or artifacts imposed from above but living energies emanating from within' (Barnard, 1983: 242–3). Hence, 'nationality is a plant of nature; a nation is as natural a plant as a family, only with more branches; the most natural state is … one nation, an extended family with one national character' (cited in Heater, 1998: 79). Further, in extolling the virtues of the diversity of cultures, Herder's aim is to repudiate the universalism of the Enlightenment which is further in pursuit of common language and good, which was developed by Fichete.

Johann Gottlieb Fichte (1762–1814), Language as the nation itself

Fichte was Kant's disciple, who gave these ideas a specifically 'German' colouring. The most explicit statement of Fichte's ideas on nationalism can be found in his famous Addresses to the German Nation, delivered between 1807 and 1808, in the wake of Prussia's defeat by France at the Battle of Jena in 1806. For Fichte, 'only the German … really has a people and is entitled to count on one, and that he alone is capable of real and rational love for his nation' (2001 [1808]: 115). In fact, the Germans are the original people, entrusted with a mission towards the rest of human kind to create the perfect state: 'it is first of all Germans who are called upon to begin the new era as pioneers and models for the rest of mankind … you will see this nation the regenerator and recreator of the world' (cited in Heater 1998: 107). But what makes the Germans so special in the eyes of Fichte? Their high culture, above all their language. 'Wherever the German language was spoken', says Fichte:everyone who had first seen the light of day in its domain could consider himself as in a double sense a citizen, on the one hand, of the State where he was born … and, on the other hand, of the whole common fatherland of the German nation … [Everywhere in Germany] the higher culture was, and continued to be, the result of the interaction of the citizens of all German states: and then this higher culture gradually worked its way down in this form to the people at large. (2001 [1808]: 125–6)

In the changing contexts, the Language does not matter only in the case of the Germans. 'Those who speak the same language', Fichte argues, 'are joined to each other by a multitude of invisible bonds by nature herself, long before any human art begins'; 'It is true beyond doubt that, wherever a separate language is found, there a separate nation exists, which has the right to take independent charge of its affairs and to govern itself … where a people has ceased to govern itself, it is equally bound to give up its language and to coalesce with conquerors. (Cited in Heater 1998: 69) Apart from these theoretical postulates the political bases that we recognize today as nationalism was firmly in place by the early nineteenth century. On the other hand, debates on nationalism continued to reflect ethical concerns and political expediencies. Hence the further discussion of nineteenth and early twentieth centuries meant to cover the Marxist and liberal positions and responses to the concept of nationalism.

The Marxist position; Communist International

The Marxist notion of nationalism is well documented and remain open. Often the writings of Marx was well put and periorically repeated interpretation of the subsequent situations and contexts by the scholars at different times. 'Of all the historical phenomena discussed by Marx', writes Avineri, 'nationalist movements and the emergence of the nation-state is the least satisfactory' (1991: 638; see also Munck 1986; Nimni 1991; Benner 199 and Forman 1998). Some scholars are of critical of Marxist position on nationalism. In the case of Nairn, who argue that 'the theory of nationalism represents Marxism's great historical failure' (1981: 329). Others disagree with him. Benner, for example, asserts that Marx and Engels have put forward strands of argument which address the national question, and that we have a lot to learn from these if we want to understand nationalism in our own times (1995: 6). Munck, on the other hand, criticizes attempts to deride those who have tried to come to grips with nationalism within the Marxist tradition, and concludes: 'It is now necessary to forge some kind of coherent Marxist approach to nationalism on the basis of these writers' (1986: 168).

An overview of the arguments that have been advanced within the Marxist tradition will not only help us make better sense of nationalism, as Benner argues, but also shed light on contemporary theoretical debates among, but not limited to, neo-Marxists. Marx (1818–83) and Engels's (1820–95) position in The Communist Manifesto (1848) was unmistakably internationalist. The memorable passages from the Manifesto are worth recalling:

> The bourgeoisie has through its exploitation of the world market given a cosmopolitan character to production and consumption in every country… In place of the old local and national seclusion and self-sufficiency, we have intercourse in every direction, universal interdependence of nations.… The working men have no country. We cannot take from them what they have not got … National differences, and antagonisms between peoples, are daily more and more vanishing, owing to the development of the bourgeoisie, the freedom of commerce, to the world market, to uniformity in the mode of production and in the conditions of life corresponding there to. *Ibid.*: 58)

Hence Marx and Engels claim that the struggle of the proletariat is first a national struggle: 'The proletariat of each country must, of course, settle matters with its own bourgeoisie' (*ibid.*: 49). More generally, Marx and Engels maintain that a common language and traditions, or geographical and historical hornet is sufficient to constitute a nation. It is true that the socialist movement adopted a pragmatic attitude towards the national question from the Second International, under the guidance of Lenin. But this conclusion needs to be qualified in two ways: first, internationalism was never completely abandoned, at least theoretically, as the ultimate goal of socialism; second, a number of influential figures, notably Rosa Luxemburg, continued to stick to an unabashedly internationalist position, at the risk of being politically marginalised within the socialist movement. A brief overview of later debates on the national question will enable us to better judge the positions of the other thinkers of socialism.

Rosa Luxemburg (1871–1919)-Nation as antagonistic interests

The views of Rosa Luxemburg on the national question were shaped under particular circumstances, more specifically, in the context of the political conflict between the Polish Socialist Party (PPS) and the Social Democratic Party of the Kingdom of Poland (SDKP; later the Social Democratic Party of the Kingdom of Poland and Lithuania, SDKPL) – which she founded – on the issue of the independence of Poland. Describing the PPS's pro-independence positions 'social patriotic', Luxemburg opposed the liberation of Poland on the grounds that the future of Polish economic development lay within Russia (Munck, 1986; Löwy, 1998).

More generally, Luxemburg believes that 'the nation as a homogenous Socio-political entity does not exist. Rather, there exist within each nation, classes with antagonistic interests and rights' (cited in Forman, 1998: 89). The national state is a specifically bourgeois formation, a necessary tool and condition of its growth. Given this, to talk about a theoretical 'right of nations' valid for all nations at all times is nothing but a metaphysical cliché, just like the so called 'right to work' advocated by nineteenth-century utopians or the 'right of every man to eat from gold plates' proclaimed by the writer Chernishevsky (Löwy, 1998: 32). According to Luxemburg, only socialism can bring about self-determination of peoples. 'So long as capitalist states exist ... there can be no "national self-determination" either in war or peace' (Luxemburg 1967 [1915]: 61).

This does not mean that Rosa Luxemburg condoned national oppression. Rather, for her, national oppression is only one form of oppression in general, which is a product of the division of societies into antagonistic classes. The task of the proletariat is to abolish the very root of the system of oppression, namely the class society. 'Since all forms of oppression are derived from the need to sustain class divisions, the emanci-pation from class societies will necessarily bring about the end of oppression of nations' (Nimni, 1991: 53). Hence Luxemburg's position was anti-nationalist, and not anti-nationality. She drew a clear line between opposition to persecution and oppression, and support for nationalism. In any case, it was not possible to decide which people suffered the Clear injustice (Forman 1998: 84). The confusion over the question of her position on nationalism and nationality was further made clear by the interference by V. I. Lenin.

Vladimir Ilyich Lenin's (1870–1924)-Right to self determination

Lenins views on the national question were diametrically opposed to those of Luxemburg. If we want to grasp the meaning of national self-determination, Lenin argues, we need to stop juggling with legal definitions or inventing abstract definitions, but examine the historical– economic conditions of national movements, which were intimately linked with the victory of capitalism over feudalism. 'From the standpoint of national relations, the best conditions for the development of capitalism are undoubtedly provided by the national state'. This leads Lenin to distinguish between two periods of capitalism, the period of the collapse of feudalism and absolutism when the national movements attract mass support and the period of the fully formed capitalist states characterised by a highly developed antagonism between the bourgeoisie and the proletariat – 'the eve of capitalism's downfall'. The proletariat should support national movements in the first phase to secure national peace and to further the cause of international revolution, and reject those in the second phase as these represent the interests of the bourgeoisie and the particular nation they belong to:

> Insofar as the bourgeoisie of the oppressed nation fights the oppressor, were always, in every case, and more strongly than anyone else, in favour, for we are the staunchest and the most consistent enemies of oppression. But insofar as the bourgeoisie of the oppressed nation stands for its own bourgeois nationalism, we stand against. We fight against the privileges and violence of the oppressor nation, and do not in any way condone strivings for privileges on the part of the oppressed nation. (*Ibid.*: 227–8)

Lenin firmly believes that the socialists would play into the hands of the bourgeoisie, feudal landlords and the oppressor nation if they fail to support the right to national self-determination. This support is not 'practical' as the critics argue. National demands are always subordinated to the interests of class struggle, and that is why 'the proletariat confines itself, so to speak, to the negative demand for recognition of the right to self-determination, without giving any guarantees to any nation, and without undertaking to give anything at the expense of another nation' (*ibid.*: 226). A final important aspect of Lenin's contribution to Marxist thinking on the national question, and probably the one with the greatest influence on contemporary theories of nationalism is his theory of imperialism. With it, Lenin adds an international dimension to his discussion of the right to national self determination. Lenins attributes to self determination and national struggle was further modified by Otto Bauer and Karl Renner, the Austro-Marxists.

Austro-Marxists-Co-operation and Co-existence

Lenin's position also differed from that of Austro-Marxists like Otto Bauer (1881–1938) and Karl Renner (1870–1950) who were trying to prevent the constituent nationalities of the multinational Austro-Hungarian Empire from seceding by granting them 'national–cultural autonomy'. This would enable national communities to be organised as autonomous units or sovereign collectives, whatever their residential location within the empire. The model proposed by Bauer and Renner stressed the need to separate the nation and the state, thus challenging the intuitive assumption that national self-determination required the establishment of independent nation-states.

Bauer's contribution to Marxist thinking on the national question was also not limited to the concept of 'national-cultural autonomy'. His monumental The Question of Nationalities and Social Democracy (2000 [first edition, 1907]) was the first attempt to theoretically engage with the issue of nations and nationalism from a Marxist perspective. For Bauer, the nation is 'a community of character that grows out of a community of destiny rather than from a mere similarity of destiny'. This community of character that is the nation is the product of various modernising processes, including the breakdown of peasant subsistence farming and the following uprooting of the rural population by capitalism, the drawing of isolated rural areas into regional economic relationships which in turn led to the homogenisation of various dialects. Bauer also claims that the national culture is shaped by the contribution of various classes. In a socialist society, conflicts among different nationalities will cease, because antagonistic relations are based upon class divisions; once class divisions are removed, national distinctions will give rise to cooperation and coexistence. This position stood distinct from the line taken by Lenin and Rosa Lexemberk. As such, the Stalin took up the debate and contradicted Bauer.

Joseph Stalin (1879–1953)-Sovereign and Equality principles

It was Joseph Stalin who took Bauer to task for his solution to the nationalities problem. In stark contrast to Bauer's, Stalin's definition of the 'nation' was unashamedly objectivist: 'a nation is a historically evolved stable community and of a common language, territory, economic life and psychological make-up manisfested in the community of culture' (cited in Heater, 1998: 64). Moreover, the nation is: a historical category belonging to a definite epoch, the epoch of rising capitalism. The process of elimination of feudalism and development of capitalism was at the same time a process of amalgamation of people into nations. For Stalin, the right to self-determination entails that only the nation itself has the right to determine its destiny, that no one has 'the right forcibly to interfere in the life of the nation, to destroy its schools and other institutions, to violate its habits and customs, to repress its language, or curtail its rights' (cited in Forman, 1998: 129).

But national sovereignty is not the only way to express this right: self-determination means that a nation can arrange its life according to its will. It has the right to arrange its life on the basis of autonomy. It has the right to enter into federal relations with other nations. It has the right to complete secession. Nations are sovereign and all nations are equal. (*Ibid.*) This defence of federalism and autonomy was to become the backbone of the official nationalities programme in the Soviet Union, which was guided by the philosophy of 'socialism in one country'. The central goal of the programme was to create the conditions which would lead to the peaceful coexistence of a variety of nations within a single proletarian state. It is pointed out that in addressing the dynamics of nationalism, Marxism failed considerably. The same is true of classical liberalism too.

4. Classical Liberalism

John Stuart Mill (1806–73)-primacy of individual

The renowned political theorist, J. S. Mill was probably the first major liberal thinker to engage directly with the practical and theoretical problems posed by nationalism. For Mill: a portion of mankind may be said to constitute a nationality if they are united among themselves by common sympathies which do not exist between them and any others – which make them cooperate with each other more willingly than with other people, desire to be under the same government, and desire that it should be governed by themselves or a portion of themselves exclusively.

This feeling of nationality may be the result of a variety of causes – race, descent, shared language and religion; but above all, it is the 'identity of political antecedents: the possession of a national history, and consequent community of recollections; collective pride and humiliation, pleasure and regret, connected with the same incidents in the past' that creates a sense of nationality (*ibid.*). Where the sentiment of nationality exists, Mill argues, 'there is a prima facie case for uniting all the members of the nationality under the same government, and a government to themselves apart. This is merely saying that the question of government ought to be decided by the governed'. Such a liberal idea of giving primacy to the individual was equally upheld by Lord Acton, within the specific historic backdrop of Europe.

Lord Acton (1834–1902). Inclusive and perfect civil society

For Lord Acton, the whole concept of the rights of nationalities is a historical novelty; they were not recognised by governments in the old

European system, nor asserted by the people. Lord Acton believes that individual freedom is better maintained in a multinational state. 'Inferior races are raised by living in political union with races intellectually superior. Exhausted and decaying nations are revived by the contact of a younger vitality.' In that sense, the greatest enemy of the rights of nationality is in fact the modern theory of nationality, which makes the state and the nation commensurate with each other. He concludes: If we take the establishment of liberty for the realisation of moral duties to be the end of civil society, we must conclude that those states are substantially the most perfect which, like the British and Austrian Empires, include various nationalities without oppressing them. Those in which no mixture of races has occurred are imperfect; and those in which its effects have disappeared ... The theory of nationality, therefore, is a retrograde step in history. (*Ibid.*: 153–4)

Apart from all these narratives and discourses, as it was mentioned elsewhere there were many further debate on nationalism by different scholars at distinct stages of time. However, a review of such details are not in the look out of this paper since the subject matter is with respect to the Indian Nationalism and its inner contradictions. At the same time, it goes without saying that vibrancy and earnest attempts made by European scholars of all time did marvelous impact on the subsequent quest for nationalism by which most of such states subscribed to the civic and secular mode of nationalism. Such a version of nationalism on these states prerequisite the developmental pattern not only in the case of democratic paces but also in ecónomic advancements.

No doubt these waves did spill over to the rest of the world. Along with this, when the states in Asia and Africa were destined with colonial legacy, their struggles for self determination and fight for freedom attained more vigorous forms and this gave the nationalist moorings a sharper edge to patriotism of the respective societies.

5. Indian Nationalism

Indian Nationalism has undergone several phases of transition. Such transions are underpinned by changing ideological and historical backdrops. It evolved from spiritual nationalism, extreme religious nationalism, cultural nationalism and nationalism based in humanism and internationalism and hyper [or injected] nationalism of the contemporary times. The historical narratives on the earlier themes are well supported by the dominant liberal ideological backdrop. As such this paper further takes the position that when liberal democracy was strong in the political discourse in India, Indian political process As well as the nationalist notions were within the limits of liberal tradition, whereby it rejected all sorts of narrow and extremist manifestations of nationalism. However, in the subsequent political contexts and developments when the liberal thinking and values began to fade away there emerged more vehement and aggressive nationalism in India. The emergence of modern Hindutva politics and their advocacy for extreme Hindu nationalism is just an expression of this historical reality.

The emergence of Indian nationalism could be brought under three distinct broader categories. The first category of writings explain about the origin of the Indian nationalism on the basis of native institutions. The second narratives rely on their explanation that Indian nationalism emerged as a result of the contact with Great Britain. Further, the third category of writings comprises of British influence but these writings regard British influence as harmful, baneful and unfavourable for India. In these variant narratives scholars are of the view that Indian nationalism was developed by the Aryans. Indian scholars like V. V. S. Aiyar and K. M. Panikkar are of the view that Aryans established states in ancient India. These scholars argue about the political unity of India during Mauryan and Gupta dynasty. In this way their version is fully focused on the Hindu states before British colonial government.

In the writings of first category, it appears that India was not a stranger to democratic institutions. These writings focus on the unification of ancient India on the basis of religion and culture. The second group of writings, emphasis on the development of Indian nationalism by the influence of British rule. The scholars of second category are of the view that Indian political ideas are the reflection of those concepts that had grown up in Britain and became part of Indian tradition. Scholars like S. W. Ali and Albion Banerji are of the view that the nationalism under, INC was the product of British rule. Tagore argues that it is to the rule and domination of England with its strictly political attitude that the development of a belief in our eventual destiny should be ascribed (McCully, 1935. 295-314). These writings limelight about the emergence of Indian nationalism because of British policies such as, education policy, economic policy, political policy and social policy etc. The third category of writings comprise scholars like Pramatha Nath Bose, H. P. Ghose, S. S. Dey and M. R. Parakh. These scholars find the reasons behind the emergence of Indian nationalism because of British policies but they are different of second group of scholars in this sense that they find British policies oppressive for Indian Nationalism is one of the most debatable topics in academic as well as political institution in world around.

Indian national movement was a product of nationalism itself in India. It is a debatable issue that did nationalism emerge at first in Europe or Indian society had the notion of nationalism before colonial period? But in spite of this debate, it has become clear that nationalism came in debate in India during colonial period. Many Indian thinkers and leaders gave their view on nationalism during colonial period. The specific discourse on nationalism during the colonial periods were fully focused on certain themes which were more or less reflective of the dominant and upcoming liberal democratic values and ethos. A brief narrative on the same would reflect the nature and core of such a discourse.

I. Spiritual Nationalism

It was Swami Vivekananda who advocated spiritual nationalism by forging the linkages between religion and nationalist sentiments in India. His concept became popular when he participated in "Parliament of Religion in 1893 at Chicago when he stated that India was the center of the world's spirituality. He had taken a critical view of the notion of spirituality and accepted that many problems in India, like untouchability and exploitation were existing, but he took a position that that these problems could be solved through spirituality. Vivekananda was not against taking ideas from other countries but he suggested that Hindus must not give up their religion. Swami Vivekananda recognised the importance of INC but was of the view that awakening of the nation should not only be limited to political and social movements. For Vivekananda, it was awakening of religion which would provide nationalism with vitality. He believed that Indian nationalism could be effective as a mass movement only if it acquired a religious content. For Vivekananda, Hinduism was tolerant and broadminded. In this way, Vivekananda tried to relate Hinduism and spirituality with Indian nationalism Gohkale (1964, 35-42). He related Hinduism with spirituality on the presumption that it stood for Universalism and brotherhood. This implies that Vivekananda's spiritual nationalism was far away from the connotation of Hindu nationalism or Hindutva ideology being practiced by the right wing political parties and fundamentalist groups in contemporary India.

Swami Dayananda Saraswathi, the founder of Aryasamaj gave an indigenous orientation to Indian Nationalism. He developed the concept of swaraj and said 'swaraj is our birth right'. He totally rejected the European notions and its influences. On the other hand he advocated a moral and ethical state, opposed to the notion of the western concept of state. Equally, he put forward the concept of Swaraj, and subsequently the term became the slogan of Indian National Congress in the Culcutta Session. He established the Arya samaj, which subsequently became the most powerful catalyst to initiate social, religious and educational movements to further indigenous nationalism. In short his notion of nationalism was purely national and the core values it carried was internationalism at par.

Bankim Chandra Chattergy, the Bengali writer and nationalist was a pioneer in Indian nationalism and was mainly responsible for the Hindu revival in the wake of freedom movement. He strongly believed that India could rise only through nationalism. He was much influenced by the European ideas and French Revolution. He belied that English education and liberal ideology could awaken and revive the Hindu society. Unlike the European forms of nationalism, he believed that Indian nationalism could take shape on the ideal of love and well being of all. All these ideas were well expressed in his novel 'Anantda Math' and through the song 'Vande Mataram'. Bankims writings gave a new lease to the revival of Indian nationalism and Hindu revivalism.[5]

Thus, the spiritual nationalism advocated by Bankim Chandra was also purely based on love and moral principles and it had nothing to do with the narrow notions nationalism. Apart from this spiritual spill over when the British colonial hegemony was taking strong roots in India, some of the intellectuals moved towards the process of mobilising the masses by appealing for the cultural revival. In this process some of them resorted to extremist and hard core options and yet some others used cultural and religious symbols.

II. Cultural and Religious Nationalism

The demarcation between cultural nationalism and religious nationalism was very much thin in earlier periods. This was primarily due to the dominance of liberal democratic values and appeal the early nationalist leaders had carried with them. Ironically some of these symbols of cultural and religious icons used for mobilisational purpose had brought in different results in two different political and ideological contexts. The period when the Indian National Congress was dominated by the liberal and moderate thinking some of the critics came out with their extreme political positions. Savarkar was a revolutionary and extremist leader of Indian national movement who first raised the question of Hindu Anti-Colonialist notion of Nationalism. He had close association with Hedgewar and Golwalkar, who were instrumental in instigating Hindu religious sentiments and rigorous organisational built up in the name of Rastriya Swayam Sevak Sangh. Both these leaders had paved the seeds for sprouting vigorous Hindu religious sentiments where by they dreamt of a Hindu Rashtra or Akhanda Bharat.

However, Savarkar was more inclined towards the anti-colonial moves and he took religion only in its literal sense alone. After the rebellion of 1857, many Indian intellectuals, philosophers, novelists, spiritual leaders, reformers and poets emerged in India who cultivated Hindu anti-colonial nationalist discourse. The ideology of this group was known as extremism. Savarkar came with the contact of extremist leaders during swadeshi movement of 1905. In 1906, he went to London to study law. Savarkar established "Abhinava Bharat Society in London which organised a lecture on nationalism on the fifteenth anniversary of the outbreak of the rebellion of 1857. Savarkar was arrested in sedition charge. The fire he bequeathed behind was further used by the contemporary political leaders of India in the name of Hindutva.

In fact, Savarkar is considered as the center of gravity of Hindu nationalism. He was the first extremist leader who did not hesitate to use violence against British government. He was one of the most important propagators of Hindu Rashtra. His view on nationalism and Hindutva can be seen in his book, 'Hindutva: Who is a Hindu?' which he wrote in 1923. For national Unity, Savarkar considered three things very important. These three things were geographical unity, racial features and common culture. Savarkar did not believe in Hindu religion but he focused on the Hindu culture. For Savarkar, Hindu is one who lives in the area beyond the Indus river, between the Himalaya and Indian Ocean.[6] Significantly Savarkar also was not looking at the people on religious basis, he prompted Hindu nationalism on the basis of his geo graphical and cultural congruences.

During Swadesi movement of 1905, leaders like Aurobindo joined the extremist wing of the INC. His political philosophy was based on Bande Mataram and had a spiritual imperative for the motherland (Singh, 1990/ 1991: 122-126). For him nationalism was not political programme but a religion that has come from God. He believed that being a nationalist one becomes an instrument of God. He exhorted the people to uphold the Snadhana Dharma. He had specified that when such dharma declines the nation itself declines. Hence it is the duty of every one to see that the Dharma is maintained properly. Infact Aurobindo's concept of nationalism in a way promoted Indian national movement in a bigger way.

Bal Gangadhar Tilak was a nationalist leader of Indian national movement. His philosophy of nationalism was rooted in revivalist orientalism. Tilak is considered as the founder of cultural nationalism in India. Tilak articulated his view on nationalism in his two famous magazines, Kesari and Mahratta. His nationalism was based on strong cultural and religious revival of Hinduism. And, for the revival of cultural nationalism, Tilak started religious Ganapathi festival in 1893 and introduced Shivaji festival in 1896. With the help of these two festivals, Tilak tried to mobilise masses. In this way, Tilak focused on cultural nationalism (Gnaneshwari, The basic difference between the approaches of Svarkar and Talak on Nationalism was that when Savarkar used religion as a catalyst for cementing Hindutva ideology through extremist options, Tilak used the symbols of Hinduism for mobilising the masses. In fact, the mobilisational strategy of Tilak was fully used by the later right wing BJP leaders in India for political mobilisation in the name of Hindutva politics. However, the idea of Liberal democracy was spreading its fragrance and its impact was so profound on the Indian elites who could get in touch with the western ideas. Such elites and intellectuals crossed the national boundaries of nationalism and thought of cultural Internationalism.

III. Cultural Internationalism

Rabindranath Tagore was a poet of Bengal who participated in Indian national movement through his writings. He wrote a book 'Nationalism' (1917), in which he expressed his view on nationalism.[7] He wrote about nationalism in the West, Japan and in India. Tagore writes about the culture and values in ancient India which lost their relevance with the passing of time. He makes distinction between the West and India. According to him, India's homes, fields, temples of worship, schools, simple laws and peaceful administration belonged to her. Tagore writes about the nation. According to Tagore "a nation is that aspect which a whole population assume when organised for a mechanical purpose (Tagore, 1917:19) Tagore names nation as the organisation of politics and commerce. Explaining about the nations, Tagore states that Mughals and Pathans were human races, not nation. In present time, we can love or hate them, fought for them or against them or we can complain that the Empire, they created, we also had equal share. But now, we have to deal not with kings or human races but with a nation-we, who are no nation ourselves. Writing about the nationalism in India, Tagore argues that our problem is not political but social. He states that this problem is not only in India but among all nations. Present politics is dominated by western ideas and India is trying to copy the same ideas.

Indians must be remember that European had their racial unity, they has insufficient natural resources, therefore, their civilisation had naturally taken the character of political and commercial aggressiveness (*Ibid.* 11-155).

Mahatma Gandhi was one of the most important leaders of Indian national movement who also have taken specific position on nationalism based on certain basic values. As it was known, Gandhi's political philosophy was first developed in South Africa. In fact, Gandhi formulated his political philosophy in South Africa and practiced it in India. Gandhi explains his view on nationalism and internationalism. He writes that he is patriotic because he is human. According to Gandhi, one cannot become internationalist without being nationalist. Gandhi never saw nationalism as an evil. He says that narrowness and selfishness are evils. Gandhi is of the view that there should be the feeling of brotherhood among men of different countries. He says that our nationalism should not be a danger for other nations.[8]

However Tagore did not agree with Gandhi's nationalist view. Tagore could see only violence and greed in nationalism. When Gandhi launched non-cooperation movement in 1920, Tagore stated that Gandhi was playing with fire. Nevertheless, Gandhi rejected violent nationalism. Gandhi used the terms like Swaraj, Swadeshi and Indian civilisation instead of nation. Gandhi believed in Internationalism. He was of the view that internationalism is possible only when peoples of different countries will organise and be able to act as one man. In this sense, Gandhi's nationalism was broad. Hardiman says Gandhi's Nationalism was broad and catholic (Hardiman, 2003: 12-17). In fact his concept on Nationalism was based on Ahimsa, Karmayoga, Ram Rajya, Tapasya and Moksha. In short, Gandhi's idea of nationalism was inclusive of all positive values. Gandhi even believed that Indian nationalism had golden opportunity to teach something new to the world. The model of a functioning multi-lingual and multi-religious nation. Thus, his nationalism was not directly hatred or fear towards another ethnic, religion. Gandhi said; "My idea of nationalism is that my country may become free, that if need be the whole of the country may die, so that the human race may live. There is no room for race hatred there. Let that be our nationalism". Thus, Gandhi too rooted his notion of nationalism in Internationalism, peace and Ahimsa.

IV. Secular Nationalism Nehru and the Left wing

Jawahar Lal Nehru's concept of Nationalism is the bi-product of his understanding of the world history as well as that of Indias past. He attempted to interpret the ideology of colonialism and anti-colonialism and woven a path fully believed in liberal democracy. As such his approach to nationalism was not a blind notion but a synthesis of socio-economic realities of the world as well as that of India. Since the modern states were closely interacting intimately with one another no nation could be an island. At the same time the old heritage of India as well as that of any nation belongs to the humanity. Thus, he provided a secular theoretical frame to nationalism itself. Therefore, he was critical of national self assertion which turned in to chauvinism, aggressiveness and hostilities towards other nations.

For Nehru, nationalism was negative manifestation. Nehru had internationalist approach on the place on nationalism. Nehru was of the view that our problems could be solved only after having worldwide thinking. Nehru was of the view that there was connection between world's events and Indian national problems. In this way, Nehru considered nationalism as negative force (Dash, 1958: 63-67). In 1939 Nehru had said, "Nationalism is in ill odour today in the West and has become the parent of aggressiveness, intolerance and brutal violence". Thus, it is evident that Nehru had contemplated the notion nationalism in a more secular and broader way where by all issue could be sorted out in an inclusive approach. This implied that he was against all narrowness, exclusiveness and selfish orientation of nationalism, which according to him would lead to dormented growth of mind. Hence he believed that Indian nationalism form its beginning will be based on universal values, peace, liberalism and rationalism.

The position of left wing socialists were not basically different from that of the views expressed by liberal democrates. In fact, they look at the concept from the anti-colonial, national class divisions. Their position was fully based on their notions of national self-determination, popular sovereignty and social equality. Their nationalist position was also embedded with anti-imperialism and national liberation movements of the period. Fundamentally the left wing nationalism was contradictory to the notions of the right wing nationalism intact.[9]

However, the Marxist perspective of the Indian nationalism was some what distinct from the earlier notions held by the other proponents of Indian nationalism. The Marxist view looks at Indian nationalism as a product of class struggle led by the urban middle class for the purpose of replacing the colonial power and to occupy the space. Finally, both the concepts of Marxism and nationalism rests in incompatible philosophical domains. Nationalism is based upon the assumption that most fundamental divisions of human kind are the many vertical cleavages that divide the people in to ethno-national groups. However, the Marxist position is that the most fundamental human divisions are horizontal class that cut across national groups.[10]

Therefore, the Indian left wing took the freedom struggle as part of the national liberation struggle taking place elsewhere in the world. In fact this generalisation of the freedom struggle put the CPI in dock that subsequently there was political allegation that the Indian left had betrayed the national freedom struggle. [11] However, the leftist position of opposition to the Quit India movement was part of its position to support the British war effort after Soviet Union was under attack.

Independence and After

The INC position on Nationalism was very vell defined by its earlier leaders and the party has maintained the track of keeping its parity while remaining in power. In this regard official posture the party following was the one which the Grand old man of India detailed pretty early itself. Dada Bhai Naoroji, during his presidential address at the congress session, 1893, Loahor had made the position very clear. In the session he said… "whether I am a Hindu, a Mohammedan, a Parsi, a Christian or any other creed, I am above all an Indian. Our country is India and our nationality is Indian"[12]. Being a liberal democratric party the INC did follow the footprints put forward by the national heroes and its own leaders of yester years. Infact, that was the beauty of Indian democracy as well. Different sections of people, the minorities, deprived sections youths, women, farmers etc across the State boundaries queued up behind the INC and it became its strength as well.

After Independence the nation was ruled by Indian national congress continuously for a period of six decades, where by the INC had maintained its liberal democratic tradition of the great freedom fighters with respect to the nationalism. As such the party was committed to look at the nation in its diversity and accepted the plurality of the nation while taking positions of nationalism. In short, the INC took its nationalist position from a secular, democrati and rational approach. The leadership changes after the assassination of Mrs Gandhi as well as Rajib Gandhi brought sea changes in the nationalist perspectives of the ruling party at the center. Though the minority non-Congress Governments came to power during the intermittent periods, they also followed the same secular nationalist path of the INC. Even the Vajpayee Government was not an exception to this.[13]

However, the fall of the Congress party led the right wing forces to come to power and as detailed elsewhere, by 2014 a new wave of BJP with strong Hindutva drive took the mantle at the center. The rise of Prime Minister Narendra Modi, in fact kept the possibility of INC bouncing back at the center almost impossible. He became the most charismatic and unchallenging leader of the party and when the next general election is round the corner in 2024, its almost sure that unless miraculous curative measures are undertaken by the INC, Prime Minister Modi will make a third time Government.

No doubt the Victory of the BJP is open and through democratic process. However, the BJP's emergence created some sort of imbalances to the democratic fabric of the nation and more precisely to the constitutional values and moralities. The ruling party could make all these possible by way of their meticulous strategies with respect to induce hyper nationalism among the masses, ridden in poverty and illiteracy.

V. Hyper Nationalism

The dawn of twenty-first century witnessed to the unusual phenomenon of Globalisation whereby the whole world has been reduced to the level of a village. Equally, erosion of boundaries and regional groups and associations also tuned out to be a reality. If these are of greater importance to a more universal and global moral well being, the phenomenon also led to the tendency of turning back to the rigid postures of parochial nationalism, at least in some regions where democratic development and paces of growth takes a back seat. The period also witnessed to the revival of fundamentalist and narrow parochial forces in the different regions where such forces took more aggressive and vigorous come back. The new realities of globalisation and its intrinsic affinity with the market forces did accelerate the trend whereby a new lease of fundamentalist groups attempt to capture either power or did influence the decision-making process on a larger proposition. The powerful presence or revival of Ku Klux Klan in the US in the name of white racialism, Talibans in Afghanistan, Nasisttrents in Germany are the new indicators.[14]

The case of South Asia and India are not an exception to this. In all these regions, a majoritarian narrative has sought to subsume each country's diverse political tendencies in to an artificial unity of masquerading as patriotism.[15] In the case of India such a narrative is questioning the earlier liberal democratic notions of nationalism. This is not a confrontation between two versions of nationalism but its between two ideologies in

Indian politics-Liberal democracy and right wing extreme Hindutva ideologies.

The continuous and deliberate narrative on Hindutva nationalism has been in effect since the inception of the BJP Government in 2014. This was a deliberate move meticulously made by the triangular nexus-Corporates-Media and Government. The present BJP government keep on pushing such narratives that the individuals or groups that criticize the Government are a threat to the unity and sovereignty of India. Equally, the mainstream media channels, controlled and indirectly influenced by the Government continue sharing pro government propaganda and biased arguments rather than neutral and independent reporting on matters related to the Kashmir issue, Anti-minority violences, farmers protest, political protests of Students in the University campuses, Dalit issues etc. Equally they use some Hindu Icons and symbols for protecting and writing the scripts for aggressive Hindutva nationalism. According to KanchaIlayya such narrative is milling around Pakistan, Muslims and Dalits and Universities.[16]

A closer observation of such narrative reveals that the BJP has been systematically trying to use some religious images and symbols for articulating the Hindutva ideology and its consolidation in to majority vote banks. Over the last decade the images like Kashmir, Article 370, National security, surgical strike, border clashes, cow, cow dung and its urine, Senkol or the ceremonial sceptre, the inauguration of parliament by a traditional Hindu rituals by the priests and their official hosting, Ayodhya and Ram Temple construction and of late its inauguration by Prime Minister Modi etc were some of the themes which speak the way the BJP try to invoke the majority community sentiments with the interior motive of consolidating the vote bank. Interestingly against the political interference of the Modi Government, Puri Sankaracharya Swami Nishchalananda Saraswati came out with open protest that what the government is doing is not desirable and unconstitutional.[17]

Equally, when the constitution speaks that spreading of science and scientific temper is the obligation on the part of the citizen, some responsible office bearers and top level leaders of the party utter absolute nonsenses in the name of Hindu beliefs. The BJP leader and former Uttarakhand Chief Minister Trivendra Signh Rawat, Madhya Pradesh Pro term Speaker Rameswar Sharma, Madhya Pradesh Culture Minister Usha Thakur BJP MP pragya Thakur etc came out in public and uttered idiotic and nonsense in tackling Corona viruses when the country was under the severe pandemic threat.[18] They used unscientific and idiotic logic through Hindu icons like cow urine, Shankh and holy smoke for getting rid of the virus. Normally, as a reaction to this often communal rift, violence and murder takes place. In such instances it's the minority community or the Dalits or other downtrodden sections who were often victimised.

Politically, the drive destabilises the democratic tradition of the nation and questions even the ethos of the constitution itself. A counter-narrative to this Parochial drive is nothing but going back to the values of Democracy upheld by the Constitutional framers and National heroes. The BJP do realise this danger and therefore, as part of their narrative of hyper nationalism, they do exhume the great freedom fighters from their graves and question their real motives. Unfortunately the drive, in some quarters led to glorify the Murder of Mahatma Gandhi and constructing a temple for Godsay in Maharashtra. Another leader who was constantly being attacked is Jawaharal Nehru. Actually, BJP wanted to de-construct these national leaders and replace them with their Hindutva ideologues and stalwarts. This is the systematic way of de-ideologizing the Indian society from its liberal democratic foundations and traditions in the name of hyper nationalism.

6. Conclusion

Thus the message is very much clear. The discourse on Indian nationalism passed through various stages and phases. It embraced internationalism, classical nationalism, aggressive nationalism, patriotism and in contemporary times hyper nationalism. During its two terms in office, BJP could successfully deploy various strategies of injecting artificial nationalism by variety of means. In a society where the plural and heterogenous millions of population live in poverty, illiteracy and unemployment, its easy to sow the seeds of hatred and division among them. Today it's very much open that BJP and Prime Minister Modi represents nothing but the Hindutva ideology. Resorting of such an ideology in a nation which is fully plural and diverse is almost impossible unless and until such diversity and pluralism is fully emersed in to a single entity. The geographical and cultural diversity of the nation naturally will put this task difficult for the party. That is why BJP's victory is often limited to the regional contexts. This reality is not fully understood by either the Congress or the other opposite parties. For, these parties are even now not coming out of their own shells of parochial and partisan weakness and interests.

Unfortunately, even Congress party some times try to emulate the BJP style of maneuvering the majority community in India, which further digs its own fall. Unless and until this realisation happens to the opposition,

BJP will rule the roof of Indian politics. Perhaps that would be at the cost of the brilliantly crafted constitution of the nation and its values and morality enshrined and ensured by its architect Dr B. R. Ambedkar. In fact Ambedkar's warning on the safety of the constitution turns out to be prophetic when he said;

"... however good a constitution may be, its sure it turn out bad because those who are called to work it happen to be a bad lot. However, bad a constitution may be, it may turn out to be good if those who are called to work it happen to be a good lot..."[19]

In this prophetic observation and keen insight in to the frame-work of our constitutional obligation, where does, really our Pime Minitser Modi fits himself in to? Only time can tell us and lets hope that we need not wait for a longer period, the common Indian people are basically secular and democratic to the core. The Lok sabha election results of 2024 underlines the same.

Notes

1. Brij B. Khare, Indian Nationalism; The political Origin, Indian Journal of Political Science, Vol. 50, No. October-December, 1989, p. 1.
2. Heimsath, C.M. [The idea of Nationalism and Hindu social reform, Princeton University. New Jercy, 1964, p. 133.
3. Hayes, C. J. H, Essays on Nationalism, New York, 1926, p. 10.
4. Anderson, B. (1998), The Spectres of Comparison: Nationalism, Southeast Asia and the World, London Verso.
5. For a detailed discussion on his view on nationalism see, Sujay Mondal, Re-visiting Hindu Nationalism;Perspectives of Bankim Chandra, Journal of Indian Council of Philosophical Research, 37[43] December 2019.
6. See for details, Jaffrelot. C, [ed.] Hindu Nationalism A Reader, Princeton University Press, 2007.
7. Tagore, Rabindranath. Nationalism. Penguin Random House India, 2017.
8. Gandhi, MK., Hind Swaraj, Raj paul & Sons, 2009, Delhi, 2015th edition. p, 211.
9. Custodi. J, [2020] 'Nationalism and populism on the left' Nations and National.
10. Joginder Singh Sanklani, Marxist Perspective on Nationalism and the National Question; A theoretical perspective. Indian Journal of Political Science, Vol. 70. No. 32009, pp. 719-25.
11. For a detailed discussion on the theme please see, Madhavan Kutty, CPI and Quit India Movement, Economic and Political Weekly, Vol. 47, Issue no 15, 14 April, 2012. Also see Prabhat Patnaik, 'The Left in Decline; A Response', EPW, 10 March 2012.
12. For details see, www. inc. in/our-values/nationalism/15/12/2023]

13. [In 1996 and 1998 to 2004 The veteran leader Atal Bihari Vajpayee was in power During the periods he did follow an inclusive policy of taking all sections of people in to confidence and did preserve the constitutional values including its secular ethos.
14. Michael O. Emerson and David Hartman, The Rise of Religous fundmentalism, Annual Review of Sociology, Vol. 32[2006] pp. 127-144.
15. Shashi Tharoor, On the Rise of Mandatory Hyper nationalism, https;//www. the week. in/columns/shashitharoor/2022/02/24.
16. See for details, The Hindu, August 20, 20][and also see, Shashi Tahroor, India became Iiberal;In the name of authenticity, we risk losing decency, The Week,. March 06, 2022]
17. The Hindu, 23/ Jan/2024.
18. See for details, Front line, June 3, 2021.
19. Constituent Assembly Debates, Official Report, Dr Ambedkar's final speech in the Constituent Assembly, Nov.25, 1949, Lok Sabha Secretari at New Delhi, 2014.

References

Anderson, B. (1991) [1983] Imagined Communities: Reflections on the Origin and Spread of Nationalism, London: Verso, 2nd edition.

Anderson, B. (2003) 'Responses', in J. Culler and P. Cheah (eds), Grounds of Comparison: Around the Work of Benedict Anderson, London and New York: Routledge, 225–45.

Avineri, S. (1991) 'Marxism and Nationalism', Journal of Contemporary History, 26(3/4), 637–57.

Bauer, O. (2000) [1924] The Question of Nationalities and Social Democracy (trans. by J. O'Donnell, ed. by E. J. Nimni), Minneapolis: University of Minnesota Press.

Beiner, R. (1999) 'Introduction: Nationalism's Challenge to Political Philosophy', in R. Beiner (ed.), Theorizing Nationalism, New York: State University of New York Press, 1-25.

Benner, E. (1995) Really Existing Nationalisms: A Post-Communist View from Marx and Engels, Oxford: Clarendon Press.

Brand, J. A. (1985) 'Nationalism and the Noncolonial Periphery: A Discussion of Scotland and Catalonia', in E. A. Tiryakian and R. Rogowski (eds), New Nationalisms of the Developed West, Boston: Allen & Unwin, 277–93.

Fichte, J. G. (2001) [1808] 'Addresses to the German Nation', in V. Pecora (ed.), Nations and Identities: Classic Readings, Oxford: Blackwell, 114–27.

Forman, M. (1998) Nationalism and the International Labor Movement: The Idea of the Nation in Socialist and Anarchist Theory, University Park, Pennsylvania: The Pennsylvania State University Press.

Hayes, C. (1931) The Historical Evolution of Modern Nationalism, New York: Macmillan.

Heater, D. (1998) The Theory of Nationhood: A Platonic Symposium, Basingstoke: Macmillan.

Kedourie, E. (1967) 'Not So Grand Illusions', The New York Review of Books, 9 (9).

Kedourie, E. (ed.) (1971) Nationalism in Asia and Africa, London: Weidenfeld & Nicolson.

Kedourie, E. (1994) [1960] Nationalism, Oxford: Blackwell, 4th edition.

Lawrence, P. (2005) Nationalism: History and Theory, Harlow: Pearson Longman.

Lenin, V. I. (2001) [1914] 'The Right of Nations to Self-Determination', in V. Pecora (ed.), Nations and Identities: Classic Readings, Oxford: Blackwell, 220–8.

Löwy, M. (1998) Fatherland or Mother Earth? Essays on the National Question, London and Sterling, Virginia: Pluto Press.

Luxemburg, R. (1967) [1915] The Junius Pamphlet: The Crisis in the German Social Democracy, Colombo: A Young Socialist Publication.

Day, G. and A. Thompson (2004) Theorizing Nationalism, Basingstoke and New York: Palgrave Macmillan.

Munck, R. (1986) The Difficult Dialogue: Marxism and Nationalism, London: Zed Books.

Nairn, T. (1981) [1977] The Break-up of Britain: Crisis and Neo-Nationalism, London: Verso, 2nd edition.

Smith, A. D. (1983) [1971] Theories of Nationalism, London: Duckworth, 2nd edition.

Smith, A. D. (1986) The Ethnic Origins of Nations, Oxford: Blackwell.

Kedourie, E. (ed.) (1971) Nationalism in Asia and Africa, London: Weidenfeld & Nicolson.

O'Leary, B. (1998) 'Ernest Gellner's Diagnoses of Nationalism: A Critical Overview, or, What is Living and What is Dead in Ernest Gellner's Philosophy of Nationalism', in J. A. Hall (ed.), The State of the Nation: Ernest Gellner and the Theory of Nationalism, Cambridge: Cambridge University Press, 40–88.

Kitromilides, P. M. (2001) 'Enlightenment and Nationalism', in A. S. Leoussi (ed.), Encyclopedia of Nationalism, New Brunswick and London: Transaction Publishers, 56–60.

Kitromilides, P. M. and G. Varouxakis (2001) 'The "Imagined Communities" Theory of Nationalism', in A. S. Leoussi (ed.), Encyclopedia of Nationalism, New Brunswickand London: Transaction Publishers, 136–9.

Kohn, H. (1965) Nationalism: Its Meaning and History, New York and Cincinnati: D. Van Nostrand Company.

Kohn, H. (2005) [1944] The Idea of Nationalism: A Study in its Origins and Background (with an Introduction by C. Calhoun), New Brunswick: Transaction Publishers, 60th anniversary edition.

Varouxakis, G. (2001) 'Mill's Theory of Nationality and Nationalism', in A. S. Leoussi (ed.), Encyclopedia of Nationalism, New Brunswick and London: Transaction Publishers, 178–82.

Chapter - 3

State Building in Sri Lanka: Is a Hazy Dream or Lofty Goal?

— Dr Nadeeka Damayanthi Mahamadachchi

1. Introduction

State-building is one of the most prominent topics discussed in national and international political forums, development discourses, and academia in the twenty-first century as a result of the numerous and severe problems caused by a variety of fields, including poor governance, reverse development, and various socio-economic and political problems in many nations (1) As defined by the Organisation for Economic Cooperation and Development (OECD), state-building is "an endogenous process to enhance capacity, institutions, and legitimacy of the state driven by state-society relations" (2). This process should be a proper combination of the establishment of new institutions and the strengthening and reforming of the existing institutions (1, 3). Furthermore, state legitimacy, the political process to deliver effective and efficient services, and state-society negotiation on the state-building strategies are essential components of the state-building process (4). Although state-building discourses consist of many aspects, including resource and technology allocation for capacity building of public sector institutions scholarships pay limited attention and engage in less research to examine factors involved in the well-functioning of government institutions in developing countries. These less focused factors are complex institutional and operational arrangements and conflicts of interest and habits of different stakeholders involved in public service delivery (5, 6). Furthermore, struggles between (political and social) elites and their impact on social changes and political authority are prominent but limitedly focused aspects of the state-building process (7). Therefore, this chapter aims to examine challenges faced by the state-building process in Sri Lanka with a particular focus on the post-1977 period.

Sri Lanka gained independence from the British Empire in 1948 and was governed by the Soulbury Constitution, until the enactment of the first Republic Constitution in Sri Lanka (Ceylon) in 1972 (8). The governance system comprises three tiers, national, provincial and local. The national level consists of the Executive President and the parliament. Both these institutions are directly elected by the citizens' votes. The Executive President is the head of the state, head of the government, chair of the board of cabinet, and the Commander-in-Chief of the armed forces. The second tier of the government consists of nine provincial councils, which is comprises of Governor appointed by the Executive President, Board of Ministers (Chief Minister and four other ministers) and elected members. The third layer of the government: local governments consists of municipal councils (24), urban councils (41), and pradeshiya sabhas (276) which were established under three different legislations of the Central Government.[2] These three type of institutions have more or less similar responsibilities and powers in their jurisdiction.

With the enactment of the Second Socialist Republic Constitution of Sri Lanka in 1977 several governance aspects as well as political factors changed remarkably. Sri Lanka is adiverse country in terms of ethnic, religious, linguistic, and other socio-cultural aspects, such as caste (9). Of the total population (21 million in 2023), approximately 75% are Sinhalese, 11% are Sri Lankan Tamils, 9. 5% are Muslims, and 4% are Indian Tamils. In addition, Sri Lankan population consists of 4. 1% of Sri Lankan Malays, 0. 2 of Burghers/Eurasians, 1% of other ethnic communities such as Veddhas (indigenous people). Moreover, around 69% of the total population are Buddhists, 14% are Hindus, 10% are Islam, and 7% are Christians (10). These variations directly or indirectly intervene in political, socio-economic, and development matters (11).

2. Attempts towards state-building in Sri Lanka

After gained the independence, the successive governments of Sri Lanka have taken various steps to build a state, including establishing the Decentralised Budget and District Political Authority systems in 1973, District Minister System in 1978, Development Councils in1981, Provincial Councils in 1987, and Divisional Secretariat systems in 1992. Furthermore, in order to facilitate providing efficient, effective, and customer-oriented public service thegovernment of Sri Lanka has enacted several acts, such as the Commission to Investigate Municipal Council Ordinance No. 29 of 1947, Urban Council Ordinance No. 61 of 1939, and Pradeshiya Sabha Act

No. 15 of 1987 Allegations of Bribery or Corruption Act No. 19 of 1994 and the Right to Information Act No. 12 of 2017. Subsequently, the government has taken steps to establish particular institutions, such as the Commission to Investigate Allegations of Bribery or Corruption and the Right to Information Commission.

2.1 Key steps towards state-building during the 1970s

In the 1970s, the government of Sri Lanka particularly focused on finding solutions for a lack of responsiveness in administration, poverty, hunger, and unemployment in the country. At the throne speech in 1970, the United Front government envisaged establishing three new institutions to address the limitations of responsiveness of public administration. These institutions were, elected employees' councils, advisory committees in government departments, and peoples committees on a territorial basis (8). Furthermore, the government established the Divisional Development Councils in 1971 to address the unemployment issue in rural areas (12). These councils were comprised of public officers from various departments, including Departments of Agrarian services, Small Industries, Rural Development, Civil Engineering, and Health Services as well as elected leaders of local-level organisations, such as rural development societies, Janatha Committees (Peoples' committees), and village councils (8). Divisional Development Councils were responsible for preparing coordinated development programmes for the area with a mainly focus on employment generation through the use of local resources. These development plans were intended to be carried out by Divisional Development Councils and District Development Councils. However, District Development Councils were not operated; instead, the government established a new institution to operate these plans at the district level: District Planning and Plan Implementation Councils (8).

In 1973, the Sri Lankan government launched the Decentralised Budget System to address the need for more public participation in planning and implementation (13). The Decentralised Budget System mainly focused on enhancing employment opportunities and (food) production in rural areas. Therefore, irrigation works and agriculture-related works were prioritised under Decentralised Budget System. Furthermore, the government introduced the District Political Authority System in 1973 to resolve the immediate food crisis in Sri Lanka (8, 14). The government had appointed a senior member of the National State Assembly of the governing party as the District Political Authority by granting him or her the authority to serve as political head of the district and the chief policy-making authority for development issues (15). The initial objectives of the District Political Authority were to provide leadership for coordinating food production activities in the district and to garner public support and cooperation. In the second phase, however, the District Political Authority commenced to supervise the activities of all government departments that received funds from the Decentralised Budget. At the third phase, the District Political Authority replaces the Government Agent as chair of the District Planning and Plan Implementation Council (8). In 1978, the United National Party government won 5/6 of the seats in Parliament and mended The First Republic Constitution enacted in 1972, resulting in vast changes to every aspect of the governing process as well as socio-economic and cultural practices in subsequent years. A new political institution: the position of Executive President, has been established by The Second Republic Constitution enacted in 1978, and the majority of political authority has become concentrated in this position. By presenting a white paper, the United National Party government launched the District Minister system in 1978. The Second Amendment to the 1972 constitution granting more formal powers to the District Ministers, including formulation of district development plans, preparing the district budget, and monitoring and evaluation of district development plan implementation (8).

2.2 Key steps towards state-building during 1980s

In the 1980s the government of Sri Lanka established two regional based political institutions that were directly involved in the state-building. These institutions were Development Councils in 1981 and Provincial Councils in 1987. The Development Councils were established by replacing 83 town councils and 549 village councils (8, 16). District Development Councils were accountable for planning district development activities, coordinating district activities, preparing district budgets, implementing district programmes, evaluating of performance of district development plans, and spending decentralised budget funds (16). As a remedy for internal (ethnic) conflicts, the Provincial Council system was introduced by the government of Sri Lanka. This was a major sign post in state-building in Sri Lanka, as it took action to devolve power, responsibilities, and functions between the Central government and provincial councils. Consequently, Central Government's functions, responsibilities, and power are divided into three lists: Reserved List (Central Government), Provincial List, and Concurrent List (both the Central Government and Provincial Councils have rights and responsibilities to be involved in matters). In addition to internal conflicts, the provincial council system is expected to address the limitations of public service delivery, and rural development. Another significant attempt towards state-building during the late 1980s was the privatisation or nationalisation of selected public enterprises by emphasising efficient, cost-effective, and accountable public service delivery (17). The deregulation of functions of Sri Lanka Telecom is an example. The privatisation of public enterprises has been continuing since the1990s.

2.3 Key steps towards state-building during 1990s

The establishment of the Divisional Secretariat system in 1992 marked a milestone in state-building in Sri Lanka because it focused on providing efficient, effective, and customer-friendly public service delivery in a single place close to the people. This system also aimed to increase accountability/ responsibility to the people and to implement national and provincial policies at the divisional level (18). The Divisional Secretariat system was established under the Transfer of Powers (Divisional Secretaries) Act No. 58 of 1992. Consequently, the workloads of 23 line ministries have been transferred to the Divisional Secretariats by circular 21/92. These Ministries were, Agricultural Development and Research, Buddhism, Cultural Affairs and News, Defence, Education and Higher education, Environmental and Parliament Affairs, Finance, Fishery and Aquaculture Resources, Food and Corporative, Health and Women's Affairs, Industries, Science and Technology, Labour and Vocational Training, Justice, Land, Irrigationand Mahaweli Development, Policy Planning and Implementation, Electricity and Energy, Portand Naval Affairs, Public Administration, Provincial Councils and Home Affairs, Social Welfare, Tourism and Rural Industries Development, Trade and Commerce, Transport and Highways and Youth Affairs and Sports. The Central Government transferred powers and responsibilities related to many of its public services from the district level to the divisionallevels (18). Of the above 23 Ministries, more than 117 functions/responsibilities had shifted toDivisional Secretariats. Furthermore, with the expansion of the Central Ministries in recent yearsthe workload of the Divisional Secretariats has expanded. Moreover, some functions of theprovincial councils also shifted to Divisional Secretariats. Therefore, Divisional Secretariats became a focal point of public service delivery at the divisional level. Currently, 331 Divisional Secretariats are operated in the country (19).

2.4 Key steps towards state-building after 2000

As emphasized in their election campaign, the 2016 coalition government took measures towards enacting a new constitution to address critical governance issues, such as power of the executive presidency, a lack of accountability, transparency, and responsiveness of the governing system, human right violations, as well as public service delivery (20). The steps towards enacting a new constitution included establishing the Parliament as a Constitutional Assembly and a Steering Committee chaired by the Prime Minister. The Steering Committee was comprised of all parliamentary party leaders and senior members of parliament. In addition the steering committee, the expert council nominated by the parliamentary parties provided assistance in a new constitutional making process (21). Moreover, the Assembly was subdivided into six subcommittees on a variety of topics, including public service, public finance and devolution (22). The Parliamentary steering committee on constitutional reforms published their interim report at the end of 2017 (21). Although this constitution-making process has been going a bit forward it didn't reach the end point. The appointment of a Public Representative Committee (popularly known as the Lal Wijenayake Committee) by the Board of Cabinet Ministers to hear citizens' voices, prepare and submit a recommendation report to the parliament to be addressed by a new constitution was a significant step in the creation of a new constitution. This committee was comprised of 20individuals, including academicians, lawyers, civil society activists, and political activists (23). The significance of the committee lies in the fact that it is the only committee appointed to hearpublic opinion on the annals of constitutional reform in Sri Lanka. The Public Representative Committee on Constitutional Reforms held 58 sittings across the country. Approximately 2, 500 individuals and organisations testified orally and in writing before the committee (23). In addition, more than 1,700 representations were made via email, postal mail, fax, and telephone messages (23). The final report of the committee addressed 22 topics, including public service, public finances and audit, power share, and devolution. The committee prepared and published the report in a very short time of period, under difficult conditions, and with extremely limited resources. The committee presented the final report to the legislature on 10th May 2016 (23).

3. Challenges in state-building in Sri Lanka

Many state-building activities in Sri Lanka face numerous obstacles in the pursuit of their objectives. These variables included political, administrative, and governance elements. Political factors include the politicisation of the governance system, a lack of interest on the part of political leaders to continue the programmes, conflicts between the diverse interests of various actors, and political instability. Administrative factors include the unclear delineation of duties and responsibilities among various stakeholders, as well as the staff's lack of access to a user friendly manual or office instruction. Corruption, a lack of accountability on the part of the government, the media, and the people, as well as communication problems between the government and the citizens, are governance issues that impede the success of state-building initiatives in Sri Lanka. In this section, however, the author concentrates more on political and administrative factors, as these are the key challenges of state-building initiatives in Sri Lanka, and governance issues are discussed interchangeably with political and administrative factors.

3.1 Political factors contribute to the failure of state-building efforts

The politicisation of the governing system and the society is a crucial factor that contributed to the failure of post-independence state-building initiatives and plans in Sri Lanka. Though successive governments had launched a number of programmes and projects to build up the state, the majority of them were introduced and initiated without a proper vision aligned with state-building, because political leaders were more concerned with maintaining their political power and status than providing solutions for issues in public service delivery and governance. For example, in order to build up more responsive public service, the United Front government established the Peoples Committee on a territorial basis in the early 1970s. However, rather than becoming a driving force to resolve local level issues in public service delivery and development planning, these committees became propelling forces in political patronage, and politicisation of public service delivery and development planning at the local level. Because instead of using theprinciple of election, committee members were appointed by the Minister based on their political affiliations (8). Further, the District Political Authority System introduced by the United Front government in 1973 also provides a great example of the politicisation of the state-building process. This system allowed the district level ruling party political leaders to interfere in the statutory work of Government Agents 3 and Divisional Assistant Government Agents 4. As a result of such a situation, staff loyalties of public service have been divided and local level development and welfare priorities have been determined by political favouritism (8). By causing the failure of state-building programmes and initiatives, this context has created an unfavourable and chaotic working environment for public officials. Moreover, unrepresented and under represented social groups being denied an impartial hearing because of political favouritism and divided staff loyalty.

Since 1977, politicisation of the public service, conflicts of diverse interests of political leaders, and political influences on state-building programmes had been increased under the United National Party government. These political factors significantly contributed to the failure of the state-building initiatives, such as the District Minister System. The District Ministers were responsible for the formulation of the district development plan, the monitoring and evaluation of its implementation, the identification of bottlenecks and the initiation of corrective action, as well as oversights of interdepartmental activities. However, rather than focusing on in their responsibilities District Ministers were predominantly involved in the matters that offered enormous opportunities for political patronage to the ruling party political henchmen, such as land, housing, irrigation, and roads (8). The District Minister system advocated a one-party position to the detriment of a large number of individuals outside the systems sphere of influence. The adopted participatory system lacked a grievance-redress mechanism for supporters of opposition political parties without access to the district minister. Moreover, the question arose as to how the district minister, a representative of an electorate (pan of a district), could genuinely represent the desires and requirement of the districts residents (8). 3 The highest level administrative officer at district level 4. The highest level administrative officer at divisional level who directly responsible to the Government Agent.

The establishment of a provincial council system in 1987 is an excellent illustration of the limited motivations of political leaders to continue or support to achieve aims of the state-building initiatives. Although the provincial council system was established as a remedy to internal (ethnic) conflict and development issues in Sri Lanka, successive governments did not demonstrate much interest or commitment to its success. For example, all provincial councils in Sri Lanka have been dissolved by 2019 and yet to be held the election. In addition, despite the fact that The Constitution has devolved responsibility for certain crucial matters of state building, such as the police to provincial councils they have not yet been implemented due to conflicts of various political interest of different groups, including the general public and political parties. Instead of resolving constitutional chaotic: overlapping power, functions, and responsibilities between the

Central Government and provincial councils or strengthening and developing the capacity of provincial councils, the government focused to strength the decentralisation of public service delivery. For example, former President Ranasinghe Premadasa established the Divisional Secretariat System in 1992 by strengthening and expanding the deconcentration system (decentralisation of the Central Governments public administration) in a devolved context (18). Although the Divisional Secretariat system provides the public with an excellent platform for easy access to the majority of Central Government and provincial council services, it has created a mess in the delivery of public services due to administrative issues that will be discussed in section 3.2 of this chapter.

The failure of multiple attempts to enact a new constitution is a significant illustration of the impact of political factors on the failure of state-building initiatives in Sri Lanka. The coalition government's effort to create a new constitution in 2016 was one example. The interimreport of the Parliamentary Steering Committee on new constitution making (2016) should be reflected consensus between political parties on critical governance issues that are required to address by a new constitution. However, various conflicts between the President and the Prime Minister as well as political parties of the coalition government had prevented to build up a consensus between political parties within the parliament (21). Consequently, the interim report of the Parliamentary Steering Committee did not show the required agreement on solutions for issues that were required to address by a new constitution.

Even with such a controversial atmosphere the government requested to draft a discussion paper based on the interim report of the Parliamentary Steering Committee and Sub-committees' reports from the selected expert panel. Subsequently, the expert panel drafted a discussion paper (Draft Zero). Although the 'Draft Zero' was expected to table in the Constitutional Assembly in late 2018, as a consequence of the constitutional crisis 5 the attempt had failed by ending the constitutional making process (20). The 'Draft Zero' paper had been leaked before it table in the Constitutional Assembly and was the subject of extensive discussion, particularly hostile criticism from anti-reform commentators in the local press on several topics, such as nature of state, power sharing, and religion (20). However, the government did not take appropriate steps to offer counter-narratives and therefore reform advocates in civil society were unaware of contents of the 'Draft Zero'paper (21). These political conflicts, which were triggered by the various personal and political agendas of national-level political leaders, had a significant influenced on the failure of enacting a new constitution that used as a key strategy for resolving the issues in state-building process as well as governance. Another major factor in the failure of Sri Lanka's attempt to enact a new constitution was the tensions that arose from citizens divergent interests, attitudes, and lack of awareness regarding government direction towards solutions to crucial challenges in state-building. Citizen strust in the false information increased as a result of the information shared by anti-reform commentators and a lack of government efforts to provide accurate information to the public. Consequently, citizens who believed the information disseminated by anti-reform commentators refrained from expressing their support for a new constitution or influencing the government and political leaders to resolve the issues in the constitution.

3.2 Administrative factors contribute to the failure of state-building efforts

Unclear demarcation of roles and responsibilities between various agencies and actors, and non-user-friendly manuals and office instructions also significantly contribute to the failure 5. On 26 October 2018, President Maithripala Sirisena appointed former president and parliament member Mahinda Rajapaksa as Prime Minister before formally dismissing the incumbent Ranil Wickremesinghe, culminating in two concurrent Prime Ministersof state-building efforts in Sri Lanka (8). The provincial council system exemplifies the difficulties caused by unclear delineation of power, responsibilities, and functions between various levels of government in state-building initiatives. Inefficient and ineffective service delivery, a lack ofaccountability, and numerous clashes between provincial and Central Government agencies on devolved functions and power are the results of unclear demarcation of responsibilities and overlapping of functions. Land, irrigation, and environment-related service delivery are the prominent illustration of this context (16, 18).

Complex institutional, legal, and administrative frameworks are other significant factors that hinder the state-building programmes. The Central Government and provincial councils have established numerous delegated agencies to provide efficient, effective, and customer-oriented service within their respective legal spheres of authority. However, in many cases over lapped responsibilities, functions, and power of these agencies resulting in the duplication of functions and the waste of resources, or the neglect of certain functions as no one takes responsibility. Moreover, this situation led to limit functions, and power of some local level agencies. For example, local government functions and role comes under their legal jurisdictions, such as rural development, poverty alleviation, and certain agricultural responsibilities were limited by various delegated authorities of the Central Government and provincial councils. The Central Governments anti-poverty initiatives, including the Janasaviya programme and the Samurdhi Development Authority, served as examples. Furthermore, instead of local governments, the Central Government and provincial councils use the Divisional Secretariat system as their field-level arms. Furthermore, due to scare of resources, including funds and human resources themajority of local governments unable to perform their duties (24). Moreover, such a situation creates conflicts between various agencies by hindering the effective service delivery. In Sri Lanka, achieving the objectives of state-building initiatives has been hampered by a lack of user-friendly office instructions and manuals, as well as ineffective communication between levels of the government and various agencies. For example, when the Central Government Ministries and other relevant agencies transferred their functions and responsibilities to the Divisional Secretariats, relevant ministries and agencies issued circulars and office instructions to perform duties at the divisional level. However, the staff of the Divisional Secretariats were unable to fathom such instructions mainly due to the non-user-friendly nature of the office manuals and the demands placed on a drained workforce by the sudden influx of a substantial amount of work (8).

4. Conclusion

Despite the fact that successive governments of Sri Lanka have taken a number of measures towards state-building, most of these efforts have been in vain due to a variety of political, administrative, socioeconomic, and cultural factors. Therefore, whatever measures are taken to create a state in Sri Lanka will remain a hazy dream until these political, administrative, and governance issues are resolved.

Notes and References

1. Fukuyama F. Preface. 2004. In: State-Building: Governance and world order in the 21st century [Internet]. Cornell University Press [ix-xvi]. Available from:http://www. jstor. org/stable/10. 7591/j. ctvrf8c1g. 3.
2. Organisation for Economic Co-operation and Development. State Building in Situationsof Fragility-Initial Findings: OECD,; 2008 14 March 2023]. Available from:https://www. oecd. org/dac/fragilestates.
3. Call CT, Cousen EM. Ending Wars and Building Peace: International Responses to War-Torn Societies. International studies perspectives [Internet]. 2008 28

March 2023]; 9(1):[1-21pp.]. Available from: https://doi. org/10. 1111/j. 1528-3585. 2007. 00313. x.

4. Organisation for Economic Cooperation and Development (OECD). Part II: Concepts and Dilemmas of State Building in Fragile Situations: From Fragility to Resilience. OECD journal on development [Internet]. 2009 28 March 2023; 9(3):[1-61 pp.]. Available from:https://www. proquest. com/docview/211874033?accountid=10910&pq-origsite=primo.
5. Fukuyama, F. The Imperative of State-Building. Journal of democracy [Internet]. 2004 23March 2023]; 15(2):[17-31 pp.]. Available from: https://doi. org/10. 1353/jod. 2004. 0026.
6. Fukuyama, F. Weak states and the black hole of public administration. 2004 [cited 13March 2023]. In: State-Building: Governance and world order in the 21st century [Internet]. Cornell University Press [cited 13 March 2023]; [43-91]. Available from:http://www. jstor. org/stable/10. 7591/j. ctvrf8c1g. 5.
7. Akchurina, V. When elites meet: The struggle for power and its social meaning. 2022[cited 17 April 2023]. In: Incomplete state-building in Central Asia: The state as social practice-Critical security studies in the Global South [Internet]. Cham, Switzerland: Palgrave Macmillan, [cited 17 April 2023]; [203-77]. Available from: https://doi. org/10. 1007/978-3-031-14182-9.
8. Nanayakkara, VK. Sri Lankan Structure of Governance. Sri Lanka; Nugegoda.: V. K. Nanayakkara; 2017.
9. Wellalage, NH, Locke, S. Corporate governance, board diversity and firm financialperformance: new evidence from Sri Lanka. International Journal of Business Governance and Ethics [Internet]. 2013 30 March 2023; 8(2):[116-36 pp.] . Available from:https://doi. org/10. 1504/IJBGE. 2013. 054416.
10. Department of Census and Statistics Sri Lanka. Census of Population and Housing. Sri Lanka: Colombo: Department of Census and Statistics-Sri Lanka; 2012.
11. Barter, SJ. ‘Second-order' ethnic minorities in Asian secessionist conflicts: problems andprospects. Asian Ethnicity. 2015;16(2):123-35.
12. Kruse, C. State structure in Sri Lanka. Centre for International Migration and Development Northern and Eastern Provincial Councils Accessed June. 2007;30:2015.
13. Lakshman, W. Developmental role and financing of sub-national units of government: the case of provincial councils in Sri Lanka. Decentralisation and Development of Sri Lanka Within a Unitary State. 2017:33-60.
14. Wijeweera, B. Policy developments and administrative changes in Sri Lanka: 1948-1987. Public Administration Camp; Development (1986-1998). 1989;9(3):287.
15. Withane S. Changing Patterns of Local Administration in Sri Lanka: Loose-Coupling between Planning and Implementation. Canadian Journal of Development Studies/Revue canadienne d’études du développement. 1984;5(2):243-55.
16. Damayanthi, MKN, Nanayakkara VK. Impact of the provincial council system on the small holder agriculture in Sri Lanka. Sri Lanka: Colombo: Hector Kobbekaduwa Agrarian Research and Training Institute; 2008.

17. Jayasuriya S, Knight-John M. Sri Lanka's telecommunications industry: from privatisation to anti-competition?; 2002.

18. Damayanthi, MKN. Devolution versus deconcentration: A study on land service delivery system in Sri Lanka. Bangladesh: North South University; 2011.

19. Centre DM. Divisional Secretariat n. d. [08 May 2023]. Available from:http:// www. dmc. gov. lk/images/pdfs/DIVISIONAL-SECRETARIAT-contact-No. pdf.

20. Ghisad A, Sahay, CD. Sri Lanka's new constitution-A politico-legal challenge Vivekananda International Foundation; 2016 [updated 2020. Available from:https://www. vifindia. org/article/2016. june/20/sri-lanka-s-new-constitution-a-politico-legal-challenge.

21. Welikala, A. Sri Lanka's (un)ending road to a new Constitution: Technical progress, political collapse 2019 [28 April 2023]. Available from: https:// constitutionnet. org/news/sri-lankas-unending-road-new-constitution-technical-progress-political-collapse.

22. Jayasekara, S. New Constitution for Sri Lanka : ten experts working on initial draft Constitution. Daily Mirror. 25 July 2018.

23. Public Representative Committee on Constitutional Reform. Report on Public Representations on Constitutional Reform. 2016.

24. Damayanthi, MKN. Challenges of Local Governments in Rural Development in Sri Lanka. Felicitation volume of Senior Professor Reverent Kandegoda Vimaladhamma Thero: Department of Philosophy, University of Kelaniya, Sri Lanka; 2017. pp. 107-20.

Chapter - 4

Accumulation and Dispossession: Neo-liberal Hindutva Nationalism in Contemporary India

— **Shashikant Pandey**

1. Introduction

Since 1970s and 80s neo-liberal shifts in the global political economy and intertwined developments like liberalisation, globalisation, and privatisation marked the end of an era of state-society relationship. Since early twentieth century Anti-colonial nationalism has been a powerful source and force for liberation throughout which mobilised the diverse and interrelated populations against colonial-imperial rule and this resulted into crystallisation of various nationalities and their further transformation into 'nation-states'. Unlike other historical antecedents of European Nationalism anti-colonial nationalism in Third World societies emerged as pivotal force that drove the struggle for independence and self-determination in the colonised world. Anti-colonial nationalism was deeply rooted in the desire to break free from colonial domination and oppression, and it has played a crucial role in the political, social, and cultural emancipation of many nations in Africa, Asia, and Latin America. Anti-colonial nationalism emerged as a response to the exploitation and dehumanisation inherent in colonial rule. Colonised peoples sought to reclaim their political and economic autonomy, identity, and dignity, which had been suppressed under foreign domination. Frantz Fanon, a seminal figure in anti-colonial thought, argued that the struggle for independence was not merely a political battle but also a profound psychological and cultural revolution. He views "national liberation, national renaissance, the restoration of nationhood to the people, commonwealth: whatever may be the headings used or the new formulas introduced, decolonisation is always a violent phenomenon". Anti colonial nationalism dismantled the entrenched structures of colonial power and reasserted and empowered the humanity of the colonised.

This paper is an attempt to identify the transition of early phases of liberal nationalism in the colonised countries, particularly in India and to contrast it with quite the contrary developments and phenomenon of ethno-cultural, majoritarian communal nationalism masquerading as Hindutva Nationalism in the times of neo-liberal transition of the political economy of India. Paper while situated in the broader discursive terrain of Gramscian concept of Hegemony, identifies the rise of communal nationalism, questioning the Hindutva's claims over Indian nationalism. An attempt is made to examine the ideological structures, constituent elements and the empowering and emancipatory potential of early nationalism in India and to understand how contemporary Hindutva Cultural Nationalism championed by the RSS-BJP along with their range of ancillary organisations, are manifestations of a much deep rooted phenomenon in the political economy of India i.e. increasing control of financialised corporate capital control over the political economy of India. It is argued how contemporary Hindutva Nationalism has emerged as one of the safest and trusted strategy in the hands of corporate capital in their quest for accumulation by dispossession. We shall understand and examine the nature of dispossession since India embarked on the path of neo-liberal globalisation and privatisation.

India since independence and particularly since 1980s has witnessed resurgence of debates and controversies around concepts of 'nation' and 'nationalism'. The decline of Indian National Congress's hegemonic one party dominnance system unleashed the social and ideological conditions and the corresponding social forces that engaged in competing, diverse and competitive ideas on the status of 'nation and nationalism' in India.

Nationalism and neoliberalism are ideologies that significantly impact global politics and economics. While they can sometimes intersect and support each other, more often, they present conflicting visions of how societies should be organised and governed. The ongoing debate between these ideologies reflects broader questions about identity, sovereignty, and the role of the state in economic and social life.

As ideology and politics of modern Indian 'nationalism' evolved and took shape during British colonial era. Since then conceptual contours of the term 'nation' and 'nationalism' has been one of the most debated political categories of Indian historical-political discourse. When Mahatma Gandhi remarked "Indian nationalism is not exclusive, not aggressive, not destructive" he was not just critiquing the western idea of nation and nationalism but was attempting to formulate a quite indigenous notion of syncretic nationalism to suit to the plurality and diversity of India's society, economy and culture under the conditions of colonialism. Political historians have characterised Gandhi's views on nation and natioionalism as "Gandhian Nationalism" which evolved over different phased of anti-colonial struggle. It had different constituents and ingredients and was a mechanism of empowering the disempowered.

On the other hand, Dr Ambedkar had quite different focus points 'of' and 'for' the idea of Indian 'nation' and 'nationalism'. For him 'justice and equality'-social and economic were the cornerstones on which a modern just nation could be built in a historically unequal and deeply hierarchical casteist society. He was highly critical of the hegemonic notions of 'nation' and nationalism. In his monograph 'Annihilation of Caste', he argued "You can not build anything on the foundation of caste. You can not build up a nation. You cannot build up a morality..."

The third stream of nationalism contesting along with liberal and radical perspectives of nationalism is popularly known as 'Hindu Nationalist movement' that had been one the three dominant currents among diverse conceptions of 'nations and nationalisms' under the conditions of coloniality. Hindutva Cultural Nationalism which resurfaced within the mainstream political discourses in 1990s particularly with the formation and ascendence of the Bharatiya Janata Party since 1980 and specially since 1989 when its parliamentary (Lok Sabha) strength rose from 2 in 1984 to 88 in 1989. Since then adherents of Hindutva and their idea of 'Hindu nation' and nationalism had been fiercely contesting to displace the 'secular, multi-cultural Indian nationalism' in favour of an 'ethno-religious' nationalism characterised as "Hindu Rashtra".

Though the idea of Hindu Nationalism took coherent organisational shape with the setting up of Rashtriya Swayam Sevak Sangh (RSS) in 1925 soon after the India's Communist Party was founded in Oct 1920, but as a movement, the idea of revivalist Hindu notion of India preceds back to early nineteenth century renaissance in West Bengal and post-mutiny Hindi speaking belt. When its consciousness was championed by many social reformers.

As Christophe Jefferlot rightly observes that "general public may have discovered Hindu Nationalism in recent years but it had of course already active in indian politics and society for decades; in fact this ism is one of the oldest ideological streams in India".

Theoretical debates around concepts 'nation' and nationalism have acquired such a complexity that in the realm of political theory it is impossible to arrive at a consensus definition of 'nation' and 'nationalism' let alone Indian Nation or nationalism. Range of theoretical perspectives from political economic or Marxian to liberal, neo-liberal, structuralisms, post-modernists, ethno-nationalists to extreme idealist cultural nationalist one, engage with understanding the "difficult dialogue" which is 'national question'.

Its true that political power that 'nationalism' has acquired in post-colonial context marks a lack of historical-political understanding of the phenomenon. The terrain of nationalism exhibits a marked duality-universality of the nationalism on the one hand and the "irremediable particularity of its concrete manifestations" on the other. It would be an examination of the extent to which 'nation' as defined by an eminent theoretician of nation and nationalism Benedict Anderson as "an imagined political community-and imagined as both inherently limited and sovereign."

The phenomenon of 'nationalism' that was considered as "one of the magnificent gifts to the rest of the world" has turned into a "dark elemental unpredictable force of primordial nature threatening the orderly calm of civilised life".

The surprising swing of nationalism to the current salience in the times of corporatist globalisation raises doubts whether nationalism in contemporary times genuinely resonates the aspirations for which 'nationalisms' had been imagined and fought for. We examine how current phase of 'nationalism' is basically a strategic tool of legitimation of corporate class interests led by global finance capital and how they deploy and continue to reinvent nationalism to suit their political strategic aims of garnering support for neo-liberal accumulation on the one hand and dispossession on the other.

2. Nationalism as emancipatory discourse Vs contemporary discourse on Hindutva nationalism as discourse on dominance and dispossession

Range of ideological perspectives and social scientific studies of the phenomenon of 'nationalism' have examined and classified nationalism from 'idealist', 'liberal', 'Marxian', 'structural', post-structuralism, modernist, and post-modernist, feminist, ethno-nationalist, subaltern, colonial, post-colonial and Dalitist perspectives, to name a few.

Suhas Palshikar in an 'Economic and Political Weekly' (EPW) article "Gandhi-Ambedkar Interface: When Shall The Twain Meet?", argues and explores how "Gandhian and Ambedkarite discourses are not antithetical." He goes on to explain that both of the leaders have been the ground setters and champions of emancipatory discourse. He opines that "At present when the legitimacy of the emancipatory discourse is being challenged and the dominant discourse upholds capitalism, it is all the more essential to broaden the scope of Gandhian and Ambedkarian discourses." Palshikar argues that there were apparent disagreements and verbal duels between Gandhi and Ambedkar and both attempted to expose each other, but less attention has been paid to the fact that both belonged to the emancipatory project and worked hard for socio-economic transformation. Unlike our times, where there are no emancipatory ideological frameworks for social transformations, Gandhian and Ambedkarite discourses were based on emancipatory ideological commitments, Palishkar argues that though immediate political interests of both leaders clashed, where Ambedkar viewed interests of communities of 'untouchables' quite distinct from the general interests and hence he was quite suspicious of 'social content' of the freedom struggle and believed that Gandhi was "not adequately sensitive to this". Ambedkar was sceptical and critical of the social content and intent of Gandhian ideology and politics, as it got represented during freedom struggle. Gandhi-Ambedkar comparison, Palshikar argues, lies in the contents of their emancipatory projects, particularly around caste question and the meaning and implications of national liberation. While Ambedkar maintained the centrality of caste question, for Gandhi, caste was not the central issue. Palshikar doesn't explain why in spite of Gandhian strategy of eradication of untouchability, caste as a system of exclusionary, discriminatory and framework of social hierarchy based on birth and lineage continues to be practiced even on our times till date. Referring to Ambedkar Palishkar outlines "Therefore, Ambedkar chose to study the caste system and critically analyze the justification it received from Hindu scriptures. His thought does not deal merely with removal of untouchability which was but one part of the anti-caste movement."

Among numerous conceptions on the ideology of nationalism, primordialist view considers national identity as 'natural and given', are presumptive, coercive, and deal mainly with sentiments and affections. (Harold Issacs, 1975). It casts nationalism in the image of 'body' and links one's national identity as extension of ones 'name', 'language', 'culture', 'religion' and 'geography.' Socio-biological perspective as an extension of primordialist view, explains 'nationalism' as natural extension of biological urge for community building and leads to conceptions of 'ethno-nationalism' (Pierre Van Den Berghe, 1981) where nationalism is linked to kinship, race and blood theories. These perspectives consider national phenomenon within the ambit of 'ethno-centricity'.

The phenomenon of communalism and the growth of Hindu nationalist movement in India and the subsequent institutionalised expression in the arena of party politics and governance preceded/followed by proliferation of large number of subsidiary organisations of militant and non-militant nature in all spheres of political life has attracted wide academic attention much before since political independence. The founding of the BJP in 1980 and its electoral success in Feb. 1998 general elections decisively challenged not only political parties but academic circles also to revise their convention wisdom on the possibility of ideology of Hindutva cultural nationalism followed by the RSS and strategy of communal mobilisation systematically undertaken by organisations affiliated to it including the BJP, gaining political power at the centre and in many of the states. The phenomenon has been truly 'Octopus' like with its tentacles in social, economic, political and cultural fields and different conceptualisations are forwarded analysing specific or interrelated aspects of political developments related to the BJP. Examining Hindu nationalists, their various representative open and clandestine organisations and strategies and their confrontation or mediation with institutions of liberal democracy, nation-state and governance in India is a difficult task.

Political parties in every country stand at crossroads where constitutional structures of formal institutional arrangements of power, organised expressions of conflicting social interests, local, regional, national or global factors and the historical memories, ideologies and prejudices intersect and shape the functioning of the political parties and party system. Sudipta Kaviraj emphasizes the study of political parties from the perspective of political sociology. Kaviraj distinguishes the nature of interest aggregation in third world countries like India where "when parties try to aggregate interests they make appeals not only to common economic interests or class but also to other identities that ordinary people commonly use to identify themselves-like caste or religious community or region or language." Terming the Jan Sangh and its successor the BJP as parties primarily restricted to north Kaviraj argues that "the BJP represent the primary political party based explicitly on the ideology of Hindu Communalism" and provides an account of "how these parties mobilised their support from social groups; but it is important to remember that these came from a period before the two major contemporary issues broke on the scene-disputes about economic liberalism and Hindu communal politics. "Kaviraj argues that the challenge to 'pluralist nationalism' of the Congress came first from the communists and then from the parties that challenged the idea by positing the alternative conception of "Hindu nationalism" and the Jan Sangh and later the BJP emerge as the primary vehicle of the idea of Hindu nation. He writes "The fortunes of Hindu nationalists constitute one of the most perplexing problem of modern Indian politics. There is first the problem of elementary characterisation of the force. Is this a fundamentalist force, like some powerful movements in modern Islam or something distinctive in character? Some analysts would hesitate to call them a 'fundamentalist' force for two reasons. The BJP seeks to use Hindu religion as its ideological base but firstly Hinduism has been marked historically by an ineradicable pluralism of doctrinal and structural forms. Therefore, there simply are no fundamental ideas of principles around which the movement could ask its adherents to rally. There is no consensus among practicing Hindus about what should constitute Hinduism fundamental texts...Secondly, fundamentalist movements are usually traditionalists, openly and intensely opposed to the forces of modernity. The Jan Sangh, the BJP position on this point is ambiguous and are strategically opportunistic on the relationship between tradition and modernity. "However, there are no ambiguity about their hostility to Muslims as a community and their characterisation of them as representing an alien presence in India. So even if there are difficulties calling the BJP fundamentalist there are none in seeing it as communal."

BJP in 80s successfully experimented with the aggressive communal strategy centred around the destruction of the Babri Masjid at Ayodhya. BJP followed radical communal strategy attacking Muslim beliefs and religious symbols directly and not indirectly i.e. their political and social arrangements only. There are inherent tensions between compulsions of electoral politics and Hindutva's ideological requirements. "In its new form the BJP faces an evident political dilemma. To use Hinduism for political purposes, it must transform historically the pluralist character, and to profess an explicitly Brahminical Hinduism would surely alienate lower castes. To advocate homogenised and caste less form of Hinduism would appear to be a travesty of what Hinduism has historically been. "For Hindu nationalists religion as a traditional force and social practice has historical adaptability and 'flexibility' and has worked as basis for construction of modern political communities on ethno-religious grounds. The secularising thrust of modernisation brings religion under the supervision of secular laws and interestingly has helped the process of self redefinition of communities through enumeration mapping, census etc. and thus transforming them into 'political agencies'. Sudipta Kaviraj disagrees with the 'simple thesis' that communalism as power of tradition is response of unwillingness of religious people to adapt to modern notions of secular democratic political practices and instead asks for a more sensitive re-look at such approach from the perspective of 'examining communalism within the discourse of modernisation and development' and inconsistencies involved therein. Independent India's constitutional arrangements rooted in the background of 'communal partition' of India, murder of Gandhi by a Hindu communalist and use of communal sentiments and communal mobilisational strategies kept the phenomenon alive which 'erupted to sudden and unexpected revival of Hindu communal politics in 1980s onwards, finding expression in social, economic, cultural and political spheres of contemporary Indian history'. No discussion of nationalism shall be complete without complex mutations these traditional ascriptive identities and practices bundled together as Hindutva and Cultural Nationalism undergo and intermingle into the political practices of contemporary India.

Thus seen from the political economic perspective entire phenomenon of contemporary Hindutva nationalism can be understood in terms of 'communalism' and a sort of "false consciousness" which has strong middle class or petit bourgeois base under the conditions of "relative economic stagnation. Its a distorted manifestation of class interests finding expressions in political arena. Bipin Chandra writes:

> "Basically communalism was one of the byproducts of colonialism, of the colonial character of the economy, of colonial underdevelopment and in recent years of the failure and incapacity of capitalism to develop the economy and society. Colonialism provided the social structure which produced communalism and in which it could grow…this was particularly true of the impact of the colonialism on the middle classes, which were in particular torn by fears, jealousies and frustration."

Bipin Chandra attributes the rise of communalism pervading in the garb of nationalism in contemporary India as competition among corporate capital, their representative bourgeois middle classes over the scarce resources and opportunities of growth caused by economic stagnation and it was the prime reason behind middle classes seeking fighting ground in the name of caste, religion or region as justificatory ground for their struggles and anxieties;

> "...the competition for jobs among individuals could be given the turn of being a struggle between two communities even though the colonial underdevelopment which had led to and intensified. This competition was affecting both Hindus and Muslims simultaneously.... in fact there were no communal interests, only individual interests masquerading as such. This is what we mean when we say that communalism neither comprehended the problem correctly nor provided the correct solution-it represented the false consciousness of the reality."

Once we analyze the range of Hindutva organisations along with the BJP in the context of historical continuity of the politics of communalism, the process and agencies which construct the "communal politics" acquire significance. Gyanendra Pandey opposes the attempt to understand 'communalism' in reductionist terms as simplified expressions of class interests. He emphasizes upon the historical understanding of the processes and agencies engaged in construction of communal imagination. Pandey underlines the processes, the circumstances under which different groups and classes engaged in historical reconstruction as part of assertion of the community. He argues that traditional fuzzier boundaries of individual communities were 'non-enumerative, abstract and without social-cultural and territorial boundaries'. Under the conditions of colonial modernity traditional abstract perception about a community underwent transformation. In the beginning there emerged "self conscious" awareness of the identities and differences between 'self' and 'the other', 'Us' and 'Them': "The new community or the enumerated community also became increasingly a part of the rationalist discourse-centrally concerned with numerical strength, well defined boundaries, exclusive rights and not least the community strength to mount purposive action in defence of their rights."

Hindutva as ideological force of political community was constructed around several religious symbols including cow. Not only upper caste Zamindar elements were adapting strategies for mobilising Hindu communities but less privileged communities were organising their own autonomous movements around cow protection initiatives in order to enhance their social status. Tracing the historical roots of construction of communal differences between Hindus and Muslims Gyanendra Pandey has identified the processes which created the binary of interests standing in confrontation with each other:

> "The point possibly applies with greater force to the Hindu community than to the Muslim because unlike the latter the Hindu community was far from being small, concentrated in any particular localities, or bound by anything in the way of a 'revealed book' or a 'united Church'. The all India united Hindu community and to a large extent all India Muslim community too] was a colonial creation. For the social and economic changes brought by colonialism, Indian efforts to defend the indigenous religions and cultures against western missionary attacks. The unifying drives of the colonial state – which was marked at the level of the administrative structure and attempted political control [Muslims must not be antagonized, Hindu sensibilities must not bet touched] and the very history of the movements like that of cow protection widely publicized as they were by the end of the nineteenth century tended to promote the idea of an all India Hindu community and an all India Muslim community which were supposedly ranged against one another for much of the time.... I would suggest that until the nineteenth century at any rate, people always had to work through caste, sect and so on..."

Thus, the rise of the 'hindutva' represent the "conservative revolution"– with majoritarian, xenophobic, paternalistic discourses and combining corporate dispossession in the name of development. Successes of the BJP in recent years has been understood in terms of its strategic combination of mobilisational tactics and successful manipulation of resources in arena of state institutions, public culture, public economy, religion, representative politics and so on.

Jairus Banaji explained aggressive fascist nationalism as "open terrorist dictatorship of the most reactionary, most chauvinist, and most imperialist elements of the finance capital.... which tries to secure the mass basis for monopolist capital among the petit bourgeoisie, appealing to peasantry, artisans, office employees and civil servants who have been thrown out of their normal course of life, particularly the declassed elements of big cities, also trying to penetrate into the working class. Along the similar lines the rise of the 'reactionary right wing' political parties in India particularly the variant of it represented by the BJP may be understood primarily in terms of the reflections of the crisis or manipulations of economy dominated and controlled by the capital or the big business. To argue the centrality of Hindutva Nationalism as a byproduct of the strategies of the political and social mobilisation by the corporate monopoly in alliance with the political elite bourgeois of India is not to deny its socio-cultural or historical origins and the corresponding culture of 'fascism' that germinates this kind of ideology. Such an ideology Jairus Banaji rightly points out that "in India the growth of fascism has been gradual, step by step process where the fascist elements penetrate all sectors of society and emerge having built up that ground work."

Understanding Hindutva Nationalism as Bourgeois nationalism, a concept rooted in Marxist theory, refers to the promotion and construction of the Hindu Rashtra by the Indian bourgeois class to further their economic interests. This strategy is particularly relevant in the context of corporate finance capital, where multinational corporations and financial institutions construct and manipulate ethno-religious nationalist sentiments to secure favourable conditions for capital accumulation and expansion. Its important to understand how bourgeois nationalism operates as a political strategy for corporate finance capital, analysing its historical context, mechanisms, and impacts.

3. The Historical Context

The term "bourgeois nationalism" emerged during the nineteenth and early twentieth centuries, coinciding with the rise of the capitalist economy and the nation-state system. Karl Marx and Friedrich Engels critiqued this phenomenon in their writings, noting how the bourgeoisie utilised nationalistic ideologies to consolidate their power and suppress class consciousness among the proletariat (Marx & Engels, 1848). This strategy involved appealing to the shared national identity of workers, thereby diverting their attention from real economic structuration of different classes, their class struggles and fostering a sense of loyalty to the bourgeoisie-dominated state. Colonial-imperial project was deeply embedded with the bourgeois national identity at home and resistance to and suppression of the urges of national self determination by subjugated people in colonies. India was no exception.

In the late from 1970s onwards and early twenty-first centuries, the dynamics of bourgeois nationalism evolved with globalisation and the dominance of corporate finance capital. Multinational corporations, in particular, began to leverage nationalist sentiments to influence political decisions and secure economic advantages. This period saw a resurgence of protectionist policies and anti-globalisation rhetoric, often framed within a nationalist discourse, which paradoxically served the interests of global capital (Harvey, 2005).

Mechanisms of Bourgeois Nationalism: Bourgeois nationalism operates through various mechanisms, including political sponsoring of political parties, lobbying, media influence, and public relations campaigns. Corporate finance capital employs these tools to shape national policies and public opinion in ways that favour their interests. At its extreme this control transforms the neo-liberal state into a corporation state where it becomes difficult to separate corporate interests from the structures and functions of the state system. We may have a quick look at some the mechanisms through which the cronyism or the nexus between corporate finance capital and forces of communal Hindutva Nationalism have mutually joined hands in glove to hide their real interests under the guise of Hindutva nationalism.

Furthermore, anti-colonial nationalism was instrumental in promoting social and economic reforms that aimed at rectifying the injustices of colonial rule. Many nationalist leaders advocated for policies that would redistribute land, resources, and wealth more equitably. For example, Julius Nyerere of Tanzania implemented the policy of Ujamaa, or African socialism, which sought to build a self-reliant and egalitarian society based on communal ownership and cooperative agriculture. Nyerere believed that true independence could only be achieved through economic self-sufficiency and social justice, arguing that "development which is not grounded in the people's culture and values, which is not owned by the people, is development which is doomed to failure".

Anti-colonial nationalism also played a crucial role in cultural emancipation. Colonial powers often sought to impose their own languages, religions, and cultural practices on colonised peoples, undermining indigenous cultures and traditions. Nationalist movements sought to revive and celebrate indigenous cultures, languages, and histories as essential components of national identity. This cultural revival was seen as a necessary step in reclaiming the dignity and pride of the colonised people. Amílcar Cabral, a leader of the liberation movement in Guinea-Bissau, emphasized the importance of cultural identity in the struggle for independence, stating, "The liberation struggle is above all a cultural act". By reaffirming their cultural heritage, colonised peoples were able to resist assimilation and assert their right to self-determination.

In conclusion, anti-colonial nationalism in Third World societies has been a powerful force for emancipation, promoting political independence, social and economic justice, and cultural revival. The legacies of these movements continue to influence contemporary struggles for equality and self-determination, highlighting the enduring relevance of the ideals of anti-colonial nationalism. Nationalism and neoliberalism are two significant and often simultaneously converging and conflicting ideologies that shape contemporary political, economic, and social landscapes. While nationalism emphasizes the interests, culture, and identity of a specific nation, often prioritizing these over international or external influences, neoliberalism champions free-market capitalism, deregulation, and reduction in government spending. Understanding the interplay between these ideologies is crucial in analyzing modern political trends and economic policies.

Nationalism is fundamentally about the sovereignty and self-determination of a nation. It is rooted in the belief that a group of people sharing common elements such as language, culture, and history should govern themselves without external interference. Nationalism often manifests in policies aimed at preserving national identity and autonomy, which can sometimes lead to xenophobia or protectionism. According to Benedict Anderson, nationalism is an "imagined community" where members of a nation perceive themselves as part of a collective despite never meeting most of their fellow members. This imagined sense of unity and common purpose can be a powerful motivator for political action and social cohesion.

Neoliberalism, on the other hand, advocates for economic policies that favour market liberalisation, privatisation, and fiscal austerity. Originating in the late twentieth century, neoliberalism seeks to enhance economic efficiency and growth by reducing government intervention in the economy. David Harvey describes neoliberalism as a "theory of political economic practices that proposes that human well-being can best be advanced by liberating individual entrepreneurial freedoms and skills within an institutional framework characterised by strong private property rights, free markets, and free trade".

This ideology has driven many governments to adopt policies that prioritize economic growth and competitiveness over social welfare and public sector strength.

The relationship between nationalism and neoliberalism is complex and often paradoxical. On one hand, neoliberal economic policies can undermine national sovereignty by subjecting national economies to the forces of global markets and multinational corporations. On the other hand, neoliberalism can be bolstered by nationalist rhetoric that frames economic liberalisation as a path to national prosperity. For instance, Margaret Thatcher's policies in the UK during the 1980s combined neoliberal economic reforms with a strong sense of British nationalism, presenting economic restructuring as a way to restore Britain's greatness.

In recent years, the rise of populist movements across the globe has highlighted the tensions between nationalism and neoliberalism. Populist leaders often harness nationalist sentiments to criticize neoliberal policies that they argue have led to economic disparity and loss of national control. For example, the election of Donald Trump in the United States and the Brexit referendum in the United Kingdom were fuelled by nationalist opposition to neoliberal trade agreements and immigration policies. These movements argue that neoliberalism benefits a global elite at the expense of ordinary citizens, eroding national identity and sovereignty. In contrast, some proponents of neoliberalism argue that global economic integration and liberalisation can foster international peace and cooperation by creating economic interdependencies. They contend that economic growth facilitated by neoliberal policies can lift nations out of poverty and create opportunities for all citizens. However, critics argue that such policies often exacerbate inequality and undermine democratic processes by concentrating power in the hands of a few.

Some of the analysts have characterised current phase of political economy as 'regime of dispossession.' Global land grab debate from where the concept evolved explaining the varieties of analytical concepts to understand observable forms and practices of dispossession. It was coined by Levien in response to the perceived inadequacy of notions such as Marx's 'primitive accumulation'—which was often deployed in these debates without consistency and clarity (Hall, 2013)—and Harvey's (2004) 'accumulation by dispossession', which Levien sees as too broad, too capital-centric and insufficiently capable of capturing the specificities of land dispossession. In india, we find deployment by the finance capital and their monopoly counterparts the entire machinery of India State with all their force to remove all obstacles in the process of accumulation in all sectors including farming. The political apparatus of Indian state has coercively redistributed landed wealth upwards and farm laws were mechanism to transfer these resources to the corporate sector albeit indirectly. Understood as a socially and historically specific constellation of state structures, economic logics tied to particular class interests and ideological justifications that generate consistent patterns of dispossession (Levien, 2013a, p. 383). The concept of regimes of dispossession is geared explaining Indian state's willingness to dispossess certain populations for certain purposes, at certain historical conjunctures, and with recourse to certain normative or ideological justifications intermixed mischievously between Hindutva majoritarianism and developmentalism of neo-liberal variety.

Hindutva, or "Hinduness," is an ideology seeking to establish the hegemony of elite segments of Hindus and the elite Bramanical imaginaries portrayed as 'Hindu way of life'. It was conceptualised by Vinayak Damodar Savarkar in the 1920s and later adopted by the Rashtriya Swayamsevak Sangh (RSS), the ideological parent of the BJP. Under BJP leadership, especially since Narendra Modi assumed power in 2014, Hindutva has transcended mere cultural pride, morphing into a potent political tool of politico-cultural hegemony.

Though the phenomenon of Hindutva based nationalism dates back to nearly a century in India, I shall examine its contemporary manifestation as a strategy of neoliberal capital attempting in the process of 'primitive accumulation' of a sort and more particularly during last ten years of Narendra Modi's regime under which this process acquired maturation. A necessary consequence of corporate accumulation and dispossession has been the sharp increase in income inequality throughout the country. World Inequality Database demonstrate that the share of the top 1% in national income, at 22.7% in 2023 is highest in the century. On the other hand Hindutva forces have continuously relied on alternative truth by suppression of the actual economic distress of the people. A misrepresentation was made in February 2024 just before parliamentary elections regarding significant increase in per capita household consumption. This narrative of developing India under Modi's regime was built keeping in mind elections and by blatant suppression of facts enumerated in the HCES report 2022-23. Report says that due to economic policies perused by this government has significantly reduced the per capita availability of food and people are forced to cut their expenditure on basic food items. This distress is much significant in rural India where there is significant decline in expenditure on basic nutrition. India ranking 111 out of 125 countries in Global Hunger Index has further worsened the scenario at the time when Hindutva nationalist forces continue to hide under the curtain of communal nationalist politics and hate politics. India's quinquennial surveys on consumer expenditure show a significant rise between 2011–12 and 2017–18 in the percentage of the population unable to access a minimum daily calorie norm per capita, which is 2,100 for urban and 2,200 for rural areas.

Neoliberal agenda of accumulation and dispossession and recasting of the role of the Indian state necessarily erodes the popular support base and legitimation quotient of ruling elites. In their attempt to control the polity and mitigate the crises emerging out of the changed role of Indian state these forces together strategically resort to ethno-majoritarian religio-communal ideology of Hindutva and its conjoined experimentation and intermediation with other caste or region based political identities.

Divisive Hindutva based cultural nationalism as an ideological ally of crony capitalists began its journey alongside Neo-Liberal shifts in Indian economy under Manmohan Singh's Congress regime. This rightward shift in the political economy has taken its course where under the Modi's tenure the relative autonomy of the public sphere or the Indian state appears to be a thing of the past.

Prabhat Patnaik rightly argues that mindless demonetisation, faulty GST, corporate waivers and concessions, homogenisation of trade rules etc are essentially "toolkit of international financial institutions." Hindutva works as a cloak for impoverishing the working class and fleecing middle classes of their holdings and possessions.

Its true that at a global plane neo-liberalism since last two decades has faced unprecedented crisis and it has worsens the overall economic distress of different segments of Indian population. We witness how under Modi's second tenure as prime minister three farm laws were enacted paving the way for corporate entry into the agricultural sector and moving towards eliminating the MSP as a remedial course for the already languishing agricultural sector. Farmers of India realised the eminent danger and through an year long struggle against corporatisation of agricultural sector they succeeded in forcing current regime to withdraw three farm laws. Unemployment in India has been at all time high and in the absence of strong industrial base and lack of employment oriented development thinking this scenario is most likely to burst in near future beyond limits. BJP's strategy of repeated resorting to identity and hate politics appears to have reached at its climax and people in nearly all states have begun realising the insignificance and futility of Hindutva model of political economy. The fundamental shift aimed at taking the political discourse from identity centric majoritarian elite agenda to the economic issues confronting Indian masses that is inflation, unemployment, corporate dispossession and increasing authoritarianism combined with neo-fascist political mobilisation of Hindutva have acquired centre-stage with various resistance movements gaining ground. The regime of corporate Hindutva dispossession of masses is evident from greater unemployment, stagnant or reduced real wages and most important reduced nutritional deprivation for the majority of poor in India. "In India this neoliberal/neofascist alliance has taken the specific form of a corporate Hindutva alliance. The Modi Government is the expression of this alliance." Writes Marxian economist Prabhat Patnaik.

Hindutva in neo-liberal times is a deflection and diversionary tactics along with a politico-cultural apparatus to control and constrict the minds and manners of political behaviour of Indian population along the lines of an imagined ethno-communal majoritarianism. It has been reinvented as a new cast for the authoritarian forces in India to sustain their political-economy of dispossession. One finds it difficult to disagree with Patnaik's explanation that "Its purpose is to bring about change in discourse so that issue of unemployment, inflation, and the economic distress are pushed to the background. Meanwhile Hindu supremacists comes to the forefront, even as the government continues to pursue an aggressive neo-liberal strategy to the benefit of the globalised capital and the domestic monopoly capital integrated with it."

Corporate forces bet on Narendra Modi as mascot of Hindutva based nationalism was not accidental. Hindutva nationalism as experimented and practiced in the name of Gujarat Model had already proven as a powerful tool in the hands of capital which provided free hand for their plunder along side majoritarian communal tactics of an aesthetic hate politics, making people unconscious of the disposing impact such a virulent ideology had on their life world.

2014 witnessed a well calibrated move by corporate neo-fascists to install BJP at the centre and to further their agenda of transfer of public assets, corporations, services, public money through range of state devised mechanisms. What ushered in the name of Hindutva nationalism was systematic attack and erosion of democratic constitutional institutions, state repression through attack on the hard won rights of common people, workers, women and peasants along with continued villainisation and othering of minorities, Adivasis and other vulnerable groups.

Hindutva based nationalism is the very anti-thesis of any version of democracy-liberal or socialist. RSS BJP combine have fostered not just the unimaginable income inequality with their K shaped economic de-growth model, but have created a stratum of criminally insensitive monopoly capitalists who sponsor and nurture the sycophantic culture of 'Supreme Leader' or Fuhrer culture with immense centralisation of power and control of political institutions and processes. Thus, India today under the spell of Hindutva nationalism is passing through a phase of 'Counter-Revolution' reversing the achievements and progress made so far since anti-colonial democratic struggles and post-colonial nation and state building. The embeddedness of the local monopoly capital with the international finance capital and corporations has eroded the foreign policy autonomy and independence of India state and there appears an understanding about global division of labour among capitalists with regards to plunder, dispossession and loot of capital, natural and public resources.

4. Tools and mechanisms

Merging Hindutva Nationalist agenda with corporate interests has been the hard choice for ruling classes in twenty-first century. Globalised finance, hardly concerned with India's economic crisis, inflation and "development" trajectory based on creating massive unemployment frowns at any strategy to increase the aggregate demand by increased public expenditure either through fiscal deficit or taxing the corporate and the rich. Under Modi's regime we have seen how government has given free hand to corporations at all levels of their operations in the economy. Hollow slogans of creating million of jobs still remain chimera for the educated unemployed and PM's talk of making 'Pakoda' as a solution further ridicules the state approach towards the problem of unemployment.

Hindutva Nationalism under the BJP is a classic example of strategic deflection from economic issues. In recent years, the political landscape of India has seen a marked rise in Hindutva nationalism, particularly under the leadership of the Bharatiya Janata Party (BJP). While this ideology has been a significant part of the BJP's agenda since its inception, its prominence has amplified during the tenure of Prime Minister Narendra Modi. This shift towards a more pronounced Hindu nationalist agenda has had profound implications on India's socio-political environment. Notably, it has served as a strategic tool for the BJP to divert public attention from pressing economic challenges facing the Indian masses. Hindutva nationalism has been utilised by the BJP to overshadow basic economic issues.

Hindutva nationalism under the BJP has been a double-edged sword. On one hand, it has solidified the party's voter base and diverted attention from economic issues. On the other hand, it has contributed to a socio-political environment where economic grievances remain unaddressed, and social cohesion is increasingly at risk. The strategic deployment of Hindutva narratives has indeed helped the BJP deflect from basic economic challenges, but the long-term implications of such a strategy necessitate careful consideration. As India moves forward, balancing cultural identity with economic progress remains a critical challenge for its leadership.

India, the world's fifth-largest economy, has been grappling with several economic challenges such as unemployment, agrarian Distress, inflation, rising inequality, and mass hunger. The unemployment rate has been a persistent issue, exacerbated by the COVID-19 pandemic. Farmers' protests highlighted the ongoing crisis and struggles in the agricultural sector. Rising prices of essential commodities have strained household budgets. The GDP growth rate has seen fluctuations, with concerns over sustaining long-term economic stability. Government is struggling hard to manage the economic indicators data through various manipulations and data fudging. In spite of these serious concerns we witness the Strategic Use of Hindutva Nationalism at its historic peak.

(a) Cultural Nationalism as a Political Strategy

The BJP has adeptly used cultural nationalism to create a narrative that prioritizes religious and cultural identity over economic well-being. This strategy resonates deeply with a significant portion of the electorate. For instance, the construction of the Ram Temple in Ayodhya, a long-standing demand of Hindutva proponents, has been a focal point of BJP's agenda. By projecting this as a historic and cultural achievement, the BJP has managed to rally substantial public support, often sidelining economic discourse. During the 2019 general elections, the BJP emphasized the completion of the Ram Temple as a significant achievement. This narrative overshadowed discussions on pressing economic issues like job creation and economic growth, helping the BJP secure a massive electoral victory.

(b) Polarisation and Divisive Politics

Hindutva nationalism has also been instrumental in creating a polarised political climate. This divisive strategy diverts public discourse from economic grievances to identity-based conflicts. The Citizenship Amendment Act (CAA) and the National Register of Citizens (NRC) are prime examples of such tactics. These policies have sparked nationwide protests and debates centered on religious identity and citizenship, effectively shifting focus from economic challenges. The CAA and NRC debates dominated headlines and public discussions in 2019-2020, coinciding with a period of economic slowdown and rising unemployment. The national conversation was predominantly about the implications of these policies on religious minorities, thereby marginalising economic issues from the public agenda.

(c) Symbolic Politics and Public Perception

The BJP has frequently employed symbolic politics to reinforce Hindutva nationalism, thereby diverting attention from economic short-comings. Initiatives like the abrogation of Article 370, which granted special status to Jammu and Kashmir, were projected as decisive moves to strengthen national unity and security. These actions, while having little direct impact on the daily economic realities of the average Indian, created a perception of strong governance and decisive leadership. The abrogation of Article 370 in August 2019 was heralded as a historic decision by the BJP. The extensive media coverage and public debates on this issue overshadowed discussions on economic indicators, such as the slowing GDP growth rate and rising unemployment figures.

(d) Media and Communication Strategy

The BJP's robust media and communication strategy has played a critical role in emphasizing Hindutva narratives over economic issues. The extensive use of social media, coupled with sympathetic media channels, has allowed the BJP to control and steer public discourse effectively. This media strategy ensures that issues aligned with Hindutva nationalism receive disproportionate attention compared to economic debates. During the COVID-19 pandemic, the migrant labour crisis highlighted the severe economic distress faced by millions. However, simultaneous media narratives focused on issues like the Tablighi Jamaat incident, which was framed as a super-spreader event linked to a Muslim group. This shifted the narrative from economic mismanagement to communal fault lines.

Consequences of Hindutva as a Deflection strategy has been that While the BJP's focus on Hindutva nationalism has been politically advantageous, it has significant repercussions for India's socio-economic landscape. One necessary impact of such a deviated discourse has been that there has been complete absence of any serious rethinking on the course of economic reforms in India. Critical economic reforms, pro-people policy orientation and policy discussions are often sidelined, delaying necessary interventions. At societal level we are witnessing social unrest, as seen in various protests and communal tensions, further destabilising economic conditions. The emphasis on religious nationalism over economic progress has badly impacted the global perception of India as a stable democracy and India has suffered in the field of foreign investment and international relations.

Corporations also control significant segments of the media, using this power to shape public discourse. Media outlets owned by large corporations often promote nationalist narratives that align with corporate interests, such as the need to protect domestic industries from foreign competition. This creates a public perception that aligns with corporate goals, reducing resistance to policies that favour corporate finance capital (Herman & Chomsky, 1988).

A necessary consequence of contemporary Hindutva Nationalism in India has been the substantial erosion of democracy – both procedurally and substantively. The influence of corporate finance capital and their representative classes on national politics has undermined the democratic institutions and processes. Directly shaping the economic policies, lobbying, media control, public relations campaigns for distorting public discourse and public policy-making has contributed towards reducing the ability of the citizens to raise their voices against dispossessing corporations and to hold them accountable for mounting malaises. This erosion of democracy is deliberately hid behind communal nationalist rhetoric and mischievous identification of corporate interests with so called national interests.

Another dangerous consequence of contemporary Hindutva Nationalism promoted by corporate finance has been the deep and often irreparable social-communal divisions and conflicts. Hindutva by definition identifies itself with an imagined majority identity of political Hinduism and marginalises minority groups resulting into accelerated tensions between different segments of society. The discourses on ascriptive and conflicting identities distracts public attention from economic issues and class based struggles and consolidates the hold and dominance of the bourgeois.

5. Conclusion

The privatisation of public assets in India since 2000 amidst the cacophony of Hindutva nationalism reflects a broader global trend towards neoliberal economic policies and rightward shift of politics. While privatisation has brought in significant investments and improved efficiency in certain sectors, it has also led to dispossession, social inequality, and challenges in governance. A balanced approach, ensuring that investments public or private serve public interest without compromising social equity, harmony, and accountability, is crucial for sustainable development. India at the crossroads needs a comprehensive check on the corporate Hindutva's agenda of accumulation and dispossession with the strong collusion of political party in power at the centre. Bourgeois nationalism, as a political strategy of corporate finance capital, reflects a complex interplay of economic interests and nationalist ideologies. By leveraging nationalist sentiments, corporate finance capital secures favourable conditions for capital accumulation and expansion, often at the expense of economic equality, democratic integrity, and social cohesion. Understanding this dynamic is crucial for addressing the challenges posed by corporate dominance in contemporary capitalist societies. Future research and activism must focus on exposing the contradictions of bourgeois nationalism and advocating for policies that genuinely serve the interests of the broader populace.

Notes

1. Fanon, F. (1961). The Wretched of the Earth. Grove Press. 2. http://ccnmtl. columbia. edu/projects/mmt/ambedkar/web/section_20. html (accessed at 6. 45 pm, 13. 08. 2017).
3. Christophe Jefferlot 'Hindu Nationalism: A Reader', Permanent black, New Delhi, 2007, p. 3.
4. Benedict Anderson, 'Imagined Communities: Reflections on the Origin and Spread of Nationalism', Verso, London, 1991 p. 5.
5. *Ibid.,* p. 6.
6. Partha Chatterjee, 'Nation and Its Fragments: Colonial and Postcolonial Histories', Oxford University Press, Delhi, 1997, p. 5.
7. Suhas Palshikar, 'Gandhi-Ambedkar Interface: When shall the Twain Meet?', Economic and Political Weekly, August 3, 1996, p. 2070.
8. *Ibid.,* p. 2070.
9. *Ibid.,* p. 2070.
10. *Ibid.,* p. 2071.
11. *Ibid.,* p. 5.
12. Kaviraj, Sudipta. Ed. "Politics in India", OUP, New Delhi, 1997, pp. 1-36.
13. *Ibid.,* p. 256.
14. *Ibid.,* p. 256.
15. *Ibid.,* pp. 259-60.
16. *Ibid.,* p. 261.
17. *Ibid.,* p. 295.
18. *Ibid.,* p. 299.
19. *Ibid.,* p. 303.
20. Pandey, Gyanendra. "Construction of Communalism in Colonial North India, OUP, New Delhi, 1990.
21. Pandey, Gyanendra. "Construction of Communalism in Colonial North India" OUP, New Delhi, 1990, excerpts cited in Kaviraj, Sudipta. Ed. "Politics in India", OUP, New Delhi, 1997, pp. 305-6.

22. Ibid, p. 306.
23. Banaji, Jairus. Sept. 2002'Political Culture of Fascism', Seminar lecture delivered at Vikas Adhyayan Kendra, Mumbai.
24. Kenneth Bo Nielsen and Alf Gunvald Nilsen, "India's Evolving Neoliberal Regime of Dispossession: From the Anti-SEZ Movement to the Farm Law Protests, Sociological Bulletin, Volume 71, Issue 4, October 2022, pp. 582-600.
25. https://thewire. in/economy/is-indias-neoliberalism-escalating-hindu.
26. *Ibid.*
27. *Ibid.*

References

Anderson, B. (1983). Imagined Communities: Reflections on the Origin and Spread of Nationalism. Verso.

Harvey, D. (2005). A Brief History of Neoliberalism. Oxford University Press.

Anderson, B. (1983). Imagined Communities: Reflections on the Origin and Spread of Nationalism. Verso.

Davis, A. (2013). Promotional Cultures: The Rise and Spread of Advertising, Public Relations, Marketing, and Branding. Polity.

Dreiling, M., & Darves, D. (2016). Agents of Neoliberal Globalisation: Corporate Networks, State Structures, and Social Movements. Cambridge University Press.

Giridharadas, A. (2018). Winners Take All: The Elite Charade of Changing the World. Knopf.

Gilens, M., & Page, B. I. (2014). "Testing Theories of American Politics: Elites, Interest Groups, and Average Citizens." Perspectives on Politics, 12(3), 564-581.

Harvey, D. (2005). A Brief History of Neoliberalism. Oxford University Press.

Herman, E. S., & Chomsky, N. (1988). Manufacturing Consent: The Political Economy of the Mass Media. Pantheon.

Marx, K., & Engels, F. (1848). The Communist Manifesto.

Piketty, T. (2014). Capital in the Twenty-First Century. Harvard University Press.

Springford, J. (2019). "The Brexit Vote: Economic and Social Implications." Journal of European Integration, 41(5), 635-652.

Summers, T. (2016). "China's 'New Silk Roads': Sub-national Regions and Networks of Global Political Economy." Third World Quarterly, 37(9), 1628-1643. Business Standard. (2010). "CIL IPO: India's Largest Public Offering." Business Standard, p. 9.

Chandrasekhar, C. P. (2004). "Privatisation in India: Limits and Constraints." Social Scientist, 32(3/4), 73.

Chandrasekhar, C. P. (2016). "The Disinvestment Story: Past, Present, and Future." Economic and Political Weekly, 51(15), 89.

GMR Group. (2006). "Delhi International Airport Privatisation." GMR Group Annual Report 2006, p. 22.

Levien, M. (2013). "Regimes of Dispossession: From Steel Towns to Special Economic Zones." Development and Change, 44(2), 55.

Levien, M. (2018). Dispossession Without Development: Land Grabs in Neoliberal India. Oxford University Press, p. 134.

Ministry of Coal. (2020). "Annual Report 2019-20." Government of India, p. 14.

Ministry of Housing and Urban Affairs. (2019). "Smart Cities Mission Annual Report." Government of India, p. 30.

Ministry of Road Transport and Highways. (2020). "National Highways Development Project: Annual Review 2020." Government of India, p. 45.

Panagariya, A. (2014). India: The Emerging Giant. Oxford University Press, p. 102.

Shiva, V. (2016). Water Wars: Privatisation, Pollution, and Profit. South End Press, p. 88, 143.

Chapter - 5

Supremacy of Religious Majoritarian Nationalism in South Asia

— **Dr Hamid Rasool**

Religious majoritarian nationalism is often referred to as religious nationalism or ethno-religious nationalism. It is a political and ideological stance that emphasizes the dominance and privileged position of a particular religious group or faith within a nation. It is characterised by the belief that the cultural, social, and political identity of a nation should be closely tied to a specific religion or religious community, with members of that faith enjoying preferential treatment and rights. The dominant religion is often considered an integral part of the national identity. This ideology may foster an exclusivist mindset, marginalising or discriminating against religious minorities. Majoritarian nationalism asserts the dominance of one religion over others within the nation,[1] and this religion is often seen as the defining characteristic of the nation. It promotes the preservation and propagation of the dominant religion's customs, traditions, and practices as a central part of national identity. Which results in the discrimination or marginalisation of religious minorities within the country, often through legal or societal means. It seeks to prioritize the interests and rights of the majority religious group in a given nation. This often involves the belief that the dominant religion should play a central role in shaping the nation's cultural, social, and political identity.[2]

This ideology places a strong emphasis on the religion followed by the majority population of a state and this religion is often seen as the foundation of the nation's identity. The proponents of religious majoritarian nationalism argue for the dominant religion to have a significant influence on the nation's culture, social norms, and political decision-making processes. This may lead to the exclusion or marginalisation of individuals who do not adhere to the majority faith and advocates for religious majoritarian nationalism may seek to consolidate political power to ensure that policies align with the values and principles of the majority religion.[3] In extreme cases, it can lead to policies that limit the rights and freedoms of minority religious groups. Such ideologies may challenge secular principles, advocating for a closer integration of religion and state, which can raise concerns about the infringement on the rights of individuals with different religious beliefs. If not managed carefully, religious majoritarian nationalism can contribute to inter-religious tensions and conflicts, as well as undermine the principles of religious freedom and pluralism.[4]

Religious majoritarian nationalism can be found in several parts of the world and is not limited to South Asia. It has been a source of political and social tension and has sometimes resulted in conflicts and violence, particularly when the rights of religious minorities are not protected, and not all forms of nationalism are inherently exclusionary or prejudiced.[5] Nationalism can take many forms, and while religious majoritarian nationalism is one variation, there are also inclusive and pluralistic forms of nationalism that celebrate the diversity of a nation's religious and cultural fabric. The issue of religious majoritarian nationalism is a complex and sensitive one in South Asia. Several factors have contributed to the supremacy of religious majoritarianism and nationalism in this region, including historical, political, and socio-economic factors.

South Asia is a diverse and complex region with a rich tapestry of religions, languages, and cultures. The concept of religious majoritarian nationalism has been a significant factor in the political and social landscape of South Asia. Whereas religious majoritarian nationalism refers to the idea that the majority religious community within a particular nation should have a dominant or privileged position in that nation's politics, culture, and society. Historically, South Asia has been characterised by a deep-seated religious and cultural divide between Hindus and Muslims. This divide was further exacerbated by the colonial rule of the British, who adopted a policy of "divide and rule" that pitted different religious and ethnic groups against each other. In the post-independence era, the issue of religious majoritarian nationalism has continued to be a source of tension in the region. In countries like India, Pakistan, Bangladesh, Sri Lanka, Nepal, and Myanmar, religious identity has often been used as a tool to mobilize political support and to justify discriminatory policies against minority communities.[6]

It has encouraged religious and ethnic tensions, with each side often seeing the other as a threat to its own identity and security. For example, India's Hindu majority has often been seen as a threat by Pakistan's Muslim majority, leading to tensions between the two states. Similarly, in Sri Lanka, tensions between the Sinhalese majority and the Tamil minority have been aggravated by nationalist sentiments.[7] In recent years, the rise of religious nationalist groups in India has further fueled the discourse of religious majoritarian nationalism in the region. Whereas religious majoritarianism has been a major factor in South Asian politics in recent years.[8] In countries like India, Pakistan, and Sri Lanka, religious majoritarianism has been used to manipulate public voting and advance the interests of political leaders by various groups and political parties.

Such groups advocate for the primacy of religious identity and are involved in promoting a climate of intolerance and discrimination against minority communities. Similar tensions are happening in Pakistan, Afghanistan, Sri Lanka, Myanmar, and Bangladesh. There are concerns about the growing influence of religious extremist groups who seek to impose their vision of religion on society and marginalise minority communities. The rise of religious majoritarian nationalism in South Asia has been an increasing trend in recent decades. This is seen in the form of hardline Hindu nationalism in India, Islamic fundamentalism in Pakistan and Afghanistan, and Buddhist nationalism in Sri Lanka.[9] These ideologies have often been used to justify oppressive measures towards religious and ethnic minorities and have been propagated through both political and social means.

In India, political parties like the BJP are promoting a religious nationalist agenda and have sought to marginalise religious and ethnic minorities. In Pakistan, Islamic fundamentalism has been used to justify the marginalisation of religious and ethnic minorities and the imposition of oppressive laws on them. Such States have implemented policies that have sought to suppress the rights of religious minorities and to promote a sense of majority supremacy.[10] In Afghanistan, the Taliban has used Islamic fundamentalist ideology to justify its oppressive rule and to enforce its version of Sharia law. This has included the destruction of religious sites and the persecution of religious minorities. In Sri Lanka, Buddhist nationalism has been used to justify the marginalisation of religious and ethnic minorities, including Muslims and Tamils.[11]

The government has implemented policies that promote the supremacy of the majority Sinhalese Buddhist population over religious and ethnic minorities. This rise of religious majoritarianism in South Asia has led to increased tensions between different religious and ethnic groups and has been used to justify oppressive measures against minority communities.[12] It has also contributed to a sense of insecurity among religious and ethnic minorities and has hindered the development of a more inclusive society.[13] India has a long history of religious pluralism, with Hinduism, Islam, Christianity, Sikhism, Buddhism, and other religions coexisting for centuries. The rise of Hindu majoritarian nationalism has gained prominence in recent years, particularly with the political ascendency of the Bharatiya Janata Party (BJP) and its affiliated organisations. The controversial Citizenship Amendment Act (CAA) and the National Register of Citizens (NRC) sparked debates about the rights and citizenship of Muslims, and concerns have been raised about the potential marginalisation of religious minorities.

Pakistan was created as a homeland for Muslims during the partition of British India in 1947. The idea of Islamic nationalism is deeply ingrained in Pakistan's identity, where the state is constitutionally required to protect the rights of religious minorities. However, over the years, there have been instances of religious intolerance, and religious minorities, including Christians, Hindus, and Ahmadis, have faced discrimination. Like Pakistan, Bangladesh was part of the former East Pakistan and became an independent nation in 1971. It was founded as a secular state, but in recent years, there have been concerns about religious minorities, particularly Hindus, facing discrimination and persecution.[14]

Sri Lanka has a predominantly Buddhist population, and tensions between the Buddhist majority and religious minorities, especially Muslims and Tamils, have flared up over the years. The Sri Lankan civil war, which ended in 2009, was marked by ethnic and religious divisions. The religious majoritarian nationalism does not represent the views of all people in these countries. Many South Asians advocate for secularism, religious tolerance, and the protection of minority rights. Furthermore, the situation in each of these countries is complex and varies over time. Political, social, and economic factors, as well as the actions of various governments, play a significant role in shaping the dynamics of religious majoritarian nationalism in South Asia. The supremacy of religious majoritarianism and nationalism in South Asia has several negative consequences, including communal violence, discrimination against minority communities, and the erosion of democratic values and institutions. Governments and civil society in the region need to work towards promoting a more inclusive and tolerant society, where diversity is celebrated and minority rights are protected.

Notes and References

1. Panikkar, K. N. "Nationalism and Its Detractors. "Social Scientist 44, no. 9/10 (2016): 3–18. http://www. jstor. org/stable/24890298.
2. Saiya N. Minority Religious Discrimination and Terrorism across Faith Traditions. In: Weapon of Peace: How Religious Liberty Combats Terrorism. Cambridge: Cambridge University Press; 2018:61-104. doi:10. 1017/9781108565127. 003.
3. Brian Girvin (2020). From Civic Pluralism to Ethnoreligious Majoritarianism: Majority Nationalism in India, Nationalism and Ethnic Politics, 26:1, 27-45, DOI: 10. 1080/13537113. 2020. 1716437
4. Poruthiyil, P. V. (2020). Religious Ethics: An Antidote for Religious Nationalism. Business & Society, 59(5), 1035-1061. https://doi. org/10. 1177/0007650317745635
5. Stausberg, Michael, Van Der Haven, Alexander and Baffelli, Erica. "Religious Minorities: conceptual perspectives". Religious Minorities Online, edited by Erica Baffelli, Alexander van der Haven and Michael Staus berg. Berlin, Boston: De Gruyter, 2023. https://doi. org/10. 1515/rmo. 23389320. Accessed 2023-12-12.
6. A Report by Human Rights Watch for the United Nations World Conference Against Racism, Racial Discrimination, Xenophobia and Related Intolerance. Durban, South Africa, September 2001.
7. Neo, Jaclyn L. 2021. "Religious Minorities in Asia: Between the Scylla of Minority Protection and Charybdis of Religious Freedom Rights?" Religions 12, no. 10: 881. https://doi. org/10. 3390/rel12100881.
8. Brian Girvin (2020) From Civic Pluralism to Ethnoreligious Majoritarianism: Majority Nationalism in India, Nationalism and Ethnic Politics, 26:1, 27-45, DOI: 10. 1080/13537113. 2020. 1716437.
9. Center for Study of Society and Secularism & Minority Rights Group International, 2017, A Narrowing Space: Violence and discrimination against.
10. Milan Vaishnav (April 04, 2019), Religious Nationalism and India's Future, Carnegie Endowment for International Peace, Washington, DC.
11. *Ibid.*
12. Thomas Carothers and Andrew O'Donohue, editors, Political Polarisation in South and Southeast Asia Old Divisions, New Dangers.
13. Neo J, Scharffs, BG. Religious Nationalism and Religious Freedom in Asia: Mapping Regional Trends in a Global Phenomenon. Asian Journal of Law and Society. 2021;8(1):1-18. doi:10. 1017/als. 2020. 53India's religious minorities, Minority Rights Group International, British Library.
14. Musferah Mehfooz (2021). Religious Freedom in Pakistan: A Case Study of Religious Minorities, Religions 2021, 12(1), 51; https://doi. org/10. 3390/rel12010051.

Bibliography

1. Anderson, Benedict. "Imagined communities: Reflections on the origin and spread of nationalism." In the new social theory reader, pp. 282-288. Routledge, 2020.
2. Bhargava, Rajeev, Muhammad Rezaur Rahman, Razia Sanwari, and Shaheed Bhagat Singh. "A Journal of Centre For Study Of Society And Secularism."
3. Brass, Paul R. Ethnicity and nationalism: Theory and comparison. New Delhi: Sage Publication, 1991.
4. Breuilly, John. Nationalism and the State. Manchester University Press, 1993.
5. Chatterjee, Partha. The nation and its fragments: Colonial and postcolonial histories. Vol. 4. Princeton University Press, 1993.
6. Chatterjee, Partha. "Secularism and toleration." Economic and Political Weekly (1994): 1768-1777.
7. Chatterjee, Partha. The nation and its fragments: Colonial and postcolonial histories. Vol. 4. Princeton University Press, 1993.
8. Jaffrelot, Christophe. "Gujarat: The meaning of Modi's victory." Economic and Political Weekly (2008): 12-17.
9. Varshney, Ashutosh. "Nationalism, ethnic conflict, and rationality." Perspectives on Politics 1, no.1 (2003): 85-99.
10. Ernest, Gellner. "Nations and nationalism." Paris, Payot (1983).
11. Ghosh, Partha Sarathy. "Ethnicity versus nationalism: The devolution discourse in Sri Lanka." (No Title) (2003).
12. Harriss, John, Craig Jeffrey, and Stuart Corbridge. "Is India becoming the 'Hindu Rashtra' sought by Hindu nationalists." Simons Papers in Security and Development 60 (2017): 2017.
13. Harriss, John, Craig Jeffrey, and Stuart Corbridge. "Is India becoming the 'Hindu Rashtra' sought by Hindu nationalists." Simons Papers in Security and Development 60 (2017): 2017.
14. Huntington, Samuel P. The clash of civilisations and the remaking of world order. Braille Jymico Incorporated, 2004.
15. Jaffrelot, Christophe. The Hindu nationalist movement and Indian politics: 1925 to the 1990s: strategies of identity-building, implantation and mobilisation (with special reference to Central India). Penguin Books India, 1999.
16. Jaffrelot, Christophe, ed. Hindu nationalism: A reader. Princeton University Press, 2009.
17. Juergensmeyer, Mark. The new cold war? Religious nationalism confronts the secular state. Vol. 5. Univ of California Press, 2023.
18. Gottlob, Michael. "India's unity in diversity as a question of historical perspective." Economic and Political Weekly (2007): 779-789.
19. Vaishnav, Milan. "From Cakewalk to Contest: India's 2019 General Election." (2018).
20. Smith, Anthony D. "National Identity University of Nevada Press." Nevada, USA (1991).

21. Palshikar, Suhas. "The BJP and Hindu nationalism: Centrist politics and majoritarian impulses." South Asia: Journal of South Asian Studies 38, no. 4 (2015): 719-735.

22. Van der Veer, Peter. Religious nationalism: Hindus and Muslims in India. Univ of California Press, 1994.

23. Vanaik, Achin. "The painful transition: Bourgeois democracy in India." (No Title) (1990).

24. Varshney, Ashutosh. Ethnic conflict and civic life: Hindus and Muslims in India. Yale University Press, 2003.

25. Varshney, Ashutosh. "Contested meanings: India's national identity, Hindu nationalism, and the politics of anxiety." Daedalus 122, no. 3 (1993): 227-261.

26. Chakrabarty, Bidyut, and Bhuwan Jha. Hindu nationalism in India: ideology and politics. Routledge, 2019.

Chapter - 6

Nationalism in South Asia: A Historical Perspective

— **Dr Raju Ojha**

Introduction

This paper analyses nationalism in South Asia in historical perspectives and it will also focus on the recent trends that led to the development of nationalism to hyper nationalism in certain extent. Nationalism is a complex phenomenon and it may have different shapes and expressions in South Asian countries. In South Asia one historical date is 1947 when India's independence from the British raj was accompanied. This date is a turning point in the construction of nationalism in South Asia. As such this paper looks in to the dynamics of nationalism in most of the states in South Asia with particular emphasis on the leading actors.

South Asia has been a true laboratory for the students of nation-building and nationalism. No other region has experienced two partitions of the magnitude of those of 1947 and 1971. The rise and growth of nationalism in South Asia was a reaction against colonial exploitation and subjugation. The new form of nationalism that became the basis of the new states in South Asia derived much of its ideology and political theory from the West but was adapted to particular circumstances and experiences. The basis of this new nationalism was an instinctive and xenophobic hatred for imperialism and symbols of imperialism. It was a simple hatred against those who had occupied their land by force, exploited their riches by force, crushed their government, and enslaved their people.

Nationalism also became a creative force which aimed at building a nation based upon the principles of liberty, independence, economic justice and nationality. It not only united the people, but also inspired them to contribute their share in the national reconstruction. The lead in this regard was given by India which produced one of the biggest mass movements in the world. The movement not only succeeded in freeing it from colonial yoke, but also left a historically developed, well thought out programme for free India. The example of India inspired other colonies such as Sri Lanka and gave raise to political consciousness in countries like Nepal, Bhutan, and the Maldives. (Ignou, 2017)

Nationalist movement spreads when people from different religions and communities begin to develop a sense of collective belongingness. Through this, an identity of a nation is characterised. This image of Bharat Mata was first created by Bankim Chandra Chattopadhyay in 1870 when he wrote 'Vande Mataram' for our motherland. During the Swadeshi Movement, a tri-colour (red, green and yellow) flag was designed in Bengal. It had eight lotuses representing eight provinces and a crescent moon representing Hindus and Muslims.

Indian National Congress was founded in December 1885 by seventy-two political workers. It was the first organised expression of Indian Nationalism on an all-India scale. In other words, Indian Nationalism grew partly as a result of colonial policies and partly as a reaction to colonial policies in fact, it would be more correct to see Indian nationalism as a product of a mix of various factors. The national movement got a new lease of life in 1928 when the British government announced the appointment of Simon Commission to study the next steps of democratic reforms in India. The Congress boycotted the commission on the ground that Indians were not represented in the Commission.

On 31 December, 1929, Congress, under the presidentship of Motilal Nehru passed a resolution for Purna Swaraj, that is, complete independence. The Civil Disobedience Movement began on 6 April 1930 by breaking the salt law. Gandhi prepared a comprehensive plan for this movement. He wanted every village to fetch or manufacture contraband salt, women to picket liquor shops, opium dens and shops of foreign cloth dealers; the young and old to spin khadi and burn foreign cloth, the Hindus to eschew untouchability, students to leave government school and government servants to resign their jobs. The government responded by issuing a number of ordinances, banning the Congress and all its branches, closing down newspapers and printing presses and arresting as many as 90,000 people.

In March 1946, the British government sent a Cabinet Mission to India. After long and detailed discussions with different political parties and organisations, the Mission rejected the Muslim League's demand to partition the country and made its proposals for an Indian federation and the setting up of a constituent assembly. The proposals were accepted both by the Congress and the League though reluctantly. In September 1946, an interim government was formed under the leadership of Jawaharlal Nehru. The Muslim League also joined the government but decided not to participate in the making of a new constitution. On 20 February 1947, the British Prime Minister announced his government's decision to quit India before June 1948. Lord Mountbatten was to be sent to India to make arrangements for the transfer of power. In the meantime, the bickering within the interim government were threatening the breakdown of the administration.

Bangladesh

The first significant event that was a landmark in the development of Bengali nationalism in Pakistan was the decision of the ruling government of Pakistan to introduce Urdu as the national language of Pakistan in disregard of Bengali wishes. Bengalis saw it as an attempt at cultural intrusion. Different strata of population came out to protest this decision. When military assault on Bengali nationalists began on 25th March, the civil disobedience and the non-cooperation movement turned into armed struggle. The brutal military action accompanied by torture, rape and murder of intellectuals destroyed the last vestiges of Pakistani nationhood in the people of Bangladesh. The heavy civilian causalities led to an unprecedented migration of Bengali people to India. What should rightfully have been an internal affair of Pakistan, thus became a major problem of India. India provided sanctuary and training facilities to the freedom fighters. Besides, it mounted a massive diplomatic offensive to being to the notice of the world the genocide in Bangladesh and its liberation struggle. Finally, Pakistan spelt its own doom by declaring war on India on 31st December. The armed struggle ended on 16th December 1971 when the Pakistani army surrendered to the joint command of the Bangladesh Liberation Army and the Indian army in Dacca. Bangladesh emerged as a sovereign independent nation.

Nepal

Nepal was a Hindu kingdom in the past and then a constitutional monarchy in the modern period for many years. Throughout this period, political parties and the although Nepal's unification as a nation and its rise as military power in the lap of the Himalayas were attained in a span of less than half a century.

Prithvi Narayan Shah, who laid the foundations of Nepal's political unification, in his Dibya Upadesh advisory refers to the country as a garden of "four castes and 36 ethnicities". That 'garden' was created not through voluntary consensus of the various communities but through the might of the sword. The country was under the feudal rule of the Gorkhali. After the Anglo-Nepali War, there was no fear of the powerful southern neighbour, as the British did not covet Nepali soil once they got access to Gorkhali manpower as mercenaries.

There were two models of nationalism prevalent during the period of colonialism. One that was called European model, which was based on ethnicity, identity, language, religion and cultural homogeneity (Gellner, 2006). The other was premised upon the historical and cultural antecedents pervasive in the Indian sub-continent dating back to ancient times and in the form a common front against the colonialism.

India

Apart from this feature, Indian nationalism was plural, non-coercive and civil. It was plural in the sense that the Indian nationalist leaders recognised the great Indian diversity but refused to consider it as a weakness or an obstacle that would have to go away in the journey towards nationhood. In other words, they consciously promoted the idea of the Indian nation as being based on cultural plurality rather than cultural monism. Perhaps the best statement endorsing India's plurality and linking it with nationalism came from Mahatma Gandhi who wrote in his weekly journal Harijan in 1940: "India is a big country, a big nation, composed of different cultures which are tending to blend with one another, each complementing the rest. If I must wait for the completion of this process, I must wait. It may not be completed in my day. I shall love to die in the faith that it must come in the fullness of time. " As is clear from Gandhi's statement, the Indian nationalist leaders fully recognised that nation making for India was a long process and far from accomplished. And that India's diversity was no obstacle.

While Indian nationalism derived its social and economic content from the objective conditions of Indian society, from the technological changes brought about by the contact with Britain, and from the consciously worked-out reform programme of the Indian National Congress, it was also to a certain extent the product of the particular character of the nationalist movement itself and of the unique method of struggle adopted by it.

Nationalist movement remained an upper and middle class affair, social and economic ideas would not have invaded it so much, and after independence, nationalism would have, probably, degenerated into a conservative, if not a reactionary, force. Under Mahatma Gandhi, the masses, both urban and rural, were drawn into the national struggle and political freedom took a new shape.

A large number of factors have contributed to the growth of nationalism in South history of the Indian sub-continent and its glorious traditions are important sources of nation almost all the countries of the region. The notions of composite culture, civilisation state their inspirations from the history and traditions of the subcontinent. The historical events, traditions, etc. have played a significant role in uniting the people into a single national The colonial rule and the quest for independence and self-rule have been important the growth of nationalism in South Asia. In fact, the ideology of nationalism was articulate countries, in the wake of struggle for independence. In Nepal and Bhutan, the absence of colonialism was taken up as a source of of national pride and identity. It gave them a sense of superiority in comparison to those countries, which were under the colonial rule. These countries although lacked the nationalist ethos which took roots during the course of struggle for independence in the state.

However, the rise of nationalism experienced in Asia today is utterly different from the past. Today, nationalism seems to be less about self-determination and more about emphasizing differences in ethnicity, gender or religion. It is an attempt to define an "us" against a "them." The idea of a nation therefore becomes exclusive to only a few. This feeling of exclusivity and national privilege is cleverly fostered by populist politicians. The idea of nationalism can be healthy if it is merely used as an ideological tool toward a broader liberating objective, and not as a political goal itself. The nationalism ideology in Mahatma Gandhi's independence movement is not the same as the extreme nationalist, racist and nativist agenda of far-right groups. Historically, third-world nationalism in different countries in Asia was progressive, for it was a resistance movement pursued in the spirit of anti-imperialism and anti-colonialism. It was inspired by an anti-colonial national consciousness, rather than by the viciousness of racial aggrandizement. It was focused on the collective aspirations of the people for liberation, rather than on an abstract devotion to a nation. (Heinrich-Böll-Stiftung, 2018)

Notes and References

Florian, B. (2018). Is Nationalism on the Rise? Assessing Global Trends, Ethnopolitics

Juego, B., Soesanto, E., & Heppe, F. (2018). Nationalism that violates the dignity of human beings deserves condemnation. Perspectives Asia, (7), 4-8.

https://th. boell. org/en/2018/11/28/perspectives-asia-7-nationalisms-and-populisms-asia

Nationalism and Populism in Asia (2018). Heinrich-Böll-Stiftung Retrieved from n. boell. org/en/2018/12/12/perspective-asia-nationalisms-and-populisms-asia.

Gellner, E. (2006). Nations and Nationalism. 2nd ed. New York: Cornell University Press.

Struggle for Independence and Nationalism in south Asia Retrieved from https://egyankosh. ac. in/bitstream/123456789/21085/1/Unit-1. pdf

Part-II

Development, Desperation and Destitution

Chapter - 7

Globalisation vs. Nationalism: Striking a Balance in a Connected World

— **Dr Veeragoni Shirisha**

1. Introduction

Living in the digital age, the popular notions of nations, nationalities, nationalism and cultures undergo a rapid changes. The frequency of communication and transportations of goods and services keep on reshaping new spheres and spaces. These changes are brought in by the phenomenal impact of globalisation and its far reaching effect in the nook and corners of the world at large. As such the world has become more interdependent, and if not reduced in to a digital village. The fact that economic impact of the globalisation brought the market closer to each societies and countries keep away the old notions of rigid stands on identities and boundaries. On the other hand, thereis consistent and persistent ways of reshaping the culture, ethnicity nationalities and nationalisms too. In a way, the new realities keep on conditioning the world in a more mature and democratic ways. But it also carry contradictory effects in terms of promoting and propagating the parochial and partisan forces at large. As such an attempt is made here to relate how the process of globalisation conditioned the popular notions of nationalism. Its true that when the process of globalisation consolidated the world in to a more transparent one, it also counter-produced a stronger market cultures market ridden equations whereby the forces attempt to go in hand with the traditional and fundamentalist forces. The remergence of such fundamentalism attempt to reshape the new forms of nationalism, either in the name of religion, ethnicity or regionalism. Thus this paper would like to see the historical context of globalisation and examine how it reshaped the world economy, culture and politics whereby the nationalism itself got reinvented in to new forms and modes. As such this paper looks at the following objectives;[1] to understand and Rise of

Economic globalisation and it's impact on Nationalism.[2] to detail the Rise of political globalisation and it's impact on Nationalism.[3] to conceptualise the role of globalisation and it's impact on socio-cultural context where by it try to re-define Nationalism in new ways modes.

2. Globalisation: Contents and contextualisation

Globalisation refers to the expansion of economic transactions and activities across political boundaries of all states. In other ways it is defined as a process involving economic openness, growing interdependence, deepening economic integration in the global economy. Equally, the phenomenon was a multidimensional one. Its reach out is not confined to one dimension alone but it stretched out to social, cultural and political domains. This being the reality, the process has been witnessed to political democracies in the developing societies. In this way it advances the technology, transport system, communication system among the different countries of the world. The process saves time and money of people and make life easier. Another way of understanding the phenomenon is to assess it in the context of culture. Once the cultural components are influenced, it stretches over to political process as well.

3. The Historic Back drop

Against the notion of the understanding of the origin of Globalisation as one emerging in recent past, the real roots of the same could be traced back to the century. In ancient time there is silk route and spice route that connected east to west. In the search of trade they found that path. In the eighteenth and nineteenth century there was industrial revolution in Britain and it is impacted widely the whole world. After the Globalisation new inventions happened. Their manufacturing industry was expanded. They needed market to sell those products. And it also provided the way for connecting the world. After the world war II, many international organisations were established like international monetary fund, World Bank, the UNO etc. These institutions also emphasized on interconnectedness of countries. Equally nation states were monitored and controlled from the legal and moral point of views for the collective good of the humanity.

4. Impact of globalisation on cultural and economic domains

Its a fact that globalisation acts as a catalyst in connecting nations and this interconnected and interdependence is directly and indirectly benefits the entrepreneurs in terms of greater economic transactions. When the producers collect raw materials at a lower cost from countries where it is available and after manufacturing they sell it to higher prices at different Market. This reciprocity and interconnectedness make the brisk transactions between and among nations. Equally now it is common that different parts of a particular component are manufactured in different countries and merged this in other country and sell it to whole world. Financial markets also are benefited by globalisation. It impacts on stock market, value of currency and investment. Due to globalisation, further, outsourcing and offshoring increases. Many businesses outsources task to countries with lower labour cost. All these aspects lower cost of production as well as the the same increases the volume of business whereby there was an almost boost of business in almost all sectors of production.

As far as the cultural dimensions are concerned, the increase in economic activities do make its own cultural reflections as well. The process of globalisatoion do interfere with the aesthetical aspects of life as well. Entertainment, media production other creative forms of art did witness to a grand change in its letter and spirit. Global mix of art from made craze demand for Corean drama, Netflix and verieties of Hollywood movies.

Apart from all these the process of globalisation is responsible for the increase in travel and tourism among the world and this leads to fusion of culture. Another major part that is influenced by globalisation is language and communication. English has become a global lingua franca, and social media platforms enable people to connect and share the idea across the border of the country. These being the positive implications, it do bring benefits brings many challenges in the context of nationalism, where as we have been witnessing to narrow and parochial mode of nationalism assuming larger significance at least in the developing world, particularly in South Asia.

5. The Rise of nationalism

Nationalism is a belief including loyalty, pride, attachment towards ones own country. It is a multifaceted and complex concept. Every country has its unique way of identifying their respective nationalism. There are many forms of Nationalism. One of them is civic nationalism. In this form of it mainly focus on pride, values and citizenship of specific country. In this kind of nationalism they connect other country through the commitment to common principles. The second one is ethnic nationalism – in this kind of nationalism, it focuses mainly upon ethnic heritage on the basis of national identity. And the third one is ultra nationalism. In this kind of nationalism people become aggressive or xenophobic. In this kind of nationalism we see dominance of one's nationalism over other. Apart from these varieties of nationalisms there are a varieties of reasons why in the globalised world nationalism found a narrow and rigid come back.

6. Resurgence of nationalism

Economic inequality is a major factor of it. There is wide disparity of wealth among different countries of the world. Due to this disparity the feeling of disenfranchisement grows and they try to protect their nation's interest. Globalisation discontent is also a prominent factor. On the one hand globalisation has brought many economic benefits on the other hand job displacement also occurs at the same time. Migration and refugees crises is also one factor of resurgence of nationalism. They strived nationalism sentiments in other countries. In the time of election and war leaders use this as a weapon to gain support particularly from the majoritarian communities.

7. The Rise of Economic globalisation and it's impact on nationalism

When interconnectedness and interdependence take place across country in the field of economy, culture and politics then it is due to the impact of globalisation At the same time nationalism is refered to a particular country's identity. Globalisation is influencing nationalism in many ways. In many scenarios, we have seen that globalisation weakened the nationalism and in other scenario it strengthens it. When countries interdependence and interconnectedness increases in the field of economy then it is termed as economic globalisation. In this kind of globalisation there is unrestricted movement of goods and services, labour among countries. Economic globalisation has impacted nationalism in negative sense due to this the disparity between countries on the basis of income, wealth has increased. Often it creates tension among different countries of the world.

We also know that economic globalisation boosts economy of every country and make the world as a market. But because of this reason people focuses on their professional benefits and forget about nation's identity. It is not good for any country's identity. They emphasizes on global identity rather than country specific identity. Overall, nationalism and globalisation are connected and we will see it's more impact in the coming years.

8. Political globalisation and it's impact on Nationalism

When there is interconnectedness of policies, politics, institutions among different countries than it is called political globalisation. After world war II many international organisations were established and that institution make the way of political globalisation across the world. Nationalism is impacted by globalisation in multiple ways. In many scenarios, political globalisation is treating as a threats to nationalism. If any country interconnected to other country than the country have to follow international rules and this weakening their sense of national sovereignty. Globalisation can spread the feeling of democracy and human values. And this can be counted as positive aspects of globalisation on nationalism. overall, we can say that political globalisation has both positive and negative impact on Nationalism.

9. Cultural globalisation and it's impact on Nationalism

When ideas and values of one country, cultural practices are inter-connected among different countries than this is termed as cultural globalisation. It is increased now-a-days because of travel and tourism, technology and communication. English has become a global lingua franca, and social media platforms enable people to connect and share ideas across borders instantaneously. Cultural globalisation is a major challenge for Nationalism of any country. In summary, we can say that globalisation and nationalism are intrinsically interrelated. It's impact varies according to the situation. Governments should Foster a sense of unity and pride in national identity while acknowledging the benefits of global cooperation. More emphasis should be on Inclusive Policies. Leaders should implement policies that bridge divides within their societies, ensuring that the benefits of globalisation are accessible to all, and that no group feels marginalized. They should Improve International Engagement. Leaders should engage constructively on the global stage, seeking collaborative solutions to global challenges rather than retreating into isolationism.

10. Strategies for Reconciling Globalisation and Nationalism

In the era of globalisation countries have to make policies that embraces diversity and they have to emphasize on inclusion within nation. This can be achieved through education, cultural exchange programme and through the many inclusive programme. In the policy government should focus to mitigate the income disparity and concern about negative impact of globalisation. Governments have to take initiative to promote national identity and sovereignty.

11. Role of International Institutions and Diplomacy

After World War II, many international organisations were established in the world. These institutions are strengthening the international corporation time to time. They encourage countries to work together. These institutions took countries together to address and solve the world wide problems like climate change, COVID pandemic etc. These institutions also solve the conflict situation among different countries through diplomacy. World Trade Organisation international monetary fund etc always support fair trade agreement between countries and try to make global economic sovereignty.

12. Critique of globalisation in the context of nationalism

Globalisation and nationalism represent two interconnected yet opposing concepts. Globalisation pertains to the growing interconnectedness and mutual reliance of economies, societies, and cultures on a global scale, whereas nationalism signifies a profound allegiance to one's nation, coupled with the aspiration for self-governance and autonomy. Critics of globalisation within the framework of nationalism contend that it weakens the sovereignty and self-reliance of nations. The increased movement of capital, goods, and services across international borders has eroded national boundaries and diminished control over economic policies. Consequently, wealth has become concentrated in the hands of a select few multinational corporations, leaving ordinary citizens and smaller enterprises at a disadvantage. Additionally, globalisation has led to a homogenisation of cultures, resulting in the loss of local traditions and practices. The propagation of Western values and consumerism has eroded cultural diversity and the distinctiveness of nations, leading to a loss of identity and belonging. Nationalists argue that globalisation has adverse social effects, including heightened inequality, social unrest, and job losses due to the outsourcing of labour to low-wage nations. They propose that addressing these issues requires restricting the influence and authority of global institutions while supporting local economic and cultural self-determination.

However, detractors of nationalism caution that it can foster isolationism, xenophobia, and ethnic conflicts. Nationalism often defines a nation based on ethnicity or race, which can lead to discrimination against minorities and immigrants. It may also encourage assertive and expansionist foreign policies as nations seek to assert their dominance and safeguard their interests. In summary, the critique of globalisation within the context of nationalism underscores the tension between the forces of global integration and the desire for national autonomy and identity.

While globalisation has brought numerous advantages, it has also counter-produced challenges that necessitate solutions to ensure equitable benefits across nations and cultures. Concurrently, nationalism must be balanced with respect for human rights and diversity to avoid the adverse consequences of ethnocentrism and exclusion.

13. Conclusion

Nationalism has played a significant role in shaping historical global events, and its trajectory in our interconnected world is a topic of extensive discussion and conjecture. On the one hand globalisation has fostered greater interdependence among nations. Equally, globalisation has facilitated the growth of multinational corporations and international trade and finance. On the other hand it diminishes the national identity and sovereignty within the country. Globalisation has opened doors to connect the country world wide and share their experiences and ideas. Due to globalisation the feeling of nationalism has eradicated and generate a sense of global citizenship among people. Major problems around the world is solved together like climate change problem, economic disparity and pandemic situation also. But in this situation national identity will loose. Governments of different nations have to develop a sense of belonging to their citizens. Otherwise national security will go in vein. Governments should be able to address citizens and offer them security by fostering a sense of unity and pride in national identity while acknowledging the benefits of global cooperation.

In this regard more emphasis should be on Inclusive Policies. Leaders should implement policies that bridge divides within their societies, ensuring that the benefits of globalisation are accessible to all, and that no group feels marginalised. They should improve international engagement. Leaders should engage constructively on the global stage, seeking collaborative solutions to global challenges rather than retreating into isolationism. In conclusion we can say that by achieving this requires a shift away from zero-sum thinking, acknowledging that one nation's interests are interconnected with those of all nations.

Ultimately, the future of nationalism in a globalised world is contingent on our individual and societal choices. Embracing an inclusive, collaborative, and forward-looking form of nationalism could help construct a more equitable and sustainable world.

Notes and References

- Sasses, S. (2006) Territory, Authority, Rights: From Medieval to Global Assemblages, Princeton, NJ.
- Smith, A. D. (1995). Nations and Nationalism in a Global Era, Cambridge.
- Arnason, J. P., 'Nationalism, Globalisation and Modernity', in M. Featherstone (ed.) (1990) Global Culture: Nationalism, Globalisation and Modernity, London and New Delhi.
- Bayly, C. A. (2004). The Birth of the Modern World 1780 1914, Oxford.
- Clark, I. (1997). Globalisation and Fragmentation: International Relations in the Twentieth Century, Oxford.
- For a survey of the debate see D. Held and A. McGrew (2007) Globalisation/ Anti Globalisation: Beyond the Great Divide, 2nd edn., Cambridge.
- For the full range of theories of globalisation see R. Robertson and K. E. White (eds.)(2003). Globalisation: Critical Concepts in Sociology, 6 vols., London and New York.
- M. D. Bordo, A. M. Taylor, and J. G. Williamson (eds.) (2003). Globalisation in Historical Perspective, Chicago and London.
- Elements of such a (historical) theory are assembled in C. A. Bayly (2004). The Birth of the modern World 1780 1914: Global Connections and Comparisons, Oxford.
- A seminal theoretical statement is offered by J. P. Arnason, 'Nationalism, Globalisation and Modernity', in M. Featherstone (ed.) (1990). Global Culture: Nationalism, Globalisation and Modernity, London and New Delhi, 20736.
- S. Sassen (2006). Territory, Authority, Rights: From Medieval to Global Assemblages, Princeton, NJ, 1. Sassen, Territory, 23.
- Clark (1997). Globalisation and Fragmentation: International Relations in the Twentieth Century, Oxford, 27. Another important theorist is James N. Rosenau, who has coined the Term 'fragmegration'. See James N. Rosenau (2003) Distant Proximities: Dynamics beyond Globalisation, Princeton, NJ, 11.
- Bayly, "Archaic" and "Modern" Globalisation in the Eurasian and African Arena, c. 1750 1850', in A. G. Hopkins (ed.) (2002) Globalisation in World History, London, 4773.
- L. Colley (1992). Britons: Forging the Nation 1707 1837, New Haven, CT. For a differently nuanced view see P. Mandler (2006) The English National Character: The History of an Idea from Edmund Burke to Tony Blair, New Haven, CT. 14. J. A. Frieden (2006) Global Capitalism: Its Fall and Rise in the Twentieth Century, New York.

Chapter - 8

Nationalism and International Integration; The Case of India's economic performance and its marked presence

— Prity Kumari

Introduction

Globalisation and nationalism, though stand distinct, often reflect and tend to be complementary and interlinked with common social outcomes and its related outputs. Globalisation stands for interconnectedness of different nations in terms of economy, society, culture etc, while nationalism is a belief of nationalist sentiments. India makes a crucial juncture in economic trajectory because of the dual forces of globalisation and nationalism. This paper tries to find out the effect of globalisation on economic growth of India and challenges posed by nationalist sentiments. It's a fact globalisation offers many new opportunities and new avenues opened for Indian economy and equally raises concerns about protecting national identity and cultural questions. Initiatives for protectionist measures like "Make in India" reflect the light on self reliance. In this mission the task ahead of India is to make balance between globalisation and emerging nationalism for safeguarding its national sovereignty. As such the nation has resorted to important policies and strategies to Navigating Nationalism and International Integration for the purpose of attaining an inclusive and sustainable economic growth. As such this paper attempts to explore how India needs to balance globalisation and emerging nationalism in order to preserve its national sovereignty, and examines important policies and strategies for navigating nationalism and international integration, and focuses on the importance of inclusive and sustainable economic growth in defence rights involving domestic industries for the sake of job creation, industrial competitiveness and strategic autonomy. Also, as we see that India has to face opportunities and challenges as it integrates globally. India should act in such a way that balances the tensions between international integration and nationalist aspirations. Such policies will not only be beneficial to the development of the country, but also have a standing in the international community. Overall, it can be said that removing the complexity of globalisation and nationalism, India can continue its economic development and thus this paper proceeds with three basic objectives.

- To understand the globalisation and nationalism in Indian context.
- To understand how globalisation has increased the sense of nationalism.
- To examine the impact of globalisationon Indian economy.

1. Interrelations and Interconnectedness of the concepts

Globalism and Nationalism are mutually coexisting objective phenomenon with inherent contradictions and interconnectedness. The relationship between the two are explored by many scholars. The theme has been the focus of many observers and led to many comments that have dominated the conflict at various levels in recent history. This question can be answered in two different ways. Who sees nations and nationalism as lost in history, creating a path to human progress that will soon collapse and make way for other structures needed to sustain global unity; and the other suggests that nationalism as the most powerful and enduring political force is nothing short of extinct – it is active in response to global challenges. Although both approaches have many differences, they understand the relationship between internationalism and nationalism. Both are fundamentally opposite to each other and therefore are determined to be long and hostile. In the first case, nationalism is expected to collapse and the latter leaves the middle stage to follow other paths up and down, as global logic requires. In the second scenario, nationalism will not persist, but will grow and strengthen in response to the destructive forces of international cooperation. Therefore, according to the words of Anthony Giddens, "the revival of nationalism and its local symbols are directly related to the power of the hostile world".

In the era of globalisation, India attracts the global attention because of its economic growth. India has adopted liberalisation, privatisation and globalisation (LPG) policy in 1990s, the LPG reform has given a wave to indian economy. This reform has opened the Indian economy globally. And Indian economy has transformed into fastest growing economies. There were many complexities in the growth journey of India, many challenges comes in the way of globalisation many of them posed by nationalism and the imperatives of safeguarding its sovereignty and identity. The interweaving of nationalism and globalisation has become a dominant feature of the Indian economy. On the one hand, globalisation has brought many benefits, such as increased trade, investment, and technological progress. India has become a major global information technology hub and day by day manufacturing and service development is growing tremendously. On the other hand, nationalist sentiment was on the rise, driven by concerns about preserving national identity, protecting local infrastructure, and reducing dependence on foreign powers. The Make in India initiative launched in 2014 epitomizes India's response to these challenges, aiming to promote domestic manufacturing and reduce reliance on imports.

2. Defining Globalisation and Nationalism

Globalisation can be defined as "the process of interaction and integration of society, that is, companies and governments from different countries as stated by Erwin (2017). Erwin is no longer globalisation has stated that this is the common terminology of the twenty-first century, in which we have seen a lot more interaction between people around the world through channels like social media and international economic interdependence. According to Giddens, "Globalisation is recognised as the intensification of social relationships that connect people around the world remote areas so that local events are shaped by frequently occurring events kilometers away and vice versa." (Giddens, 1990). According to Holm and Sorensen (1995: 1–7): Globalisation can be defined as an economic, political, social and cultural intensification cross-border relations.

On the other hand, nationalism as defined in the Merriam-Webster dictionary is "loyalty" and dedication to the nation; in particular: a feeling of national consciousness exalting the nation above all and with an emphasis on promoting your culture and interests, unlike other nations or transnational groups. This was mentioned by Erwin (2017). "Nationalism is the idea of identifying with a nation and adhering to that point of view a nation and its culture are superior to others. Nationalism does not identify with just one thing country and its culture, is rather a largely psychological phenomenon. Erwin (2017) added that in the modern era, nationalism has become associated with idealised concepts what a nation should look like, usually based on how it has functioned in the past. As mentioned Kacowicz (1998), the term "nationalism" refers to the feeling of attachment to someone different from that of the members of the nation and the feeling of pride that the nation has in itself. Nationalism itself is an international ideology that can be used to promote and defend: specific culture and way of life

(Godfrey, 2008). This was stated by Abdulsattar (2013), Nationalism is the basis of modern society and social solidarity.

3. Globalisation and the Promotion of Nationalism, National Extremism

Today, culture has become a new source of conflict and an important dimension the struggle between the global and the local. (Godfried, 2008). According to Giddens, "The Directly related to this is the revival of local nationalism and the emphasis on local identity. globalising influences that they oppose" (Giddens: 1994, cited in: Natalie: 2010). Abdulsattar (2013) stated that since globalisation is an external force that pushes in the case of localities that led to a reduction in national understanding, they responded in a very local way face this pressure decisively, adopting a stronger national sense. More communication and interactions lead to greater awareness of individual identity and cultural differences, leading to by the increasing emphasis on ethnic, cultural and national differences, which will lead to a greater number of conflict (Abdulsattar, 2013). Due to globalisation, minorities in many countries are like this mobilise to demand justice and respect, and established communities often oppose them demands (Riggs, 2012) and this is an example of how globalisation has increased the power sense of identity, culture, faith among various social and religious groups. Relaxing (1993) state that to preserve culture, traditions, language and national movements they are motivated by a certain community, wanting to guarantee its existence. Here it comes the concept of "fundamentalism", which refers to groups that resist not only globalisation but also the structure of the globe as a whole (Abdulsattar, 2013). According to Robertson "Resistance to contemporary globalisation, for example, the radical side of mainstream Islam. This movement would be seen as opposition not only to the unified system, but also to the system itself, the concept of the world as a series of cultural equals." (Robertson, 1996). Therefore, Fundamentalism opposes and provokes the idea of homogeneity of cultures and nationalities extreme nationalism (Abdulsattar, 2013).

4. Globalisation and its Impact on Indian Economy

Chakraborty and Basu (2002) used a vector error correction mechanism (VECM) structural cointegration model to examine the relationship between FDI and GDP growth in India over the period 1974–1996. Empirical results show that in the long run there is a two-way relationship between FDI and GDP, while in the short run there is a one-way relationship between GDP and FDI flows in a country.

Calvo and Robles (2003) examine the relationship between FDI, economic freedom and economic growth in a sample of 18 Latin American countries using a panel data set covering the period 1970–1999. The study shows that FDI has a positive impact on economic growth and is an effective channel for the transfer of technology, know-how and management skills to these countries. However, to reap the benefits of FDI, countries must achieve a minimum level of development and provide greater freedom to economic operators.

According to Frenkel et al. (2004), FDI is identified as an important factor for the sustainable growth of developing economies, which mainly involves the transfer of capital from developed and emerging economies to these countries for the benefit of the whole world. FDI can accelerate growth in countries by creating jobs in host countries, reducing the savings gap and huge investment demand, and sharing management knowledge and skills through upstream and downstream linkages in host countries.

Maqsood and Azam (2010) stated that all countries must improve human capabilities by increasing investment in the education and health sectors. Increasing human capacity will certainly increase the country's productivity and economic growth. Batarseh and Ananzeh (2015) investigate the causal relationship between economic growth and FDI during the period 1975-2013 in Jordan. Using cointegration, the Granger causality test and the error correction model, the study found a unidirectional relationship between economic growth and FDI in Jordan, not the other way around.

Using quarterly data for 2001-2010 and applying VECM and the cointegration method, Szkorupova (2014) examines the causal relationship between FDI, exports and GDP in Slovakia. The study confirms a sporadic and unidirectional relationship between FDI and GDP growth in the mentioned country.

5. Impact of Globalisation on Indian Economy

In the modern world, the main objective of every country is to ensure continuous improvement in the living standards of the masses. Policies and strategies are adopted that help promote economic growth without any fluctuations in business. Each country places primary emphasis on enriching human and social capital, innovation and entrepreneurship skills, and the accumulation of physical capital. With the wave of globalisation and liberalisation, the importance of international capital flows in generating economic activity has increased. Currently, resource-deficit countries are creating policies and providing incentives to attract FDI to accelerate economic growth.

Some recent studies have highlighted the role of FDI in the economic growth of developing countries. Borensztein (1998) states that the impact of foreign direct investment (FDI) on a country's economic growth depends on the level of education (human capital) of the host country. There is also evidence of an agglomeration effect in host countries as FDI becomes a source of inward investment growth. Findlay (1978) postulates that FDI increases the rate of technological progress in the host country through contagion effects from more advanced technologies and management practices used by foreign companies. Giirsoy and Kalyona (2012) stated that FDI is a means by which technology and physical capital can be transferred from developed countries to developing countries, which can increase their rate of growth and development, as was the case of Georgia. However, FDI is most attracted to countries that have a sound social infrastructure in the form of well-functioning state institutions, stable governments, sound economic policies and an adequate level of physical infrastructure. Hall and Jones (1999) believe that FDI helps developing countries to import improved technology and know-how, increase productivity and ensure maximum utilisation of their resources. Alfaro etal. (2004) suggest that the functioning of local financial markets must be properly regulated to reap the benefits of FDI in the short and long term. Blomsrtom et al. (1992, pp. 1-36) found that the lower the initial per capita income compared to the US (1960), the faster the subsequent growth. In this way, developing countries can benefit from FDI, improved technology and knowledge developed by other countries.

However, FDI flows have a more positive impact on countries with higher income levels. Developing countries, therefore, need to reach a minimum level of development in order to make the most of the investments of foreign companies. Like other developing countries, FDI can play a central role in India's economic development. After three decades of domestic politics since independence, Rajiv Gandhi realised in the mid-1980s how important it was to open up his economy and take advantage of the wave of globalisation and liberalisation. The liberalisation process gained momentum after India faced an economic crisis in 1991-1992 and decided to change its economic policy. Policy has changed significantly and many incentives have been created to attract FDI. In addition, trade policy changes have been introduced to increase exports and open import channels for essential machinery and other related materials. A large market and cheap labour have made the country an attractive destination for FDI, not only for traditional trading partners, but also for many industrialised economies in Asia. FDI, exports, imports and foreign remittances have grown at an ever-increasing pace and played an important role in the economic development of the country. There is a wealth of literature on the role of FDI in the economic development of developing countries facing resource and technology constraints. It was similar in the case of India, and when the economy opened, the dynamics of the gross domestic product (GDP) showed an upward trend, as can be seen in Figure 1.

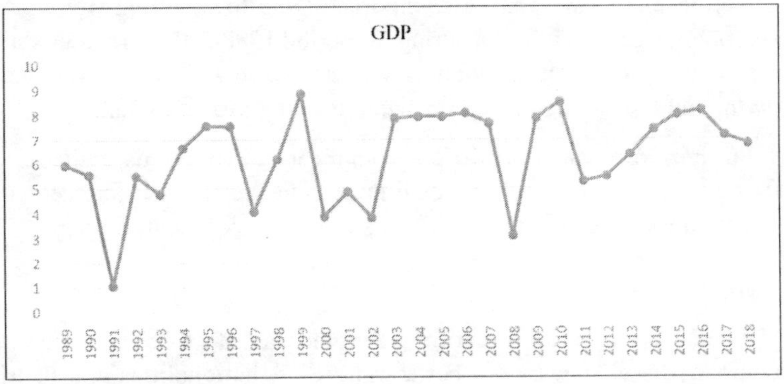

Source: World Development Indicators, World Bank.

Figure 1: GDP Growth Rate.

It should be noted that after the economy opened to the world, imports grew faster than exports. There are many reasons for the rapid increase in imports relative to exports, including: demand for large machines, advanced technological devices, technical knowledge and low competitiveness of domestic products on the world market. The dynamics of exports, imports, FDI and remittances from abroad are presented in Figure 2.

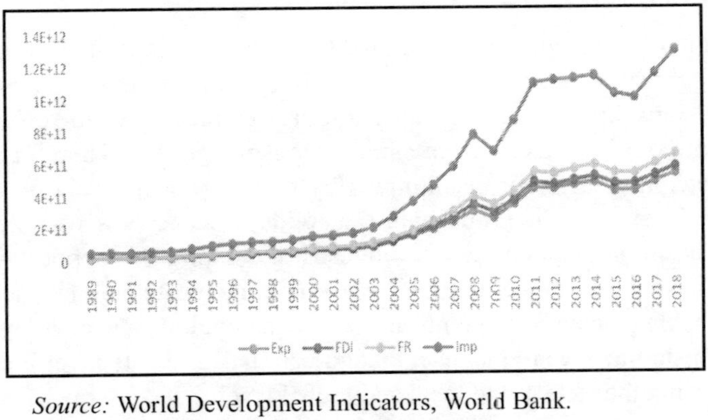

Source: World Development Indicators, World Bank.

Figure 2: Growth of Exports, FDI, Foreign Remittances and Imports.

Figure 2 shows that imports have grown at a much faster pace than exports, foreign remittances and FDI. Recently, many researchers have tried to investigate the relationship between variables. Recently, time series analysis using the Autoregressive Distributed Lag (ARDL) bounds testing method has become popular among researchers examining relationships between variables. In this study, the same approach was used to analyze the relationship between exports, imports, FDI inflows, foreign remittances and economic growth of India during the period 1988-2018. Previous studies have examined the relationship between one or two variables and economic growth, and few studies take into account all factors of globalisation.

Furthermore, this study differs from recent and previous studies on the use of advanced econometric techniques. India, as an emerging economy, has gone through many ups and downs in its development journey.

6. Conclusion

Finally, it can be said that the strengthening of globalisation and the accompanying changes were born, minorities, nationalities and districts woke up and came. They are more aware of the dangers arising from globalisation. This resulted in a greater national feeling than the respond to the power of globalisation in the protection of cultures, traditions and nationalities from falling apart due to globalisation or taking on a new global structure (Abdulsattar, 2013). Thus, the fear of the power of globalisation gave birth to this expression "Xenophobia", where people fear that their nationality and traditions will disappear in view of globalisation and therefore people tend to retain their customs and traditions or restore old traditions in which they retain their identity (Abdulsattar, 2013). Finally it's here.

It has been suggested that globalisation has the capacity to overcome the aggressive nationalism it engenders emphasizing isolation and uncertainty. In addition, globalisation creates incentives to resolve and prevent conflicts arising from simultaneous integration. Therefore, build character in educational institutions by reviving local media promoting national values, celebrating national holidays and events with zeal and enthusiasm, strengthening local industries, creating job opportunities in order to stop the brain drain, it is necessary to inculcate moral values and a sustainable globalised economy and society maintaining the interdependent relationship between globalisation and nationalism for the welfare of the people and the state at the local and global level.

The results indicate that there is a positive and significant relationship between FDI, imports and economic growth in the long run. In the short term, imports play a more important role in the country's economic growth, as the results above show. In the case of exports and remittances abroad, there is a significant negative relationship between these two variables and economic growth. These results suggest that exports and foreign remittances need more time to have a positive impact on India's economic growth. The study by Pereira and Xu (2000) and Sultanuzzaman et al. (2018) also found that exports had a negative impact on economic growth. Given the countries' trade policies and export structure, this means that it takes longer for exports and remittances than imports and foreign direct investment to have a positive impact on the country's economic growth. From the above study, it is clear that India should focus more on foreign direct investment and imports, which can lead to comparative advantages in export-oriented industries, export-led growth strategy and development path for other sectors of the economy. Furthermore, the composition of exports needs to be improved towards higher value-added products that will help improve the country's long-term development. The country's policymakers should promote foreign direct investment to reduce barriers, encourage joint ventures between domestic and foreign companies, and increase exports to achieve stronger effects to accelerate the growth of the Indian economy.

This article represents a breakthrough in analyzing the impact of globalisation on India's economic growth. However, the finding is limited to a few variables and other variables such as exchange rate, inflation and human capital may be included in future work.

Notes and References

Ahmad, N., Hayat, M. F., Luqman, M., & Ullah, S. (2012). The causal links between foreign direct investment and economic growth in Pakistan. European Journal of Business and Economics, 6. http://doi. org/10. 12955/ejbe. v6i0. 137

Alfaro, L., Chanda, A., Kalemli-Ozcan, S., & Sayek, S. (2004). FDI and economic growth: The role of local financial markets. Journal of International Economics, 64(1), 89–112.

Azam, M. (2013). Foreign direct investment, financial deeping and economic growth in Azerbaijan and Kazakhistan: A comparative empirical study. The Empirical Economic Letters, 12(6), 611–618.

Azam, M. (2016). Does governance and foreign capital inflows affect economic development in OIC countries? Journal of Economic Cooperation and Development, 37(4), 21–50.

Azam, M., & Ahmad, M. (2015). Role of human capital and foreign direct investment in promoting economic growth: Evidence from Commonwealth of independent states. International Journal of Social Economics, 42(4), 98–111.

Batarseh, A., & Ananzeh, L. (2015). The casual relationship among foreign direct investment, domestic saving and economic growth in Jordan during the period (1975-2013). International Journal of Business and Management, 10(1), 173–179.

Behname, M. (2012). Foreign direct investment and economic growth: Evidence from South Asia. Atlantic Review of Economics, 2, 1–14.

Blomsrtom, M., Lipsey, R., & Zejon, M. (1992). What explains developing country growth[Working Paper No. 4132]. National Bureau of Economic Research.

Borensztein, E., Gregorio, J. D., & Lee, J. (1995). How does foreign direct investment affect economic growth? Journal of International Economics, 45(1), 115–135.

Calvo, M. B., & Robles, B. S. (2003). Foreign direct investment, economic freedom and growth: New evidence from Latin-America. European Journal of Political Economy, 19(3).

Cambazoglu, B., & Karaalp, S. (2014). Does foreign direct investment affect economic growth? The case of turkey. International Journal of Social Economics, 41(6), 434–449.

Chakraborty, C., & Basu, P. (2002). Foreign direct investment and growth in India: A cointegration approach. Applied Economics, 34(9), 1061–1073.

Engle, R. F., & Granger, C. W. (1987). Co-integration and error correction.

Frenkel, M., Funke, K., & Stadtmann, G. (2004). A panel analysis of bilateral FDI flows to emerging economies. Economic Systems, 28(3), 281–300.

Giirsoy, F., & Kalyona, H. (2012). Foreign direct investment and growth relationship in Georgia. International Journal of Economics and Financial Issues, 2(3), 267–271.

Hall, R. E., & Jones, C. I. (1999). Why do some countries produce so much more output per worker than others? Quarterly Journal of Economics, 114(1), 83–11.

Iqbal, M. S., Shaikh, F. M., & Shar, A. H. (2010). Causality relationship between foreign direct investment, trade and economic growth in Pakistan. Asian Social Science, 6(9), 82–89.

esentation, estimation, and testing. Econometrica: Journal of the Econometric Society, 251–276.

Findlay, R. (1978). Relative backwardness, direct foreign investment, and the transfer of technology: A simple dynamic model. The Quarterly Journal of Economics, XCII(1), 1–16.

Feridun, M., & Sissoko, Y. (2011). Impact of FDI on economic development: A causality analysis for Singapore, 1976-2002. International Journal of Economic Sciences and Applied Research, 4(1), 7–17.

Lall, S., & Narula, R. (2004). Foreign direct investment and its role in economic development: Do we need a new agenda? The European Journal of Development Research, 16(3), 447–464.

Maqsood, A., & Azam, M. (2010). The role of human capital in economic development: Evidence from Pakistan: (1961-2009). Interdisciplinary Journal of Contemporary Research in Business, 2(4), 220–234.

MacKinnon, J. G. (1996). Numerical distribution functions for unit root and cointegration tests. Journal of Applied Econometrics, 11(6), 601–618.

Mawugnon A. K., & Qiang, F. (2011, November). The relationship between foreign direct investment and economic growth in togo (1991–2009). In Proceedings of the 8th International Conference on Innovation and Management (ICIM 2011) Vol. 73, E1269 E. Kitakyushu, Japan, November 30–December 2, 2011.

Narayan, P. K. (2005). The saving and investment nexus from China: Evidence from cointegration tests. Applied Economics, 37, 1979–1990.

Pacheco-López, P. (2005). Foreign direct investment, exports and imports in Mexico. World Economy, 28(8), 1157–1172.

Pesaran, M. H., Shin, Y., & Smith, R. J. (2001). Bounds testing approaches to the analysis of Level relationships. Journal of Applied Econometrics, 16, 289–326.

Reza, S., Fan, H., Reza, T., & Wang, W. (2018). The impact of foreign direct investment inflows on economic growth: Evidence from Bangladesh. Journal of Business and Retail Management Research, 12(2), 212–223.

Sultanuzzaman, M. R., Fan, H., Akash, M., Wang, B., & Shakij, U. S. M. (2018). The role of FDI inflows and export on economic growth in Sri Lanka.

Szkorupova, Z. (2014). A casual relationship between foreign direct investment, economic growth and exports for Slovakia. Procedia Economics and Finance, 15, 123–128.

Thangamani, B., Xu, C., & Zhong, C. (2010). Determinants and growth effect of FDI in South Asian economies: Evidence from a panel data analysis. International Business Research, 4(1), 43–50.

Tiwari, A. K., & Mutascu, M. (2011). Economic growth and FDI in Asia: A panel-data approach. Economic Analysis and Policy, 41(2), 173–187.

Zachariadis, T. (2006). On the exploration of causal relationships between energy and the economy. University of Cyprus Working Papers in Economics.

Chapter - 9

Nationalism and Development in India; The case of Modi Administration

Shiwangi Singh, Mohan Lal Meena & Vikas Patel

1. Introduction

The paper refers to development and nationalism over the last two tenure of the Prime Minister Narendra Modi under the Modi administration. The Government and establishment used nationalism as the justification for development to achieve high rates of growth, but it also breeds exclusives and hostility frequently in order to unite a political core. During the Modi period, popular nationalism has also dialectically reshaped the objectives and patterns of development. During the Modi era, India has seen a focus on nationalism and development. The Modi government has emphasized the importance of a strong, united, and self-reliant India, while also pushing for economic growth and development. On the nationalist front, the Modi government has taken several steps to promote a sense of pride in Indian culture and heritage. For instance, there has been a push to revive traditional practices and promote the use of Indian languages.

Additionally, the government has implemented policies aimed at promoting Hindu nationalism, which has led to some controversy and criticism. In terms of development, the Modi government has implemented several initiatives aimed at boosting economic growth and improving living standards for Indians. Some of the key programme include the quote; Make in India and quote; campaign, which aims to promote manufacturing in India, and the and quote; Digital India and quote; campaign, which seeks to expand access to digital technologies across the country. The government has also launched several infrastructure projects, such as the construction of new highways and railways, aimed at improving connectivity and stimulating economic growth. However, there have been some criticisms of the Modi governments approach to development. Some have argued that the governments policies have not done enough to address issues such as poverty and inequality, and that the benefits of economic growth have not been distributed evenly. There have also been concerns about environmental damage and the impact of development on indigenous communities. Overall, the Modi era has been characterised by a focus on nationalism and development, but therehave been both successes and challenges in these areas.

The politics of casteism, succession, corruption, and appeasement have given way to the politics of development, growth, unification, and nationalism in the country. By empowering the disadvantaged groups in our society, from the poor and backward classes, Dalits and minorities, tribals and oppressed classes, to women and youth, this amazing journey has strengthened democracy in its truest sense. Altering the Indian psyche from one of the quote; nothing is possible in this country and quote; to one of the quote; everything is possible if the government and the people have the will and commitment and quote; hasalso been a journey. It also demonstrates that any challenge can be overcome and any issue can be resolved if a leader has a broad objective, a sustainable policy and programme, intention, and devotion. Then there are several path breaking schemes like Jan Dhan Yojana, Ujjwala Yojana, Kisan Samman Nidhi, Ayushman Bharat Yojana, Gareeb Kalyan Yojana, Swachh Bharat Yojana, Awas Yojana, Jal Jivan Mission, Digital India, Gram Vikas Yojana, Goods and Services Tax, which not only empowered citizens but also strengthened our economy and made India resilient and self-reliant (Atmanirbha). Schemes such as Atmanirbhar Bharat, Vocal for Local, Gati Shakti Yojana, PLI (production linked incentive) catapulted India to the top of the global world order. Previous administrations lacked the resolve to address enduring issues, so everything was left to chance. It all came down to PM Modi's innovative and tenacious strategy to solving issues. His firm resolve led to the scrapping of Article 370, construction of the grand Ram Temple in Ayodhya, abolition of instant Triple Talaq, passing of the Citizenship Amendment Act and surgical strikes on terror camps across the border. Citizens lives were made easier, and government effectiveness increased.

The confidence and support of Indians gained the key success under PM Modi. People today are aware that the central government is dedicated to Sabka Saath-Sabka Vikas, Sabka Vishwas-Sabka Prayas and works for their wellbeing. He is dedicated to transforming India and creating a nation where everyone is united, content, and wealthy. Its time to regurgitate India is a prosperous and happy country by working diligently. Cultural nationalism is a political and social movement that emphasizes the cultural identity and heritage of a particular nation or group of people. It is based on the idea that a shared culture, language, and history are important aspects of national identity, and that preserving and promoting these cultural values is essential to maintaining a strong and cohesive society. Cultural nationalism can take many different forms, from promoting traditional art, music, and literature, to advocating for the use of a particular language or dialect in public life. It is often closely linked with concepts such as patriotism, pride in ones country or region, and a desire to maintain cultural traditions and customs.

While cultural nationalism can be a positive force for promoting cultural diversity and preserving important cultural traditions, it can also be used to promote exclusionary and discriminatory practices, particularly towards minority groups or immigrants who do not share the dominant culture of a society. As such, it is important to approach cultural nationalism with a critical eye and to ensure that it is not used as a means of promoting intolerance or division. Cultural nationalism shared culture and language are used to identify the nation rather than ideas of common ancestry or race. The appearance of common and political idea's establish on the local spiritual and cultural, traditions of the Indian subcontinent have been referred to as Hindu nationalism as a whole. The phrase "Hindu nationalism" is often translated in a crude manner. It is more appropriately called "Hindu polity." Hindutva, which means "Hinduness," is the most popular and prevalent brand of Hindu nationalism in India today. (Vinayak Damodar Savarkar) coined the term "Hindutva" to describe a political philosophy in 1923. The fundamental tenet of Hindu nationalism is the belief that the country exists and that all of its citizens have some things in common. In a diverse nation like India, this might get out of hand. The concept of a pre-existing Hindu country and a sense of national pride in ones language, culture, and homeland are the foundations of cultural nationalism. It is rare to demote to the Modi brand of nationalism as "Hindutva," which is more widely known (loosely translated as Hindu-ness). Examples include the current government's efforts to promote Sanskrit in schools and its efforts to promote yoga and Ayurveda both inside andoutside of India.

One of the pioneers in the twentieth century to make an attempt at a comprehensive definition of the term "Hindu" in terms of what he called Hindutva, or "Hinduness," was Savarkar. The name "Hindutva" was first used by Savarkar, a nonreligious rationalist, in an effort to distance it from any religious associations that had come to be associated with it. While defining the term "Hindu" Savarkar said, "He who considers India to be both his Nation andHoly land." Thus, Hindutva ("Hindu-ness") or Hindu was defined as distinct from Hinduism.[2] This definition only recognised native religious denominations as Hindu and excluded the Abrahamic religions (Judaism, Christianity, and Islam).

Nationalism Since 2014

The concept of & quote; Hindutva, & quote; which emphasizes the cultural and religious identity of India's majority Hindu population, is the foundation of the nationalism advocated by Prime Minister Modis administration. Some have criticized the government's approach to nationalism asbeing exclusive and polarising because it can marginalise minority populations like Muslims and other religious groups. The term nationalism refers to a political ideology thatemphasizes the interests of a particular nation, often in opposition to globalisation or internationalism. Since 2014, there have been several instances of nationalism gaining prominence in various parts of the world. Here are some notable examples:

India

In India, the rise of Hindu nationalism and the election of Narendra Modi as Prime Minister in 2014 has led to a resurgence of Indian nationalism. Modis government has pursued policies that emphasize India's cultural heritage and promote Indian nationalism. The abrogation of Article 370 of the Indian Constitution, which granted special status to the stateof Jammu and Kashmir, and the building of the Ram Mandir in Ayodhya, which was a major campaign pledge of the ruling party, are two of the key policies and initiatives implemented by the Modi government that have been linked to nationalism such as through the Make in India and Aatma Nirbhar Bharat Abhiyan initiatives, with the aim of promoting national prideand self-reliance.

United States

In the United States, the election of Donald Trump as President in 2016 was seen by many as a victory for nationalism. Trump's and quote; America First and quote; policies and his opposition to immigration and globalism were seen as nationalist in nature.

United Kingdom

The Brexit referendum in 2016, which resulted in the United Kingdom's decision to leave the European Union, was seen as a victory for nationalism. Many who supported Brexit argued that the UK needed to regain control over its own affairs and that this could only be achieved through leaving the EU.

Russia

In Russia, President Vladimir Putin's government has pursued policies that emphasiz Russian nationalism and the country's historical greatness. Putin has also been accused of promoting a form of neo-imperialism, which seeks to restore Russia's influence in the world.

China

In China, the government has pursued a policy of the quote; Chinese Dream, which emphasizes China's historical greatness and the need to assert its influence in the world. This has been accompanied by a rise in Chinese nationalism and a more assertive foreign policy. Overall, the rise of nationalism since 2014 has been driven by a variety of factors, including economic inequality, globalisation, and a sense of cultural identity under threat. While nationalism can provide a sense of belonging and purpose for some, it can also lead to intolerance and conflict if taken to an extreme.

Economic Nationalism

The Aatma Nirbhar Bharat Abhiyan

One of the main aim of this cultural revolution is to make one's country strong. An economics trategy known as Aatma Nirbhar Bharat Abhiyan, or the quote; Self-Reliant India Mission, was introduced by the Indian administration in May 2020. The strategy aims to make India self-sufficient in a number of industries, including manufacturing, technology, and agriculture, among others. With the intention of lowering India' s reliance on imports and fostering domestic production, the Aatma Nirbhar Bharat Abhiyan strategy has been promoted as a type of economic nationalism. The policy's proponents contend that in order to ensure India's sovereignty and independence, it is essential to develop a strong and independent economy. However, detractors of the policy contend that it is excessively centered on protectionism and isolationism and that it may result in a decline in foreign investment and trade, which could be detrimental to India's long-term economic development. Additionally, they contend that because domestic production may not be as effective as imported goods, the strategy may result in higher prices for consumers. The Aatma Nirbhar Bharat Abhiyan policy has been marketed as a type of economic nationalism, but it is still unclear how it will affect India's long-term economic growth andrelations with other nations.

Economic Nationalism: Make in India

Another economic initiative introduced by the Indian government in 2014, Make in India, seeks to support domestic manufacturing and draw in foreign capital. India's competitiveness in the international market is to be increased, and the strategy aims to establish India as a hub for global manufacturing. The Make in India initiative, which emphasises the value of domestic output and lowers India's reliance on imports, has been compared to the Aatma Nirbhar Bharat Abhiyan policy. In order to boost national pride and foster a feeling of nationalism, the policy also aims to promote Indian brands and products. Economic nationalism is a political and economic ideology that prioritizes the interests of a country's domestic economy and industry over international trade and globalisation. The idea behind economic nationalism is that protecting domestic businesses and industries from foreign competition can help to create jobs, foster economic growth, and ensure national security.

The goal of the initiative is to make India a global manufacturing hub by creating an environment that is conducive to business and investment. The Make in India initiative is often seen as an example of economic nationalism in action. By promoting domesticmanufacturing, the Indian government hopes to create jobs, boost economic growth, and reduce the country's reliance on imported goods. The initiative also includes measures to simplify and streamline regulations, reduce bureaucratic red tape, and improve infrastructure, all of which are intended to make India a more attractive destination for foreign investment.

However, some critics argue that economic nationalism and protectionism can have negative consequences, such as limiting competition, reducing innovation, and driving up prices for consumers. They also argue that a reliance on domestic manufacturing can lead to inefficiencies and reduced competitiveness in the global market. Economic nationalism is a political and economic ideology that prioritizes the interests of a country's domestic economy and industry over international trade and globalisation. The idea behind economicnationalism is that protecting domestic businesses and industries from foreign competition can help to create jobs, foster economic growth, and ensure national security.

Conclusion

Overall, while the Modi government's approach to nationalism has been criticized by some for being exclusionary and divisive, it has also been seen as a way to promote a sense of national pride and unity among India's majority Hindu population. The impact of these policies on India's diverse society and long-term social cohesion remains a topic of debate.

Notes and Reference

1. Savarkar, Vinayak Damodar: Hindutva, Bharati Sahitya Sadan, Delhi 1989 (1923).
2. Savarkar, Vinayak Damodar: Hindutva, Bharati Sahitya Sadan, Delhi 1989 (1923).
    - Savarkar, Vinayak Damodar. Hindutva, Bharati Sahitya Sadan, Delhi 1989 (1923).
    - McDonald, Ian. & quote; Physiological Patriots'? The Politics of Physical Culture and Hindu Nationalism in India. & quote; International Review for the Sociology of Sport 34. 4 (1999): 343-358.
    - Kinnvall, Catarina. Globalisation and religious nationalism in India: The search for ontological security. Vol. 46. Routledge, 2007.
    - Athreya, Aditi. & quote; Cultural nationalism in India. & quote; Anthropol 4. 165 (2016): 2332-0915.
    - Biswas, Debajyoti, and John Charles Ryan, eds. Nationalism in India: Texts and Contexts. Routledge, 2021.
    - Siddiqui, Kalim. & quote; A critical study of 'Hindu Nationalism'in India. & quote; Journal of Business and Economic Policy 3. 2 (2016): 9-28.
    - Anand, Dibyesh. Hindu nationalism in India and the politics of fear. Springer, 2016.
    - Shani, Giorgio. & quote; Towards a Hindu Rashtra: Hindutva, religion, and nationalism in India. & quote; Religion, State & amp; Society 49. 3 (2021): 264-280.
    - Kumar, Sunil. & quote; Contribution of Western Culture in Nationalism of India. & quote; Thematic Journal of History 1.1 (2017).

Chapter - 10

Nationalism and Development in South Asia

— Dr Vinay Chandra Pathak

Introduction

Nationalism is an ideology promoting nationhood, a strong sense of collective identity and solidarity among a wide population on the basis of their common language, culture, heritage, religion, or citizenship in a state. It is important to distinguish between two types of nationalism which are sometimes called; civic nationalism and ethnic nationalism. Nationalism as a term was mentioned for the first time in 1409 at Leipzig University. It was not before the end of the eighteenth century that it began to be used in the sense of national egoism. A person's great love for their nation can be referred to as nationalism. It is often associated with the belief that a particular nation is better than any other nation. This kind of fierce nationalism is a powerful and potentially volatile force. Nationalism is primarily a political principle, which holds that the political unit and the national unit should be congruent...Nationalist sentiment is the feeling of anger aroused by the violation of the principle, or the feeling of satisfaction aroused by its fullment.

A nationalist movement is one actuated by a sentiment of this kind. (Ernst Gellner, Nations and Nationalism, 1983) Nationalism not only creates a sense of national identity. It presents the state as the most important form of political organisation for a people. Nationalism encourages the vie that 'nations' should be governed by a 'state' made up of members of that nation. National self-determination really strengthens the validity of the state as an expression of 'nationhood'. This is not a new idea: 'All nations and reasonable men prefer to be governed by men of their own country and nation, who share the same language as them...rather than by strangers.' If this desirable state could not be achieved peacefully then it was to be prosecuted by war, if necessary. (Boyd and Harisson, 2018) (Miller, 2023) discussed how nationalism in South Asia is often associated with and defined as anti-colonial nationalism, as the South Asian elites vied to gain political and economic freedom from the British, seek self-rule and parallelly develop the idea of what it means to be a nation.

Development has several aspects: economic growth (mainly through industrialisation), political restructuring (improving administrative effectiveness and democratic participation), and sociocultural modernisation (which some do, and others do not, equate with Westernisation). In examining the relationship between nationalism and development, we have found these two factors embedded in a larger system, so that the causal connections between them are mediated by other factors-especially the presence or absence of democracy. We have also needed to distinguish between various types of nationalism-civic and ethnic-and of development-sustainable and unsustainable. At present, ethnic nationalism seems to be a greater threat to peace, security, and development than civic nationalism. (Spencer & Becher, 2001) Nationalism is certainly related to economic development, but it is largely an inward interactive process, promoting National social as well as economic growth, e.g. America First. All development processes have a tendency to expand and Nationalism seeks expansion since it brings prosperity and affluence in its own way. Expansion, however, depends on adequacy of available resources, which may, in case of inadequacy, be acquired by borrowing or begging, in both cases falling in the debt trap. The newly developing countries including Pakistan present a case in example.

Nationalism assumes a nation capable of forming a national and developmental class coalition and defining a national development project. When a society is deeply divided into social classes, the bourgeoisie tends to unite around a liberal economic policy regime. When it senses an external threat, or when it manages to define a national development project, the nation imposes itself to civil society and a developmental class coalition forms. In such times, the two ruling classes – the capitalist and the techno-bureaucratic classes – divide into fractions, and manufacturing businessmen, workers and the public techno-bureaucracy form a developmental coalition in a struggle against a rentier-financier coalition formed by rentier capitalists, financiers and the senior private-sector techno-bureaucracy that manages major corporations. (Bresser-Pereira, 2018)

The developmental coalition gives rise to a popular and national economic Nationalism, and economic nationalism in particular, has informed most Asian nation-states since the Second World War. While patrimonial tendencies—the tendency of leaders to treat national resources as their patrimony—have periodically been parasitic on economic strategy, by and large the pursuit of national advantage has been the primary thrust of Asian nation-states. Import substitution industrialisation or export-oriented strategies have sometimes been sequential, but they often have been subtly combined, especially in East Asian nations, from the 1960s. Economic nationalism in the era of post-Cold War globalisation continues to prevail, although with considerably different approaches as Asian nations have come to accept global integration and seek to make their domestic firms more competitive in the global market.

An academic conception of South Asia which emerged typically in the 1950s. American academia, driven by the requirements of US foreign policy in the post-war world. This optic aggregated spaces from a geopolitical point of view, disregarding political and cultural differences—which may be significant for their inhabitants, but unimportant for the framing of American strategy. There is considerable literature on the history of this notion which shows how a term prompted by military calculation slowly morphed into a respectable disciplinary entity in academic scholarship. Gradually its geopolitical connotation was replaced by a different content, as postcolonial states grew and required more serious academic scrutiny. There was a concern to avoid study of the region exclusively centred on India, or one of the other post-colonial states. It should encourage more comparative research; but comparative analysis is plagued by an ambiguity in its self-definition. There is still a great deal of uncertainty about whether the starting point should be the historic similarity of the societies or the dissimilarities of their contemporary political systems.

At a much prior stage, Bankim Chandra had understood that since one of the fundamental issues of Indian legislative issues was the need of social attachment, it was this that should have been given more attention than maybe patriotism itself. Undoubtedly, an essential to patriotism was the nearby recognizable proof of the person with a specific network and the separation of the enthusiasm of the specific network from different networks. Subsequently, a few of the prior patriot pioneers were seeing union as a piece-feast measure. However, the elements of imperialism itself made conditions for solidarity. South Asian states are undergoing a fundamental transformation with ethno-political conflict. At the core of ethno-political conflict are issues about state power and the distribution of economic and other material resources. The settlement of these conflict has entailed a political process of negotiating how to alter radically the way in which state power is organised and distributed which, in turn, is resulting in democratisation of the political community, pluralisation of the state and sharing of state sovereignty.

Nehru's ideas were implemented during the first decades of the Republic through the Five Year Plans of the Planning Commission, which he chaired. Other South Asian countries also developed national plans that stressed self-sufficiency, national markets, growth, and reduction of poverty and inequality. To be sure, these plans were not anti-market, but rather pro-national market (Ludden, 2005). The Nehruvian model of a mixed economy and a secular, democratic (bottom-up) political system remained a powerful imaginary of the nation that also became deeply entrenched as different interests and path dependencies became fixed into it.

The last wave of nationalism in India came with the BJP, who appealed to the middle and lower-middle classes suffering from the economic transformation in the country. The party was able to win hearts and votes through a populist rhetoric underlining religion and tradition. Prime Minister Narendra Modi represented the country's best chance at much-needed economic reforms. That would have been true…so long as Modi kept focused on the economics, as he largely did throughout his first term from 2014-2019. During those years, Modi was able to radically simplify the country's arcane tax system and institute a comprehensible goods and services tax. By modernising the country's bankruptcy laws, Modi helped transform India into a serious destination for foreign investment. Significant infrastructure investment in roads, airports, public transportation and sanitation improved the lives of literally hundreds of millions of people in just the span of a few years.

Modi was able to channel India's gains from globalisation into actionable policy; for the first time in generations, India had a leader who seemed to transcend the country's sclerotic and corrupt politics to tangibly improve the lives of everyday Indians. Even his policies that didn't pan out as expected—like pulling 86% of the country's hard currency out of circulation in an ill-fated attempt to quash the country's black market—still underscored that India was being led by a politician with both ambition and strategic vision. (Bremmer, 2019) The most basic meaning of nationalism is the use of this way of categorizing human populations, both as a way of looking at the world as a whole and as a way of establishing group identity from within.

In addition, nationalism usually refers not just to using the category of nation to conceptualize social groups but also to holding that national identities and groups are of basic importance (and often that loyalty to one's own nation should be a commanding value). Nationalism is thus simultaneously a way of constructing groups and a normative claim. The two sides come together in ideas about who properly belongs together in a society and in arguments that members have moral obligations to the nation as a whole—perhaps even to kill on its behalf or die for it in a war. (Calhoun, 1993) Hyper nationalism can be highly disruptive, it advancing the interests of one group above all else—even at the expense of others. Hyper nationalism is illiberal and intolerant and doesn't accept those outside the narrowly defined nation as equal. Extreme nationalism, the belief in the superiority of one's nation and the desire to make it strong. This "us versus them" mentality, often rooted in ideas of racial and national superiority, can lead to dangerous and violent ends.

Notes and References

Boyd & amp; Harrison (2018). Understanding political ideas and movement. Manchester University Press.

Bremmer, I (2019). I Argued That Narendra Modi Was India's Best Hope for Economic Reform. Things Have Changed. Time Magazine https://time. com/5753624/india-narendra-modi-nationalism/

Bresser-Pereira, L. C. (2018). Economic Nationalism and Developmentalism, Fiscaoeconomia, Special Issue (1), 1-27.

Calhoun, C. (1993). Nationalism and Ethnicity. Annual Review of Sociology, 19, 211–239.

Centre for Social and Economic Progress. (2023). Nationalism, Great Power and Conflict in South Asia. https://csep. org/wp-content/uploads/2023/04/ Nationalism-great-power-and-conflict-in-south-asia. pdf

Duara, P. (2019). Nationalism and Development. In: Asian Transformations: An Inquiry into the Development of Nations. Edited by Deepak Nayyar, Oxford University Press.

Spencer. (2022). Development and Nationalism. Retrieved from https://www. mettaspencer. com/?Papers:Academic_papers:Development_and_Nationalism.

Chapter - 11

Nationalism and Political Violence

— Dr Deo Krishna Choudhary

1. Introduction

Nationalism is an idea and movement that holds that the nation should be congruent with the state. As a movement, it presupposes the existence and tends to promote the interests of a particular nation, especially with the aim of gaining and maintaining its sovereignty over its perceived homeland to create a nation-state. It holds that each nation should govern itself, free from outside interference (self-determination), that a nation is a natural and ideal basis for a polity, and that the nation is the only rightful source of political power. It further aims to build and maintain a single national identity, based on a combination of shared social characteristics such as culture, ethnicity, geographic location, language, politics, religion, traditions and belief in a shared singular history, and to promote national unity or solidarity. Nationalism, therefore, seeks to preserve and foster a nation's traditional culture. There are various definitions of a "nation", which leads to different types of nationalism. The two main divergent forms identified by scholars are ethnic nationalism and civic nationalism.

Beginning in the late eighteenth century, particularly with the French Revolution and the spread of the principle of popular sovereignty or self determination, the idea that "the people" should rule is developed by political theorists. Three main theories have been used to explain the emergence of nationalism: Primordialism (perennialism) developed alongside nationalism during the romantic era and held that there have always been nations. This view has since been rejected by most scholars, and nations are now viewed as socially constructed and historically contingent.

Modernisation theory, currently the most commonly accepted theory of nationalism adopts a constructivist approach and proposes that nationalism emerged due to processes of modernisation, such as industrialisation, urbanisation, and mass education, which made national consciousness possible. Proponents of this theory describe nations as "imagined communities" and nationalism as an "invented tradition" in which shared sentiment provides a form of collective identity and binds individuals together in political solidarity.

A third theory, ethnosymbolism explains nationalism as a product of symbols, myths, and traditions, and is associated with the work of Anthony D. Smith. The moral value of nationalism, the relationship between nationalism and patriotism, and the compatibility of nationalism and cosmopolitanism are all subjects of philosophical debate. Nationalism can be combined with diverse political goals and ideologies such as conservatism or socialism. In practice, nationalism is seen as positive or negative depending on its ideology and outcomes. Nationalism has been a feature of movements for freedom and justice, has been associated with cultural revivals, and encourages pride in national achievements. It has also been used to legitimize racial, ethnic, and religious divisions, suppress or attack minorities, undermine human rights and democratic traditions and start wars, being frequently cited as a cause of both World Wars.

The terminological use of "nations", "sovereignty" and associated concepts were significantly refined with the writing by Hugo Grotius of De jure belli ac pacis in the early seventeenth century. [how?] Living in the times of the Eighty Years' War between Spain and the Netherlands and the Thirty Years' War between Catholic and Protestant European nations, Grotius was deeply concerned with matters of conflicts between nations in the context of oppositions stemming from religious differences. The word nation was also applied before 1800 in Europe in reference to the inhabitants of a country as well as to collective identities that could include shared history, law, language, political rights, religion and traditions, in a sense more akin to the modern conception.

Nationalism as derived from the noun designating 'nations' is a newer word; in the English language, dating to around 1798. The term gained wider prominence in the nineteenth century. The term increasingly became negative in its connotations after 1914. Glenda Sluga notes that "The twentieth century, a time of profound disillusionment with nationalism, was also the great age of globalism. Academics define nationalism as a political principle that holds that the nation and state should be congruent. According to Lisa Weeden, nationalist ideology presumes that "the people" and the state are congruent.

2. Intellectual origins

Anthony D. Smith describes how intellectuals played a primary role in generating cultural perceptions of nationalism and providing the ideology of political nationalism:

> Wherever one turns in Europe, their seminal position in generating and analysing the concepts, myths, symbols and ideology of nationalism is apparent. This applies to the first appearance of the core doctrine and to the antecedent concepts of national character, genius of the nation and national will.

Smith posits the challenges posed to traditional religion and society in the Age of Revolution propelled many intellectuals to "discover alternative principles and concepts, and a new mythology and symbolism, to legitimate and ground human thought and action". He discusses the simultaneous concept of 'historicism' to describe an emerging belief in the birth, growth, and decay of specific peoples and cultures, which became "increasingly attractive as a framework for inquiry into the past and present and an explanatory principle in elucidating the meaning of events, past and present".

The Prussian scholar Johann Gottfried Herder (1744–1803) originated the term in 1772 in his "Treatise on the Origin of Language" stressing the role of a common language. He attached exceptional importance to the concepts of nationality and of patriotism "he that has lost his patriotic spirit has lost himself and the whole world about himself", whilst teaching that "in a certain sense every human perfection is national". Erica Benner identifies Herder as the first philosopher to explicitly suggest "that identities based on language should be regarded as the primary source of legitimate political authority or locus of political resistance". Herder also encouraged the creation of a common cultural and language policy amongst the separate German states.

3. Emergence of nationalism

Scholars frequently place the beginning of nationalism in the late eighteenth century or early nineteenth century with the American Declaration of Independence or with the French Revolution. The consensus is that nationalism as a concept was firmly established by the 19th century. In histories of nationalism, the French Revolution (1789) is seen as an important starting point, not only for its impact on French nationalism but even more for its impact on Germans and Italians and on European intellectuals. The template of nationalism, as a method for mobilising public opinion around a new state based on popular sovereignty, went back further than 1789: philosophers such as Rousseau and Voltaire, whose ideas influenced the French Revolution, had themselves been influenced or encouraged by the example of earlier constitutionalist liberation movements, notably the Corsican Republic (1755–1768) and American Revolution (1775–1783).

Due to the Industrial Revolution, there was an emergence of an integrated, nation-encompassing economy and a national public sphere, where British people began to mobilise on a state-wide scale, rather than just in the smaller units of their province, town or family. The early emergence of a popular patriotic nationalism took place in the mid-eighteenth century and was actively promoted by the British government and by the writers and intellectuals of the time. National symbols, anthems, myths, flags and narratives were assiduously constructed by nationalists and widely adopted. The Union Jack was adopted in 1801 as the national one. Thomas Arne composed the patriotic song "Rule, Britannia!" in 1740, and the cartoonist John Arbuthnot invented the character of John Bull as the personification of the English national spirit in 1712.

The political convulsions of the late eighteenth century associated with the American and French revolutions massively augmented the widespread appeal of patriotic nationalism. Napoleon Bonaparte's rise to power further established nationalism when he invaded much of Europe. Napoleon used this opportunity to spread revolutionary ideas, resulting in much of the 19th-century European Nationalism.

Some scholars argue that variants of nationalism emerged prior to the eighteenth century. American philosopher and historian Hans Kohn wrote in 1944 that nationalism emerged in the seventeenth century. In Britons, Forging the Nation 1707–1837, Linda Colley explores how the role of nationalism emerged about 1700 and developed in Britain reaching full form in the 1830s. Writing shortly after World War I, the popular British author H. G. Wells traced the origin of European nationalism to the aftermath of the Reformation, when it filled the moral void left by the decline of Christian faith; nineteenth century.

The political development of nationalism and the push for popular sovereignty culminated with the ethnic/national revolutions of Europe. During the nineteen0th century nationalism became one of the most significant political and social forces in history; it is typically listed among the top causes of World War. Napoleon's conquests of the German and Italian states around 1800–1806 played a major role in stimulating nationalism and the demands for national unity. English historian J. P. T. Bury argues:

> Between 1830 and 1870 nationalism had thus made great strides. It inspired great literature, quickened scholarship, and nurtured heroes. It had shown its power both to unify and to divide. It had led to great achievements of political construction and consolidation in Germany and Italy; but it was more clear than ever a threat to the Ottoman and Habsburg empires, which were essentially multi national. European culture had been enriched by the new vernacular contributions of little-known or forgotten peoples, but at the same time such unity as it had was imperiled by fragmentation. Moreover, the antagonisms fostered by nationalism had made not only for wars, insurrections, and local hatreds—they had accentuated or created new spiritual divisions in a nominally Christian Europe.

21st century

The rise of globalism in the late twentieth century led to a rise in nationalism and populism in Europe and North America. That trend was further fueled by increased terrorism in the West (the September 11 attacks in the United States being a prime example), increasing unrest and civil wars in the Middle East, and waves of Muslim refugees, especially from the Syrian Civil War, flooding into Europe (as of 2016 the refugee crisis appears to have peaked). Nationalist groups like Germany's Pegida, France's National Front and the UK Independence Party gained prominence in their respective nations advocating restrictions on immigration to protect the local populations.

Since 2010, Catalan nationalists have led a renewed Catalan independence movement and declared Catalan independence. The movement has been opposed by Spanish nationalists. In the 2010s, the Greek economic crisis and waves of immigration have led to a significant rise of Fascism and Greek nationalism across Greece, especially among the youth.

In Russia, exploitation of nationalist sentiments allowed Vladimir Putin to consolidate power. This nationalist sentiment was used in Russia's annexation of Crimea in 2014 and other actions in Ukraine. Nationalist movements gradually began to rise in Central Europe as well, particularly Poland, under the influence of the ruling party, Law and Justice (led by Jarosaw Kaczyñski). In Hungary, the anti-immigration rhetoric and stance against foreign influence is a powerful national glue promoted the ruling Fidesz party (led by Viktor Orbán). Nationalist parties have also joined governing coalitions in Bulgaria, Slovakia, Latvia and Ukraine.

In India, Hindu nationalism has grown in popularity with the rise of the Bharatiya Janata Party, a right wing party which has been ruling India at the national level since 2014. The rise in religious nationalism comes with the rise of right-wing populism in India, with the election and re-election of populist leader Narendra Modi as Prime Minister, who promised economic prosperity for all and an end to corruption. Militant Buddhist nationalism is also on the rise in Myanmar, Thailand and Sri Lanka.

In Japan, nationalist influences in the government developed over the course of the early twenty first century, largely from the far right ultra-conservative Nippon Kaigi organisation. The new movement has advocated re-establishing Japan as a military power and pushed revisionist historical narratives denying events such as the Nanking Massacre.

A referendum on Scottish independence from the United Kingdom was held on 18 September 2014. The proposal was defeated, with 55.3% voting against independence. In a 2016 referendum, the British populace voted to withdraw the United Kingdom from the European Union. The result had been largely unexpected and was seen[by whom? as a victory of populism. citation needed] As the promise of continued European Union membership was a core feature of the anti-independence campaign during the Scottish referendum, there have been calls for a second referendum on Scottish independence.

Brazilian Former President Jair Bolsonaro, sometimes called the "Tropical Trump", with United States President Donald Trump.

The 2016 United States presidential campaign saw the unprecedented rise of Donald Trump, a businessman with no political experience who ran on a populist/nationalist platform and struggled to gain endorsements from mainstream political figures, even within his own party. Trump's slogans "Make America Great Again" and "America First" exemplified his campaign's repudiation of globalism and its staunchly nationalistic outlook. His unexpected victory in the election was seen as part of the same trend that had brought about the Brexit vote. On 22 October 2018, two weeks before the mid term elections President Trump openly proclaimed that he was a nationalist to a cheering crowd at a rally in Texas in support of re-electing Senator Ted Cruz who was once an adversary. On 29 October 2018 Trump equated nationalism to patriotism, saying "I'm proud of this country and I call that "nationalism." In 2016, Rodrigo Duterte became president of the Philippines running a distinctly nationalist campaign. Contrary to the policies of his recent predecessors, he distanced the country from the Philippines' former ruler, the United States, and sought closer ties with China (as well as Russia).

In 2017, Turkish nationalism propelled President Recep Tayyip Erdoðan to gain unprecedented power in a national referendum. Reactions from world leaders were mixed, with Western European leaders generally expressing concern while the leaders of many of the more authoritarian regimes as well as President Trump offered their congratulations.

Many political scientists have theorised about the foundations of the modern nation-state and the concept of sovereignty. The concept of nationalism in political science draws from these theoretical foundations. Philosophers like Machiavelli, Locke, Hobbes, and Rousseau conceptualised the state as the result of a "social contract" between rulers and individuals. Max Weber provides the most commonly used definition of the state, "that human community which successfully lays claim to the monopoly of legitimate physical violence within a certain territory". According to Benedict Anderson, nations are "Imagined Communities", or socially constructed institutions.

Many scholars have noted the relationship between state-building, war, and nationalism. John Etherington argues nationalism is inherently exclusionary and thus potentially violent, while Jeffrey Herbst posits that external threats can foster nationalist sentiment: "External threats have such a powerful effect on nationalism because people realise in a profound manner that they are under threat because of who they are as a nation; they are forced to recognize that it is only as a nation that they can successfully defeat the threat". With increased external threats, the state's extractive capacities increase. He links the lack of external threats to countries in Sub-Saharan Africa, post independence, to weak state nationalism and state capacity. Barry Posen argues that nationalism increases the intensity of war, and that states deliberately promote nationalism with the aim of improving their military capabilities. Most new nation-states since 1815 have emerged through decolonisation.

Adria Lawrence has argued that nationalism in the colonial world was spurred by failures of colonial powers to extend equal political rights to the subjects in the colonies, thus prompting them to pursue independence. Michael Hechter has argued similarly that "peripheral nationalisms" formed when empires prevented peripheral regions from having autonomy and local rule.

4. Political violence

Political violence is violence which is perpetrated in order to achieve political goals. It can include violence which is used by a state against other states (war), violence which is used by a state against civilians and non-state actors (forced disappearance, psychological warfare, police brutality, targeted assassinations, torture, ethnic cleansing, or genocide), and violence which is used by violent non-state actors against states and civilians (kidnappings, targeted assassinations, terrorist attacks, torture, psychological and/or guerrilla warfare). It can also describe politically motivated violence which is used by violent non-state actors against a state (rebellion, rioting, treason, or coup d'etat) or it can describe violence which is used against other non-state actors and/or civilians. Non action on the part of a government can also be characterised as a form of political violence, such as refusing to alleviate famine or otherwise denying resources to politically identifiable groups within their territory.

Due to the imbalances of power which exist between state and non-state actors, political violence often takes the form of asymmetric warfare where neither side is able to directly assault the other, instead relying on tactics such as guerrilla warfare and terrorism. It can often include attacks on civilian or otherwise non-combatant targets. People may be targeted collectively based on perception of being part of a social, ethnic, religious, or political group; or selectively, targeting specific individuals for actions that are perceived as challenging someone or aiding an opponent.

Many politically motivated militant, insurgent, extremist, and/or fundamentalist groups and individuals are convinced that the states and political systems under which they live will never respond to their demands, and they thus believe that the only way to overthrow and/or reshape the government or state accordingly to their political and/or religious worldview is through violent means, which they regard as not only justified but also necessary in order to achieve their political and/or religious objectives. Similarly, many governments around the world believe that they need to use violence in order to intimidate their populaces into acquiescence. At other times, governments use force in order to defend their countries from outside invasions or other threats of force and coerce other governments or conquer territory.

5. Types of political violence

Political violence varies widely in form, severity, and practice. In political science, a common organising framework is to consider the types of violence which are used by the relevant actors: violence between non-state actors, one-sided violence which is perpetrated by a state actor against civilians, and violence between states.

Stathis Kalyvas identifies eleven types of political violence: Interstate war, Civil war, Terrorism, Political assassination, Military coup, Mass protest/Rebellion, Intercommunal violence, Organised crime/Cartels, Ethnic cleansing, Genocide, and State repression.

5. Violence between non-state actors

Fighting between non-state actors without state security forces playing a direct role in the conflict.

6. Ethnic conflict

An ethnic conflict is fought between ethnic groups. While at times a specific ethnic group may have the backing (whether formal or informal) of the state (or conversely, a specific ethnic group may be targeted by the state), ethnic conflict can also take place between two groups without the direct intervention of the state, or despite the state's attempts to mediate between groups.

7. One-sided violence by non-state actors

1. Stochastic terrorism

Terrorism can be directed by non-state actors against political targets other than the state (e. g. Stabbing attacks at gay pride parades in Jerusalem, Charlie Hebdo shooting). Because terrorism is a tactic often used by the weaker side of a conflict, it may also fall under violence between a state and non-state actor.

While there lacks a concrete definition of terrorism, the United States Department of Defence however defines terrorism as, "the calculated use of unlawful violence or threat of unlawful violence to inculcate fear; intended to coerce or to intimidate governments or societies in the pursuit of goals that are generally political, religious, or ideological. " What is and is not considered terrorism is itself a controversial political question, as states have often used the label of terrorism to exclusively demonize the actions of their enemies while obscuring "legal" violence administered by the state (e. g. The Troubles, communist rebellion in the Philippines, 2014 Israel–Gaza conflict).

2. One-sided violence by the state

Mass murder & By states

The use of force by an organised armed group, be it a government or a non-state group, which results in the deaths of civilians is considered one-sided. According to the Human Security Report Project, a campaign of one-sided violence is recorded whenever violence against civilians committed by one group results in at least 25 reported deaths in a calendar year.

3. Genocide

One form of political violence is genocide. Genocide is commonly defined as "the deliberate and systematic destruction, in whole or in part, of an ethnic, racial, religious, or national group", although what constitutes enough of a "part" to qualify as genocide has been subject to much debate by legal scholars. Genocide is typically carried out with either the overt or covert support of the governments of those countries where genocidal activities take place. The Holocaust is the most cited historical example of genocide.

4. Torture

Torture is the act of inflicting severe pain (whether physical or psychological) as a means of punishment, revenge, forcing information or confession, or simply as an act of cruelty. Torture is prohibited under international law and the domestic laws of most countries in the twenty-first century. It is considered a human rights violation and is declared unacceptable by Article 5 of the UN Declaration of Human Rights. Signatories of the Third Geneva Convention and Fourth Geneva Convention have officially agreed not to torture prisoners in armed conflicts. National and international legal prohibitions on torture derive from a consensus that torture and similar ill-treatment are immoral, as well as impractical. Despite international conventions, torture cases continue to arise such as the 2004 Abu Ghraib torture and prisoner abuse scandal committed by military police personnel of the United States Army. Organisations such as Amnesty International and the International Rehabilitation Council for Torture Victims monitor abuses of human rights and reports widespread violations of human torture by states in many regions of the world. Amnesty International estimates that at least 81 world governments currently practice torture, some of them openly.

5. Capital punishment

Capital punishment is the sentence of death upon a person by the state as a punishment for an offence. This does not include extrajudicial killing, which is the killing of a person by governmental authorities without the sanction of any judicial proceeding or legal process. The use of capital punishment by country varies, but according to Amnesty International 58 countries still actively use the death penalty, and in 2010, 23 countries carried out executions and 67 imposed death sentences. Methods of execution in 2010 included beheading, electrocution, hanging, lethal injection and shooting.

6. Famine

Famine can be initiated or prolonged in order to deny resources, compel obedience, or to depopulate a region with a recalcitrant or untrusted populace.

7. Police brutality

Police brutality is another form of political violence. It is most commonly described in juxtaposition with the term excessive force. Police brutality can be defined as "a civil rights violation that occurs when a police officer acts with excessive force by using an amount of force with regards to a civilian that is more than necessary". Police brutality and the use of excessive force are present throughout the world and in the United States alone, 4, 861 incidences spelling? of police misconduct were reported during 2010. Of these, there were 6, 826 victims involved and 247 fatalities.

5. Violence between a state and a non-state actor

At least one of the warring parties involved is the government of a state.

(i) Rioting

A riot can be described as a violent disturbance by a group of individuals formed to protest perceived wrongs and/or injustice. These can range from poverty and inequality to unemployment and government oppression.

They can manifest themselves in a number of ways but most commonly in the form of property damage. Riots are characterised by their lack of predictability and the anonymity of their participants. Both make it difficult for authorities to identify those participating.

Riots have been analyzed in a number of ways but most recently in the context of the frustration aggression model theory, expressing that the aggression seen in most riots is a direct result of a groups frustration with a particular aspect of their lives. Widespread and prolonged rioting can lead to and/or produce rebellion or revolution. There are also a number of different types of riots including but not limited to police riots, race riot, prison riots, and sport riot.

(ii) Revolution

In political science, a revolution is a fundamental and relatively sudden change in political power and political organisation which occurs when the population revolts against the government, typically due to perceived oppression (political, social, economic) or political incompetence.

In a revolution political violence is usually common. The use of political violence is usually to fulfill a revolutionary objective, and in times of civil strife to challenge the status quo. The goals of political violence can be varied such as to strengthen the position of a group, or to weaken an opposing side.

(iii) Civil war

A civil war, also known as an intrastate war, is a war fought within the same state or country between organised groups. Less commonly, it can also be fought between two countries that have been created from one previously unified state. Often these conflicts involve one group wishing to take control of a region or expressing dissatisfaction with the government. There is typically a desire to overthrow the existing power or at least change some of their policies. In many cases, an outside power may intervene on behalf of one side if they share their ideology or condemn the methods/ motives of their opponents.

(iv) Counter-insurgency

Counter-insurgency, another form of political violence, describes a spectrum of actions taken by the recognised government of a state to contain or quell an insurgency taken up against it. There are many different doctrines, theories, and tactics espoused regarding counter-insurgency that aim to protect the authority of the government and to reduce or eliminate the supplanting authority of the insurgents. Because it may be difficult or impossible to distinguish between an insurgent, a supporter of an insurgency who is a non-combatant, and entirely uninvolved members of the population, counter-insurgency operations have often rested on a confused, relativistic, or otherwise situational distinction between insurgents and non-combatants. Counter-insurgency operations are common during war, occupation and armed rebellions.

(v) Electoral violence

Electoral violence includes any acts or threats of coercion, intimidation, or physical harm perpetrated to affect an electoral process or that arise in the context of electoral competition. It is used to influence the outcome of elections; to delay, disrupt or derail polls; and to protest election results or suppress protests against election results. Electoral violence is used to influence the outcome of elections because parties cannot win through fraud alone and because candidates cannot rely on fraud agents to perpetrate fraud for them because fraud is hidden and violence is not.

(vi) War between states

War is a state of organised, armed, and often prolonged conflict carried on between states, nations, or other parties typified by extreme aggression, social disruption, and usually high mortality. War should be understood as an actual, intentional and widespread armed conflict between political communities, and therefore is defined as a form of political violence. Three of the ten most costly wars, in terms of loss of life, have been waged in the last century: the death toll of World War II, estimated at more than 60 million, surpasses all other war death tolls by a factor of two. It is estimated that 378,000 people died due to war each year between 1985 and 1994.

5. Consequences

In the aftermath of political violence, there are many changes that occur within the state, society, and the individual.

(a) Macro

Social science literature that examines how political violence affects the region, state, nation, and society on a macro and general ways.

(b) State-building

Charles Tilly argues that "war making", eliminating rivals outside a territory, "state making", eliminating rivals within a territory, "protection", protecting subjects within a territory, and "extraction", extracting resources to "[carry] out the first three activities", are what defines a state. [64] All four activities depend on the state's ability to use and monopolize violence. In other words, politically and non-politically motivated violence is necessary in state-building and building fiscal capacity.

(c) Micro

There are a growing number of social science studies that examine how political violence affects individuals and households. It is important to keep in mind that what happens at the individual and household level can affect what happens at the macro level. For example, political violence effects an individual's income, health, and education attainment, but these individual consequences combined can effect a state or nation's economic growth. In other words, the macro and micro consequences of political violence do not occur in a vacuum.

(d) Political impacts

There are empirical studies that link violence with increases in political participation. One natural experiment examines the effect of being abducted by Joseph Kony's LRA on political participation. An abducted male Ugandan youth, or in other words a former child soldier, had a greater probability of voting for Uganda's 2005 referendum and being a community mobilizer/leader than a male Ugandan youth who was not abducted.

However, this effect is not just contained to Uganda. Another natural experiment on the effects of the Sierra Leone civil war found that victimized households, household whose members were killed, injured, maimed, captured, or made refugees, were more likely to register to vote, attend community meetings, and participate in local political and community groups than households that did not experience violence.

(c) Economic impacts

A study on the effects of the Sierra Leone civil war found that victimized households, household whose members were killed, injured, maimed, captured, or displaced, did not have long-term impacts on owning assets, child nutrition, consumption expenditures and earnings.

Notes and References

Billig, Michael (1995). Banal Nationalism. London: Sage. ISBN 978-0803975255.

Delanty, Gerard; Kumar, Krishan, eds. (2006). The Sage Handbook of Nations and Nationalism. London: Sage Publications. ISBN 978-1412901017.

Hayes, Carlton J. The Historical Evolution of Modern Nationalism (1928) the first major scholarly survey.

Hobsbawm, Eric J. (1992). Nations and Nationalism Since 1780: Programme, Myth, Reality (2nd ed.). Cambridge: Cambridge University Press. ISBN 978-0521439619.

Hobsbawm, E.; Ranger, T. (1983). The Invention of Tradition. Cambridge, UK: Cambridge Univ. Press.

James, Paul (1996). Nation Formation: Towards a Theory of Abstract Community. London: Sage Publications. ISBN 978-0761950721.

James, Paul (2006). Globalism, Nationalism, Tribalism: Bringing Theory Back In. London: Sage Publications.

Kohn, Hans. The Idea of Nationalism: A Study in Its Origins and Background (1944; 2nd ed. 2005 with introduction by Craig Calhoun). 735 pp; an often-cited classic.

Kymlicka, Will (1995). Multicultural Citizenship: A Liberal Theory of Minority Rights. Oxford: Clarendon Press. ISBN 978-0198279495.

Leoussi, Athena S., ed. (2001). Encyclopedia of Nationalism. New Brunswick, N. J: Transaction Publishers. ISBN 978-0765800022.

Miller, David (1995). On Nationality. Oxford: Oxford University Press. ISBN 978-0198280477.

Motyl, Alexander, ed. (2001). Encyclopedia of Nationalism. San Diego: Academic Press 2 vol. ISBN 978-0122272301.

Mylonas, Harris; Tudor, Maya (2023). Varieties of Nationalism: Communities, Narratives, Identities. Cambridge University Press. doi:10. 1017/9781108973298. ISBN 9781108973298. S2CID 259646325.

Mylonas, Harris; Tudor, Maya (2021). "Nationalism: What We Know and What We Still Need to Know". Annual Review of Political Science. 24 (1): 109–132.

Snyder, Louis L. (1990). Encyclopedia of Nationalism. New York: Paragon House. ISBN 978-1557781673.

Paul Hollander. Political Violence: Belief, Behavior, and Legitimation, Palgrave Macmillan, 2008.

Philip Herbst. Talking terrorism: a dictionary of the loaded language of political violence, Greenwood Publishing Group, 2003.

Chapter - 12

The Interrelationships of Nationalism, Political Violence, Environmental Issues and Public Policy

— **Bir Abhimanyu Kumar & Rajiv Kumar**

1. Introduction

The intricate interplay between nationalism, political violence, environmental issues, and public policy forms a complex and multifaceted landscape that profoundly influences global and local dynamics. Nationalism, defined by the promotion of distinct national identities and the prioritisation of national interests, often exerts a significant impact on political agendas and policy decisions. This nationalist fervour can lead to political violence, encompassing a range of actions such as terrorism, armed conflict, and state repression, as groups and individuals struggle for power, control, and recognition within and across national boundaries. Environmental issues, including degradation and resource scarcity, frequently serve as catalysts for conflict (Ehrlich, Gleick & Conca, 2001, September). The competition for dwindling resources, such as water, arable land, and energy supplies, can exacerbate existing tensions and fuel nationalist sentiments. These environmental stressors do not merely provoke violence but are also exacerbated by it. Warfare, sabotage, and other forms of political violence directly harm the environment, while disruption of governance structures and conservation efforts indirectly compounds degradation. Public policy emerges as a crucial arena for addressing these intertwined challenges. Policies that promote environmental sustainability, ensure equitable resource distribution, and facilitate conflict resolution are vital in mitigating the adverse effects of nationalism and political violence (Kamat & Mathew, 2003). Effective public policy can act as a preventative measure, curbing the potential for environmental degradation to incite conflict and ensuring that nationalist agendas do not undermine environmental and social stability (Banerjee, S. (2021).

Understanding the intersections of nationalism, political violence, and environmental issues is essential for developing holistic public policies. Policymakers must adopt integrated approaches that address the root causes of conflict, promote environmental stewardship, and foster social and political stability (Embree, 2018). This comprehensive and inclusive strategy is crucial for advancing sustainable development, peace, and stability in an increasingly interconnected world. The following discussion explores the relationships between nationalism, political violence, environmental issues, and public policy. It highlights the importance of integrated approaches and underscores the need for policies that consider these interdependencies to effectively address the complex challenges facing contemporary societies (Rai, 2013).

2. Nationalism and Its Influence on Public Policy

Nationalism is a political ideology and social movement characterised by identification of a group of people with a nation. It emphasizes the interests, culture, and values of a particular nation, often in opposition to foreign influences or control. Nationalism fosters a sense of belonging and identity among members of the nation, promoting unity and solidarity. Key characteristics of nationalism include a shared language, culture, historical experience, and often a common religion or ethnicity. Nationalism can manifest in various forms, ranging from civic nationalism, which is inclusive and based on shared values and political participation, to ethnic nationalism, which is exclusive and based on common ancestry and cultural heritage (Chandra, 2010).

3. How Nationalism Shapes Political Agenda

Nationalism significantly influences political agendas by prioritizing the interests and values of the nation-state above other considerations. Nationalist leaders and parties often advocate for policies that strengthen national sovereignty, promote economic self-sufficiency, and preserve cultural heritage. This can lead to the implementation of protectionist economic policies, restrictive immigration laws, and cultural preservation initiatives. Nationalist agendas frequently emphasize the need for strong defence and security measures to protect the nation from external threats and internal subversion. Moreover, nationalism can shape foreign policy, leading to assertive or aggressive stances towards other nations perceived as threats or rivals (Pal, 1910).

4. Nationalist Policies and Their Impacts

One notable example of nationalism shaping public policy is the "America First" agenda during the Trump administration in the United States. This policy prioritized American economic and security interests, leading to the implementation of protectionist trade measures, such as tariffs on imported goods, and restrictive immigration policies, including travel bans and family separation at the border (Jaffrelot, 1999). While these policies aimed to protect American jobs and national security, they also resulted in trade tensions with other countries, increased costs for consumers and businesses, and significant humanitarian and ethical concerns (Ram-Prasad, 2000).

Another example is the rise of Hindu nationalism in India, exemplified by the Bharatiya Janata Party (BJP) under Prime Minister Narendra Modi. The BJP's policies have focused on promoting Hindu cultural values, enacting citizenship laws that favor non-Muslim immigrants, and implementing economic policies aimed at self-reliance, such as the "Make in India" initiative (Ganguly, 2015). These policies have fostered a sense of national pride and economic growth but have also led to increased social tensions, particularly with the Muslim minority, and challenges to India's secular democratic framework (Chacko, 2019). These studies illustrate how nationalist policies can profoundly impact a country's economic, social, and political landscape. While nationalism can promote unity and national pride, it can also lead to exclusionary practices, economic protectionism, and increased domestic and international tensions. Understanding the influence of nationalism on public policy is crucial for comprehending the broader implications of this powerful ideology (Jaffrelot, 2021).

5. Terrorism, Armed Conflict, State Repression

Political violence encompasses a range of actions and behaviours that are intended to achieve political goals through coercion, intimidation, or force. Three primary forms of political violence include terrorism, armed conflict, and state repression. Terrorism involves the deliberate use of violence against civilians or non-combatants to instill fear, achieve political objectives, or influence public opinion (Chakma, 2022). It is often characterised by attacks on symbolic targets and aims to create widespread panic and disruption. Armed conflict refers to organised violence between armed groups, including civil wars, insurgencies, and interstate conflicts. Armed conflicts typically involve combatants using military force to achieve political, territorial, or ideological objectives (Vadlamannati, 2011). These conflicts can have devastating humanitarian consequences, resulting in casualties, displacement, and long-term social and economic instability. State repression encompasses actions taken by governments to suppress dissent, opposition movements, or perceived threats to state authority. This may include censorship, surveillance, arbitrary arrests, torture, and extrajudicial killings. State repression is often justified as necessary for maintaining law and order or national security but can infringe on civil liberties and human rights (Staniland, 2017).

6. Root Causes of Political Violence

The root causes of political violence are multifaceted and often interconnected. Socioeconomic inequalities, political grievances, ethnic or religious tensions, and historical grievances can contribute to the emergence and escalation of violence (Kuszewska, 2022). Economic disparities, lack of political representation, and perceptions of injustice or discrimination can fuel grievances and motivate individuals or groups to resort to violence as a means of addressing their grievances or asserting their interests (Chaurasia, et al., 2021).

(i) Political Violence Influenced by Nationalism

Nationalism frequently plays a significant role in motivating and justifying political violence. Studies illustrate how nationalist ideologies can mobilise individuals or groups to engage in violent actions in pursuit of nationalistic goals (Bofill, 2021). For instance, ethnonationalist movements seeking autonomy or independence may resort to armed struggle against central governments perceived as oppressive or illegitimate. In some studies, nationalist rhetoric and historical narratives fuel intergroup conflicts, leading to cycles of violence and retaliation (Dhattiwala & Biggs, 2012). An example is the conflict in Northern Ireland, where ethnonationalist sentiments among Catholic Republicans and Protestant Unionists contributed to decades of sectarian violence known as "The Troubles." The struggle over national identity and sovereignty between these groups, exacerbated by historical grievances and discrimination, led to bombings, assassinations, and armed confrontations. Understanding the types, root causes, and specific contexts of political violence influenced by nationalism is crucial for developing strategies to prevent and mitigate such conflicts. Addressing underlying grievances, promoting inclusive governance, and fostering dialogue and reconciliation are essential for building sustainable peace and stability in societies affected by political violence (Habermas, 1990).

(ii) Environmental Degradation and Resource Scarcity

Environmental degradation and resource scarcity are critical issues that can exacerbate social, economic, and political tensions, potentially leading to conflict. Environmental degradation refers to the deterioration of the natural environment through human activities such as deforestation, pollution, and habitat destruction. This degradation reduces ecosystem services, threatens biodiversity, and undermines the resilience of ecosystems to support human livelihoods. Resource scarcity involves the inadequate availability or access to essential resources such as water, arable land, minerals, and energy. Population growth, urbanisation, unsustainable agricultural practices, and climate change contribute to the depletion and unequal distribution of resources, intensifying competition among individuals, communities, and nations (Barbier, 2021).

7. How Environmental Stressors Lead to Conflict

Environmental stressors can contribute to conflict through various pathways. Competition over scarce resources can escalate tensions and trigger violent confrontations between different social groups, ethnicities, or nations. Resource scarcity often exacerbates existing social inequalities and disparities, leading to grievances and grievances that may erupt into conflict. Environmental degradation can also undermine livelihoods and exacerbate poverty, driving marginalised communities to engage in illegal activities such as poaching, illegal logging, or land grabbing, which can lead to conflicts with authorities or other groups. Moreover, environmental disasters such as droughts, floods, and hurricanes can displace populations, strain resources, and create conditions conducive to social unrest and conflict (Fischer, 2018).

8. Examples of Conflicts Driven by Environmental Issues

Numerous conflicts around the world have been influenced by environmental degradation and resource scarcity. In Darfur, Sudan, for example, competition over increasingly scarce water and grazing land fueled tensions between nomadic herders and settled farmers, contributing to violent clashes and the Darfur conflict. In Syria, a combination of prolonged drought, mismanagement of water resources, and socioeconomic grievances contributed to civil unrest and ultimately escalated into the Syrian Civil War (Schwab, 2023). In the South China Sea, disputes over fishing rights, oil and gas reserves, and control of strategic waterways have heightened geopolitical tensions among countries in the region, leading to naval standoffs and potential conflicts over maritime territories. These examples illustrate how environmental issues can act as catalysts for conflict, exacerbating social divisions, economic disparities, and political instability. Addressing environmental degradation and resource scarcity through sustainable management practices, equitable resource distribution, and conflict prevention strategies is essential for mitigating the risks of conflict and promoting peace and stability in vulnerable regions (Morton, 2016).

9. Direct Effects of Warfare and Sabotage on the Environment

Political violence, including warfare and sabotage, has profound and often devastating direct effects on the environment. Warfare typically involves the use of military force, weapons, and explosives, which can cause immediate and long-term damage to ecosystems. Bombings and artillery fire can destroy forests, wetlands, and agricultural lands, leading to habitat destruction, soil erosion, and loss of biodiversity. The use of chemical weapons or defoliants can contaminate soil and water sources, posing serious health risks to humans and wildlife. Sabotage involves deliberate acts of destruction or disruption aimed at infrastructure, industrial facilities, or natural resources. For example, attacks on oil pipelines, refineries, or mining operations can result in oil spills, toxic chemical releases, and water pollution. These incidents not only harm the environment directly but also compromise human health, livelihoods, and ecosystem integrity (Feuer, 2023).

10. Indirect Effects Through Disrupted Governance and Conservation Efforts

Political violence can indirectly exacerbate environmental degradation by undermining governance structures and conservation efforts. Conflict disrupts administrative institutions, law enforcement agencies, and environmental management authorities, reducing their capacity to enforce environmental regulations and protect natural resources. Government resources and attention may be diverted towards security and military operations, neglecting environmental monitoring, conservation programmes, and sustainable development initiatives. In regions affected by prolonged conflict, conservation efforts such as wildlife protection, habitat restoration, and ecosystem management are often suspended or compromised. The absence of effective governance and law enforcement can lead to increased poaching, illegal logging, and unsustainable resource extraction, further depleting natural resources and undermining biodiversity conservation efforts (Thondhlana, et al., 2020).

11. Environmental Degradation Caused by Political Violence

The impacts of political violence on the environment are evident in various conflict zones around the world. In the Democratic Republic of Congo (DRC), ongoing armed conflicts have led to widespread deforestation driven by illegal logging and charcoal production, threatening the habitat of endangered species such as mountain gorillas. The use of landmines and unexploded ordnance in conflict areas poses risks to wildlife and prevents communities from accessing and utilising natural resources safely. In Iraq, the 1991 Gulf War and subsequent conflicts resulted in extensive oil spills and contamination of freshwater resources due to sabotage and destruction of oil infrastructure. The environmental consequences of these incidents have persisted for decades, affecting local ecosystems, agriculture, and public health. These studies underscore the complex interplay between political violence and environmental degradation. Addressing the environmental impacts of political violence requires not only immediate mitigation measures but also long-term strategies for peacebuilding, governance reform, and sustainable development. Effective environmental management, conservation efforts, and international cooperation are essential for restoring ecosystems, promoting resilience, and fostering peace in conflict-affected regions (Lee, 2016).

12. The Role of Public Policy in Mitigating Conflicts

Public policy plays a crucial role in addressing the multifaceted challenges posed by conflicts exacerbated by environmental issues and political violence. Effective public policies are essential for mitigating the root causes of conflict, promoting environmental sustainability, ensuring equitable resource distribution, and fostering peace and stability. Environmental sustainability policies are critical for mitigating conflicts that arise from environmental degradation and resource scarcity. These policies aim to conserve natural resources, protect ecosystems, and promote sustainable development practices. By addressing the drivers of environmental degradation such as deforestation, pollution, and habitat loss, environmental sustainability policies help reduce competition and conflict over scarce resources. Moreover, they contribute to long-term environmental resilience and enhance the capacity of communities to adapt to environmental changes. Equitable resource distribution policies are essential for addressing socio-economic inequalities that can contribute to conflict. These policies aim to ensure fair access to essential resources such as water, land, and minerals, thereby reducing grievances and tensions among different social groups. By promoting inclusive economic growth and reducing disparities, equitable resource distribution policies contribute to social stability and prevent conflicts arising from resource competition and inequality (Gilmore & Buhaug, 2021).

13. Conflict Resolution Strategies in Public Policy

Public policy can incorporate conflict resolution strategies that promote dialogue, mediation, and reconciliation among conflicting parties. Diplomatic efforts, peacebuilding initiatives, and reconciliation programmes can help address underlying grievances, build trust, and facilitate peaceful resolution of conflicts. By addressing the root causes of political violence and fostering cooperation among stakeholders, conflict resolution strategies contribute to sustainable peace and stability (Stephenson Jr & Pops, 1989).

14. Examples of Effective Public Policies

Several examples illustrate the effectiveness of public policies in mitigating conflicts and promoting peace:

1. **Environmental Peacebuilding Initiatives:** Programmes that integrate environmental conservation with peacebuilding efforts, such as promoting sustainable land management practices in conflict-affected areas, have been successful in reducing resource-based conflicts and fostering cooperation among communities.
2. **Water Management Agreements:** International agreements and treaties on transboundary water resources, such as the Mekong River Commission and the Nile Basin Initiative, facilitate cooperative management of shared water resources, reducing tensions and potential conflicts among riparian countries.
3. **Land Tenure Reform:** Policies that address land tenure issues and ensure secure land rights for marginalised communities can prevent land disputes and conflicts over land ownership, promoting social stability and economic development.

4. **Peacebuilding Funds:** Governments and international organisations often establish funds to support peacebuilding activities, including community reconciliation, disarmament, and reintegration programmes, which help reduce violence and promote sustainable peace in conflict-affected regions.

In decision, public policy plays a pivotal role in mitigating conflicts exacerbated by environmental issues and political violence. By promoting environmental sustainability, equitable resource distribution, and conflict resolution strategies, public policies contribute to building resilient and peaceful societies. Effective implementation of these policies requires collaboration among governments, civil society organisations, and international actors to address the complex challenges of conflict prevention and resolution (Roberts & Finnegan, 2013).

15. Integrated Approaches to Addressing the Interconnections

Addressing the interconnections between nationalism, political violence, environmental issues, and public policy requires holistic and integrated approaches that recognize the complex and intertwined nature of these challenges. Such integrated approaches are essential for developing comprehensive strategies that effectively mitigate conflicts, promote sustainable development, and foster peace and stability. Holistic policy-making is crucial for addressing the root causes and interrelated impacts of nationalism, political violence, and environmental degradation. Rather than treating these issues in isolation, holistic policies consider their interconnectedness and aim to develop integrated solutions that promote social cohesion, environmental sustainability, and inclusive development. This approach acknowledges that nationalist sentiments can exacerbate political tensions and environmental degradation, while environmental degradation can fuel grievances and conflict. By adopting a holistic perspective, policymakers can develop policies that address multiple dimensions of complex problems, leading to more effective outcomes (Dahlmann & Bullock, 2020).

16. Strategies for Integrating

Integrating nationalism, political violence, and environmental considerations in public policy involves several strategic approaches:

1. **Conflict-sensitive environmental management:** Policies and programmes that take into account the environmental impacts of

political violence and conflict, and incorporate conflict-sensitive approaches to natural resource management.

2. **Promotion of inclusive governance:** Policies that promote inclusive decision-making processes, respect diverse cultural identities, and address grievances related to nationalism and political exclusion.
3. **Environmental peacebuilding:** Initiatives that promote environmental cooperation and sustainable development as pathways to peacebuilding and conflict prevention.
4. **Education and awareness:** Policies that promote education and awareness about the interconnectedness of nationalism, political violence, and environmental sustainability, fostering informed public discourse and promoting tolerance and cooperation.

Benefits of Comprehensive and Inclusive Public Policy

Comprehensive and inclusive public policy offers several benefits in addressing the interconnections between nationalism, political violence, and environmental issues:

1. **Conflict prevention:** By addressing the root causes of nationalism and political violence, such policies help prevent conflicts from escalating and promote stability and peace.
2. **Environmental sustainability:** Policies that integrate environmental considerations promote sustainable resource management, reduce environmental degradation, and enhance ecosystem resilience.
3. **Social cohesion:** Inclusive policies that respect cultural diversity and promote social equity contribute to fostering inclusive societies and reducing social tensions.
4. **Effective governance:** Comprehensive policies strengthen governance frameworks, enhance institutional capacity, and improve coordination among stakeholders, thereby improving the effectiveness and efficiency of public administration.

In assumption, integrated approaches to addressing nationalism, political violence, environmental issues, and public policy are essential for promoting sustainable development and peace. By adopting holistic policy-making strategies, policymakers can develop solutions that address the root causes of conflicts, promote environmental sustainability, and build resilient societies capable of addressing complex challenges effectively.

Collaboration among governments, civil society organisations, and international actors is crucial for implementing and sustaining these integrated approaches over the long term (Daniels, Ustyuzhantseva & Yao, 2017).

17. Lessons Learned from Past Experiences

From the studies and interventions analysed, several key lessons emerge for policymakers and practitioners. Integrated approaches are essential for addressing the interconnections between nationalism, political violence, and environmental issues, necessitating policies that simultaneously consider social, economic, and environmental dimensions. Community involvement and empowerment are crucial, as policies that empower local communities, respect cultural diversity, and promote inclusive governance are more likely to reduce conflict and foster sustainable development. Effective interventions also require long-term commitment and flexibility, with adaptability to changing circumstances and continuous engagement with stakeholders, including governments, civil society organisations, and affected communities. Additionally, the importance of international cooperation cannot be overstated, as addressing transboundary environmental issues and conflicts often necessitates coordination and support from regional and global stakeholders.

Conclusion

This paper has explored the intricate interconnections between nationalism, political violence, environmental issues, and public policy. Nationalism, characterised by the promotion of distinct national identities and interests, often shapes political agendas and can lead to political violence as groups vie for power and recognition. Environmental degradation and resource scarcity frequently act as catalysts for such conflicts, while political violence exacerbates environmental problems through direct actions like warfare and sabotage, and indirectly by undermining governance and conservation efforts. Public policy plays a crucial role in navigating these challenges by promoting environmental sustainability, equitable resource distribution, and conflict resolution.

The analysis highlights the necessity of integrated approaches in policy-making to effectively address the multifaceted challenges posed by the intersection of nationalism, political violence, and environmental issues. Holistic policy-making that considers these interconnections can lead to more comprehensive and effective solutions. Strategies such as conflict-sensitive environmental management, inclusive governance, and environmental peacebuilding demonstrate the benefits of integrated approaches. Such policies not only mitigate the immediate impacts of conflicts but also contribute to long-term sustainability and stability by addressing root causes and promoting social cohesion.

Future research should continue to explore the complex relationships between nationalism, political violence, and environmental issues, with a focus on developing more nuanced and context-specific understandings. There is a need for interdisciplinary studies that combine insights from political science, environmental studies, and conflict resolution to develop comprehensive strategies for addressing these challenges. Policy development should prioritize the creation and implementation of integrated approaches that address multiple dimensions of these issues. This includes promoting international cooperation and support for transboundary environmental and conflict resolution initiatives, enhancing community involvement and empowerment in policy-making processes, and ensuring long-term commitment and flexibility in the implementation of policies. In conclusion, the intertwined nature of nationalism, political violence, environmental issues, and public policy necessitates a comprehensive and inclusive approach to policy-making. By integrating these considerations, policymakers can develop more effective strategies to foster sustainable development, peace, and stability in an increasingly interconnected world.

Notes and References

Banerjee, S. (2021). Warriors in politics: Hindu nationalism, violence, and the Shiv Sena in India. Routledge.

Barbier, E. B. (2021). The evolution of economic views on natural resource scarcity. Review of Environmental Economics and Policy, 15(1), 24-44.

Bofill, H. L. (2021). Law, violence and constituent power: the law, politics and history of constitution making. Routledge.

Chacko, P. (2019). Marketizing Hindutva: The state, society, and markets in Hindu nationalism. Modern Asian Studies, 53(2), 377-410.

Chakma, A. (2022). Does state repression stimulate terrorism? A panel data analysis on South Asia. Journal of Policing, Intelligence and Counter Terrorism, 17(2), 200-217.

Chandra, B. (2010). The rise and growth of economic nationalism in India: Economic policies of Indian national leadership, 1880-1905. Har Anand Publications.

Chaurasia, H., Debnath, P., Srivastava, S., & Purkayastha, N. (2021). Is socioeconomic inequality boosting intimate partner violence in India? An overview of the National family health survey, 2005–2006 and 2015–2016. Global Social Welfare, 8(3), 263-277.

Dahlmann, F., & Bullock, G. (2020). Nexus thinking in business: Analysing corporate responses to interconnected global sustainability challenges. Environmental Science & Policy, 107, 90-98.

Daniels, C. U., Ustyuzhantseva, O., & Yao, W. (2017). Innovation for inclusive development, public policy support and triple helix: perspectives from BRICS. African Journal of Science, Technology, Innovation and Development, 9(5), 513-527.

Dhattiwala, R., & Biggs, M. (2012). The political logic of ethnic violence: The anti-Muslim pogrom in Gujarat, 2002. Politics & Society, 40(4), 483-516.

Ehrlich, A. H., Gleick, P., & Conca, K. (2001, September). Resources and environmental degradation as sources of conflict. In Pugwash occasional papers: 50th Pugwash conference: eliminating the causes of war, Vol. 2, pp. 108-138.

Embree, A. T. (2018). Utopias in conflict: Religion and nationalism in modern India (Vol. 3). University of California Press.

Feuer, A. (2023). Environmental Warfare Tactics in Irregular Conflicts. Perspectives on Politics, 21(2), 533-549.

Fischer, A. P. (2018). Pathways of adaptation to external stressors in coastal natural-resource-dependent communities: Implications for climate change. World Development, 108, 235-248.

Ganguly, S. (2015). Hindu nationalism and the foreign policy of India's Bharatiya Janata Party. Transatlantic Paper Series, 2.

Gilmore, E. A., & Buhaug, H. (2021). Climate mitigation policies and the potential pathways to conflict: Outlining a research agenda. Wiley Interdisciplinary Reviews: Climate Change, 12(5), e722.

Habermas, J. (1990). Citizenship and national identity (pp. 491-515). Cambridge, MA: MIT Press.

Jaffrelot, C. (1999). The Hindu nationalist movement and Indian politics: 1925 to the 1990s: strategies of identity-building, implantation and mobilisation (with special reference to Central India). Penguin Books India.

Jaffrelot, C. (2021). Modi's India: Hindu nationalism and the rise of ethnic democracy.

Kamat, S., & Mathew, B. (2003). Mapping political violence in a globalised world: The case of Hindu nationalism. Social Justice, 30(3 (93), 4-16.

Kuszewska, A. (2022). Selected root causes and the structure of human rights violations. In Human Rights Violations in Kashmir, pp. 13-46. Routledge.

Lee, B. X. (2016). Causes and cures VIII: Environmental violence. Aggression and Violent Behavior, 30, 105-109.

Morton, K. (2016). China's ambition in the South China Sea: is a legitimate maritime order possible? International Affairs, 92(4), 909-940.

Pal, B. C. (1910). The spirit of Indian nationalism. Hind Nationalist Agency.

Rai, S. M. (2013). Gender and the political economy of development: From nationalism to globalisation. John Wiley & Sons.

Ram-Prasad, C. (2000). Hindu Nationalism and the international relations of India. In Religion and international relations, pp. 140-197. London: Palgrave Macmillan UK.

Roberts, E., & Finnegan, L. (2013). Building Peace around water, land and food: Policy and practice for preventing conflict. Geneva: Quaker United Nations Office.

Schwab, R. (2023). Escalate or negotiate? Constraint and rebel strategic choices towards rivals in the Syrian civil war. Terrorism and political violence, 35(4), 1007-1026.

Staniland, P. (2017). Armed politics and the study of intrastate conflict. Journal of Peace Research, 54(4), 459-467.

Stephenson Jr, M. O., & Pops, G. M. (1989). Conflict Resolution Methods and the Policy Process. Public Administration Review, 49(5).

Thondhlana, G., Redpath, S. M., Vedeld, P. O., van Eeden, L., Pascual, U., Sherren, K., & Murata, C. (2020). Non-material costs of wildlife conservation to local people and their implications for conservation interventions. Biological Conservation, 246, 108-578.

Vadlamannati, K. C. (2011). Why Indian men rebel? Explaining armed rebellion in the northeastern states of India, 1970–2007. Journal of Peace Research, 48(5), 605-619.

Chapter - 13

National Consciousness and The Kuka Movement: The Genesis of Non-Violence and Non-cooperation Movement in India's Struggle for Independence

— Dr Khushwant Kaur

1. Introduction

In the intricate tapestry of India's struggle for independence, the Kuka Movement emerges as a vibrant thread weaving through the very soul of our nation. This is not just a historical exploration but an intimate journey into the heart of the nationalist consciousness that galvanised a diverse nation. Led by the visionary Satguru Ram Singh Ji, the Kuka Movement pioneered the non-cooperation and non-violence movement that left an indelible mark on India's quest for freedom, a mark that resonates with sacrifices, resilience, and an unwavering commitment to our cultural identity.

2. Embracing the Motherland

जननी जन्मभूमिश्च स्वर्गादपि गरीयसी

"Janani JanmabhûmishchaSwargâdapiGarîyasî"

The Sanskrit shloka from the Hindu epic Ramayana which means, "The mother and the land of birth is more exalted than even heaven". This Sanskrit shloka elevates the motherland to the status of a mother and declares that the birthplace is better and greater than heaven. Just as a mother gives birth and nurtures her children, enduring many hardships. Just as a mother does not fail to sacrifice her own happiness for the happiness of the child. In the same way, the birthplace produces grains like a mother and despite facing many natural calamities, the motherland always nurtures its children. Our motherland is a celebration of the sacred connection between the people and their birthplace, a connection deemed holier and more profound than the very concept of heaven. It lays the foundation for understanding the deep-rooted emotions Indians harbour for their land. Motherland embraces and nurtures its children and sustains them even while enduring multitude of vicissitudes and calamities.

3. The Essence of Nationalist Consciousness

Our Vedas, Puranas and religious scriptures have been praising the glory of both, the mother and the motherland, for centuries. Since the Vedic period, the sacred land of India has been revered and worshiped like a mother. This is the reason that despite such a long history of struggle, all Indians are still tied together and feel a deep connection like children born to one mother. The feeling of connection is a form of consciousness. Consciousness is a broad concept under which there is an infinite ocean of experiences whose depth is not easy to measure. The concept of nationalist consciousness is not just an abstract ideology. It is a binding force that unites us as a nation. The profound attachment to our country becomes evident, fuelling a collective willingness to sacrifice for its protection, welfare, and progress. This emotional context becomes crucial in deciphering the motivations behind the Indian independence movement.

This article presents the awakening of the consciousness of Indians trapped in the shackles of slavery, which inspires them to sacrifice everything for the national interest. The Indian independence movement is the result of nationalist consciousness. As a result of nationalist consciousness, the countrymen became aware of the geographical, religious, political, economic, historical, cultural and social unity of their country. Countless patriots happily sacrificed their lives to realise the dream of an independent India and the dawn of freedom came in the lives of Indians after a long night of slavery.

4. A Tryst with Colonisation

As we navigate the historical landscape, the metaphor of an expanding octopus aptly captures the Islamic and British colonisation of India. Missionary activities, cultural erosion, genocidal on versions, and the deliberate dismantling of our religious heritage becomes apparent. These were not just external but threats to our very identity, setting the stage for patriots to rise and reclaim what was rightfully ours. Countless patriots wrote the story of the country's independence in golden letters with their sacrifices so that Indians could regain their lost identity and be of being Indians and of their Indian cultural heritage. The saga of sacrifices had a deep impact on the consciousness of the sleeping Indians resulting in rising clamor for an independent India from every corner of India. Every religion and sect have made an incomparable contribution to this story. In awakening the nationalist consciousness, the rebellion of heroines like Rani Velu Nachiyar, Kuyili and Rani Chennamma, as well as the Sanyasi Rebellion, Fakir Rebellion, Paika Rebellion, Ahom Rebellion, Kuka Rebellion, Gadkari Rebellion, Santhal Rebellion, Munda Rebellion, Bhil Rebellion, Kol Rebellion Revolution of 1857, military revolution etc. have had a very important contribution.

5. The Kuka Movement: A Clarion Call for Liberation

Dependence is a curse which deeply hurts the conscience of man due to which man loses his importance as well as his identity. The nationalist consciousness of the Sikhs was led by Satguru Ram Singh Ji, the Guru of Namdhari sect of Sikhs. He was the originator of the 'Kuka Movement'. He inspired people to awaken their spiritual consciousness and exhorted them to abandon the frustrated ideologies of the society. He continuously strove towards the upliftment of the country and society. Satguru Ram Singh Ji had said that when a community becomes subjugated or enslaved, the spiritual progress of the people of that community cannot take place. Due to hindered spiritual progress, that community becomes extremely weak socially and economically and its contribution in the development of the nation becomes negligible due to which the development of the nation gets hampered. S. S. Ahluwalia writes that Satguru Ram Singh understood that the freedom struggle cannot be won without raising moral standards in society. Because of this realisation he made honesty and truth the central focus.[1]

Kuka Movement was a clarion call for the rise of nationalistic conscience, guided by the enlightened teachings of Satguru Ram Singh Ji. It is not just a historical account but a vivid portrayal of a spiritual awakening of a nation and its people. Satguru Ram Singh Ji, a visionary leader, placed moral standards at the forefront of the freedom struggle, pioneering non-cooperation and boycott as potent weapons against the British. Satguru Ram SinghJi explained to the people the importance of awakening spiritual consciousness to free the country from the shackles. He taught about the importance of adopting values like good conduct, truth, simplicity, honesty, dutifulness and altruism as transforming them into invincible weapons of the freedom struggle. He was among the first who sounded the trumpet of freedom. According to Wikipedia, Satguru Ram Singh was the first leader who employed non-cooperation and boycott of British goods and services as a political weapon against the British through the Kuka Rebellion. Guruji awakened the consciousness among people to live with self-respect and also inspired them to develop devotion and heroic spirit, love for the country, mutual brotherhood, tolerance and living together.[2]

After Satguru Ram Singh ji was put under house arrest, he declared, "I will create Ram Singhs in every house. The spark of independence that I have lit will become a conflagration that will destroy your rule." (Translated; see pg. 49)

6. Battling the Storm

'Sant Khalsa' or Kuka started the non-cooperation movement under the leadership of Satguru Ram Singh Ji, under which they announced complete boycott of the British rule and raised the cry of freedom. Adopting (reliance of self, on indigenous products), the Kukas took the lead in fighting the war of independence by following the path of truth and non-violence. To make the Non-Cooperation Movement successful, the Kukas boycotted the English administrative and judicial system, the English postal system, the railway system for transportation, the English education system, the English medical system. They even boycotted the roads built by the British. The boycott of all types of goods made in British factories and the boycott of government jobs shook the British colonial rulers to its foundation.

Tracking the export and import of textiles, Rajni Pamdutt reported that, from 1814 to 1835, the consumption of imported textiles from Manchester mills had increased from 10 lakhs yards to 5 crores 10 Lakh yards. In the same duration, the exports of Indian handloom textiles precipitously reduced from 77 Lakhs 50 thousand yards to 20 Lakh 6 thousand yards only. Satguru Ram Singh ordered the boycott of imported textiles as he realised that only by eschewing foreign made textiles could the livelihoods of local handloom weavers be ensured. The impact of the boycott can be gauged from the reaction of the British as the boycott threatened the economic viability of their colonial enterprise.[3]

Tara Singh Anjan writes in his book 'Satguru Ram Singh Ji Te Kuka Lahar'[3] that Satguru Ram Singh Ji ordered the Kukas to live harmoniously and to resolve minor mutual differences in the Lok Panchayat. To make the

Swadeshi movement successful, he emphasized on adopting indigenous education instead of English education. He started a private postal system for Kukas. Kukas were ordered to travel on foot, by bullock carts or horse carts, instead of the railways. Kukas were ordered to boycott English clothes and wear plain white cotton clothes, and instead of taking up government jobs, they were asked to work in local small scale industries and agriculture. The Kuka movement was propagated not only in the country but also abroad.

Satguru Ram Singh Ji taught people the lesson of equality and inspired them to work for social upliftment by rising above caste and creed. He tried to eliminate this deep gap of discrimination and bind the Indian society in the thread of unity. Kapoor Singh ICS writes that the British government wanted to keep the entire country enslaved forever by implementing its 'divide and rule policy'. Hence, the British opened slaughterhouses at various places with the aim of dividing the society on the basis of religion. Under the leadership of Satguru Ram Ji, the Kukas took up the cause of cow protection and gave a befitting reply to the British rule by freeing the cows from the slaughterhouse. According to Wikipedia,

The social harmony of the region was largely under threat due to the issue of cow slaughter. In the late nineteenth century, the support of colonial administration to kine-killing had become publicly evident, and was reported in a number of newspapers like Aftab-i-Punjab (Lahore), Wasir-ulMulk (Sialkot), Koh-i-Nur (Lahore), which explicitly stated that "kine-killing" was done by the orders of the authorities who 'desired that disharmony should prevail' between Hindus and Muslims.[4]

The brutal response from the British government, the sacrifices of the Namdhari Sikhs during the heroic protests against cow slaughter stand as testament to the movement's resilience. Each act of defiance became a spark that fuelled the flames of India's fight for freedom.

7. A Ripple Beyond Punjab

The British government's escalating concern and their futile attempts to suppress the movement echo in the resonance it found beyond Punjab. It wasn't just a regional upheaval; it was a collective roar for freedom. A small spark lit by Satguru Ram Singh Ji had taken the form of a huge revolution – a conflagration. The Kuka wave was not limited to Punjab but became the voice of the entire country. The Kuka wave had shaken the British government. Satguru Ram Singh ji had become a big threat to the British, hence the demand for his arrest started gaining momentum in the

British government. Bishan Singh lists in his book Baghi Kuka, the frisson among the British regarding the activities of Satguru Ram Singh Ji. Major Mike Andreo wrote that Guru Ram Singh's teachings has destabilised the British rule. Kaim Ali reported to his superiors that Guru Ram Singh was a dangerous man and the British should arrest him. Lahina Singh sent reports that the entire country has started following Guru Ram Singh, the government should make suitable arrangements. Genda Muqbar, District Commissioner of Jalandhar city, sent a report that Guru Ram Singh has made preparations to fight a war with an army of 1.25 lakhs and is getting ready to kill the British… and in his second report, he said that Narangwal Sardar Mehtab Singh is vigorously exhorting the Kukas to expel the British at the earliest. (Translated from Punjabi)[5]

The Kuka movement was becoming a big challenge for the British rule. The British government tried to brutally suppress this revolution. In order to crush the Kuka movement, the panicky British government martyred Kukas by making them stand in front of the cannons and blowing them up, hanging them, etc. But despite their best efforts, the British government was not able to stop this Kuka wave of revolution. According to Wikipedia;

The British wanted to extinguish every spark that was a threat to their power. To eliminate the Namdhari Sikhs, nine cannons were procured from the native states and installed at the parade ground of Malerkotla. Seven cannons were fired seven times, in which 49 Namdhari Sikhs were martyred by cutting them into pieces for freedom. A 12-year-old child, Bishan Singh, was also included in this group, who was martyred by the soldiers by beheading him. On 18 January 1872, 16 other Sikhs were martyred by being blown up by cannons. Thus, in the Malerkotla incident, 10 Sikhs were martyred while fighting, four were serving the punishment of black water, 65 Sikhs were martyred with cannons and one Sikh with swords. (Translated).[6]

8. Satguru Ram Singh Ji's Enduring Legacy

The sacrifices made during this movement, chronicled in the annals of history, became the bedrock of India's freedom struggle. Satguru Ram Singh Ji emerges not just as a historical figure but as a luminary whose teachings continue to illuminate our pursuit of independence. Satguru Ram Singh Ji awakened in the hearts of his disciples and countrymen the dormant national consciousness and suggested the path of liberation through breaking the shackles of subjugation by adopting Swadeshi and completely boycotting every symbol of the unjust and tyrannical British rule. By imbibing the ideals of simple life and high thoughts, Satguru Ram Singh ji led the country's march to freedom and sounded the trumpet of freedom.

Dr Madan Rathi gives the social background of colonial Punjab, where "social laws" were being altered by the colonizers and the rising "social vices, religious hypocrisy and political slavery" were being exacerbated by the policies of British, in his article 'Kuka Movement in Punjab: An Overview.'[7] The social and nationalistic renaissance due to Kuka Movement was duly highlighted by Dr Rajendra Prasad, the first president of independent India, in an article published in 1935 wrote that Satguru Ram Singh Ji "considered political freedom as a part of religion...(and) the principles of boycott and non-cooperation, which Mahatma Gandhi introduced so vigorously in our freedom movement were expounded by Guru Ram Singh for the Namdharis." (emphasis added)

Shaheed Bhagat Singh has written about Kuka Freedom Movement in his biography and remarked that the British had realised that the religious movement would acquire fearful political dimensions. Subhash Chandra Bose said that Guru Ram Singh had given "the banner of freedom to Indians" and was the "first leader of the peaceful non-cooperation movement in India." While India's first Prime Minister, Pandit Jawaharlal Nehru, said in 1939 that, "No Indian can deny the importance of efforts put in by Sat Guru Ram Singh Ji...in achieving freedom for the motherland. Congress merely followed the path shown by him and attained independence." (emphasis added). Finally, in 2008, the Government of India recognised the freedom fighters of Kuka Movement, a portrait of Satguru Ram Singh Ji was unveiled in the parliament of India. In 2013, a postage stamp was released as an ode to Kuka Movement.[8]

The inspiring path shown by Satguru was adopted and followed by countless other freedom fighters. In fact, the idea of non-violence and non-cooperation originally originated from the Sikhs, which was later followed by many including, Baba Kharag Singh in Punjab, and later copied by Mohandas Karamchand Gandhi in the struggle for independence. Ultimately, because of the sacrifices of Satguru Ram Singh Ji, Namdhari Sikhs, and countless brave children of Mother India, the country's dream of independence came true. According to Vishwa Namdhari Sangat's book Azadi Sangram De Mahan Hero, Satguru Ram Singh was the shining star of India's freedom struggle and a religious leader. By winning not only freedom but also giving life to people, morality is the first revolution. Which will always survive in human history. (Translated).[9]

The origin of the word "Kuka" is theorised to have a political origin derived from "Kook" (a war cry for freedom).[10] Satguru Ram Singh Ji had said, "The torch of freedom struggle that I have kindled in the hearts of people, will not only keep burning but spread to all nooks and corners of this country. The more you try to extinguish it, the more violently it will flash. No one can extinguish it till independence is achieved."

In essence, the spirit of the Kuka Movement breathed life into our collective pursuit of liberty. It was not just dry impersonal historical facts and figures, but the emotions, sacrifices, and unwavering determination, that define the soul of India's quest for independence.

References

1. https://archive. org/details/KukaLehar/page/n202/mode/1up, pg. 27
2. https://hi-m-wikipediaorg. translate. goog/wiki/रामिसं
3. https://archive. org/details/KukaLehar/page/n202/mode/1up, pg. 25
4. https://en. wikipedia. org/wiki/Ram_Singh_Kuka
5. https://archive. org/details/inqalabi-kuka/page/n39/mode/2up
6. https://hi. wikipedia. org/wiki/]
7. https://rntujournals. aisect. org/assets/upload_files/articles/7f05eb2ed3aa60e7d81f26f370f5d76 b. pdf
8. https://kukasikhs. com/kukasikhs-wp/?page_id=1113
9. https://archive. org/details/ajadi-sangram-de-mahan-hero/page/n5/mode/2up
10. https://archive. org/details/kuka-movement-fs/page/34/mode/1up, Pg. 19

Chapter - 14

Indian Nationalism; The Ethical and Political Questions

— Dr Ashita R

1. Introduction

Nationalism is a multifaceted, intricate phenomenon that has long impacted human history and politics. While nationalism is exclusive to the present era, several of its components have historical roots. The ancient Hebrews, who saw themselves as both a chosen people that is, a people superior to all others and a people with a shared cultural past, are most likely the source of nationalism. The Roman Empire, which established a strong, centralised monarchy and fostered the development of regional languages and artistic forms, replaced these sentiments of ethnocentrism, which are akin to nationalism, with far more universal identities. Nation against nation was sparked by the religion wars. Subsequently, via the conceptions of the French Revolution led to the conclusion that people should form governments that provide equality to everyone. This was the first time in history that a government was formed in line with the general desire of the people, and nationalism found its first political manifestation.

As a bridge between city-states and empires, nations frequently become instrumental to defend themselves. All that a nation is a certain kind of civilisation. On the other side, nationalism refers to the presence of national beliefs, especially the conviction that the "nation" is the only thing deserving of being pursued.

The concept that all of human civilisation is organised into separate, independent entities known as nations is the foundation of nationalism. A group of people that speak the same language, have a similar culture, have a shared destiny, and have a shared past is referred to as a country. Thus, nationalism may also refer to the shared values that unite citizens of a country and foster a new kind of society. This is linked to the notion of self-determination, which holds that each nation should have the authority to decide its own destiny and that people's allegiance should be directed toward their country. Thus, nationalism also refers to the belief that a country ought to have the freedom to self-govern and to make its own decisions.

2. Historical backdrop

The nationalistic movement is rather new. Even though individuals have always had a strong loyalty to their home country and the customs of their ancestors, nationalism did not gain widespread acceptance until the late 1700s. Many people believe that the American and French revolutions of the eighteenth century were the first significant examples of nationalism. Nationalism expanded over central, eastern, and southeast Europe in the 1800s and into the newly formed Latin American nations. Asia and Africa saw the rise of nationalism in the first part of the twentieth century.

Pre-twentieth Century Nationalism

The Puritan Revolution of the middle of the 1600s in England gave rise to the first authentic manifestations of nationalism. The English nationalism of the eighteenth century, embodied in the "social contract" political theory of John Locke and Jean Jacques Rousseau, would shape nationalism in America and France for the remainder of the century. Influenced by ideas of liberty put forth by Locke, Rousseau, and other contemporary French philosophers, British colonists in North America gave rise to American nationalism. In the late 1700s, American colonists were inspired to take up arms by the political ideas of Thomas Jefferson and Thomas Paine. They started fighting for liberty and individual rights. The impact of the emerging American nationalism was evident in the French Revolution of 1789, which culminated in the American Revolution of 1775 and the Declaration of Independence in 1776. In France nationalism also came to represent a universal adherence to the progressive idea of a future of freedom and equality rather than the authoritarianism and inequality of the past.

twentieth Century Movements

The period of twentieth century witnessed the emergence of new form of nationalism shaped largely by World War I and World War II. After the World War I Adolf Hitler introduced a new brand of nationalism. Authoritarian governance, racial purity, and the legendary splendors of

Germany's pre-Christian history are discussed in Germany. The majority of the post-World War II surges in nationalism were fueled by independence movements following decolonisation. People developed national identities to set themselves apart from their oppressors as they battled to escape their European colonists. All of these new patriotic identities, whether rooted in culture, religion, politics, or the European Cold War, had some connection to the quest for independence. Following World War II, Europe saw a broad decline in nationalism as a result of the creation of multinational economic, military and political organisations.

3. Nationalism: Definitional tasks

Although nationalism is typically understood to be a sentiment, it is much more than that. Emerging from the human gregarious impulse and reinforced by the logical need for self-governance, nationalism has evolved into a dynamic force in contemporary politics. It promotes the feeling that every man owes his first and last duty to the nation and that the –nation state is the ultimate unit of human an organisation".

In international society, nationalism is by far the greatest dynamic force. Nationalism constitutes both the foundation of a sovereign state system and a powerful determinant factor of supernational movement".

Nationalism is an ideology that places the nation at the centre of its concerns and seeks to promote its well being. According to nationalists, a nation cannot survive without a sufficient degree of three generic goals which are national autonomy, national unity and national identity. Nationalism can be defined on the bases of these three goals. "An ideological movement for attaining and maintaining autonomy, unity and identity for a population which some of its members deem to constitute an actual or potential "nation".

In the words of Jawaharlal Nehru "Nationalism essentially an anti-feeling". Above all, nationalism is an attitude, an act of consciousness. It is an ideology that asserts, among other things, that every nation has the right to its state and that the nation serves as the only acceptable foundation for the state. It also maintains that the nation, ethnicity, or national identity is a fundamental unit of human life.

4. Rise of Indian nationalism

Nationalism in India emerged as a sentiment against the colonial rule against the Britishers. The colonial period faced many socio-economic and cultural agitations which promoted a national identity and pride among Indians. To achieve independence, people participated in the movement irrespective of their caste, religion, cultural, and socio-economic disparities the agitations against the Britishers gave a new dimension to the concept of nationalism.

The late nineteenth century marked the beginning of the foundation of the Indian National Congress; its principal objective was to unify the people in India under one umbrella and fight against the colonial regime. In the initial period, the INC was a moderate organisation focused on constitutional reforms. In later years The Indian National Congress lost, its moderate nature and was replaced with a more radical reform of nationalism in India. The partition of Bengal in 1905 by the British Government was a turning point in Indian politics. The division of Bengal into a religious line by the British government was seen as a deliberate attempt to weaken the growing nationalist movement in the country. Boycotts and other forms of mass protest against this strategy marked the start of the nationalist movement's more militant phase. Bengal's partition in 1905 contributed to the rise of extreme nationalist factions within the Indian National Congress. The Indian National Congress's radical factions launched a boycott of British goods and promoted the Swadeshi movement as part of its radical programmes. The movement aimed to achieve economic self-sufficiency. The 1920s to 1940s are regarded as the Gandhian era of nationalism.. Gandhian nationalism is primarily grounded in the nonviolence, civil disobedience, and Satyagraha. Consequently, nationalism emerged in India as a liberal elite movement that aimed to cooperate with the British to effect political change. Funda-mentally, this kind of nationalism was conservative and non-revolutionary. Following Bengal's division in 1905, a new surge of nationalism with a distinctly more radical nationalist agenda arose. Gandhi, in the end, became a nationalist leader who gained the trust of the people and created the momentum that neither radicals nor liberals could. Gandhi, however, continued to take a cautious and nonviolent stance in his quest for freedom from British domination in spite of the backing of the general public.

5. Post Independent period

(i) The Nehruvian Nationalism

The period of the 1960s and '70s evolved with the ideology of Nehruvian Nationalism. Regarding the question of the antiquity of the Indian nation, they argued that India could not be a nation; it was only a group of communities and sub-regions. The thinkers were equating the rise of nationalism with the emergence of modern states. It presumes that India was not a nation-state before the nineteenth century. The struggles for independent India unified the whole nation and gave a new outlook to the nation-state. The independent movement was a multi–sector, a multi-linguistic, multi-communal, and multi-regional struggle which galvanised the people of India and giving kindled in them a feeling of nationalism. This ideology of nationalism emphasized that the Indian freedom struggle was a secular, plural, and multi-class struggle where many sub-nationalities took part and finally consolidated itself as a nation-state in 1947.

(ii) Communalist Nationalism

They never believed in the concept of nationalism; according to them, nations are the creations of the capitalist state and will wither away with the rise of communism. They believe in class consciousness, their primary allegiance towards the class, not the nation.

(iii) Hindu Nationalism and the rise of BJP

The Hindu right has always existed in independent Indian politics, although it was marginal until the 1970s. They managed to unite fierce opponents of Nehru's secularism under their organisational banner. The 1980 emergence of Jana Sangh as the centerpiece of the BJP's new form was a part of the "revisionist" ideological stance, which was a skillful and subtle break from the RSS's radicalism. The BJP was the critics Nehru's pro-Islamic stand and they considered Nehru as anti-Hindu.

The Bharatiya Janata Party (BJP) claimed that India is a Hindu country, which is embodied by the term "Hindutva," and criticized Nehru's policies. The Hindutva ideology promoted pluralism and unity under the slogan "one nation, one culture, and India first," while arguing that Islam and Christianity are foreign to India. The 1990s witnessed the emergence of the BJP, as the Hindu right's call was answered by the urban middle class. During this time, neoliberal economic policies and Hindu fundamentalism, two opposing ideas, merged and found a voice in a significant portion of India's political establishment. In 1984, the party had only two members in the Eighth Lok Sabha. However, in the 1989 election, it gained 85 seats, and in 1991 they achieved 119 seats in 1984, but increased its total to 85 in the 1989 election and to 119 in 1991.

The period of 1990s was crucial for the BJP's growth. Influenced by socio-political issues like the Mandal Commission and Ram Janmabhoomi, in the Tenth Lok Sabha elections in 1991, by 1996, the BJP had become the largest party in the Lok Sabha, although its government was short-lived. In 1998, the BJP-led National Democratic Alliance (NDA) narrowly lost a confidence vote. However, the Thirteenth Lok Sabha election in 1999 marked a turning point, with the NDA completing a full five-year term. The year 2014 marked a turning point. Under Narendra Modi's leadership, the BJP won a decisive majority with 282 seats and in 2019 Loksabha election also BJP has got the largest majority in the House with 303 seats and the BJP-led National Democratic Alliance (NDA) won 353 seats. The Political exponent clearly signifies BJP's predominance.

6. Challenges to Indian Nationalism

Indian nationalism emerged in the late eighteenth and early nineteenth centuries as an anti-colonial and secular movement. It marked the beginning of the nation-building process and encompassed various fields like literature, science, art, and religion. This movement contributed to the development of a "Modern India" that was progressive in politics, religion, and socio-economics.

However, the meaning of nationalism has transformed over time, especially in India. It has now become a political tool that can be wielded to quash dissent. The politicisation of nationalism has led people to equate it with religion, resulting in divisive and hostile attitudes between communities. This, in turn, has led to violence and further discord. Mahatma Gandhi believed that nationality should be a source of unity rather than division. For Mahatma Gandhi, nationalism meant the prosperity of the human race, that the country should be free, but not at the cost of human lives. He despised racial discrimination and communal hate. The nationalism that Mahatma Gandhi envisioned for India is vastly different from what is present today. Instead of promoting humanity, modern India is plagued by religious intolerance and division. Nationalism has evolved to become more than just love for one's country, with today's "hyper-nationalism" being particularly toxic. This has been fuelled by politicians and the media, who have made nationalism the top priority. However, manipulating nationalism is a dangerous game that can lead to anarchy within a nation. It is important to remember that nationalism was a major factor in the partition of India, which resulted in the deaths of millions of innocent people.

Nationalism and its challenges are evident in Indian soil in different periods under different situations. In the post-independent era, various regions in India demanded separate statehood for themselves. The North

Eastern states like Nagaland, Mizoram, etc fought with the Indian government for their separate state entity. The Khalistan Movement was a big jolt to the Indian history. The demand for the Khalistan movement was a separate state for Sikh people. But the Indian Government suppressed the movement with an iron hand, which in resulted mass killings of Sikhs across the nation.

In today's Indian political scenario, religion plays an enormous role. It is used as a political weapon to determine one's nationalistic sentiments towards the nation. Religious fundamentalism is one of the greatest threats to the very existence of Indian nationalistic sentiments. Right-wing politics is a political and cultural force in Indian society. Their policies are focused on the Hindutuva agenda. In order to attain their goals, these groups developed a term called hyper nationalism or neo-nationalism. This kind of nationalistic element is evident in India's political scenario, such as the building of Ram Mandir in Ayodhya, the removal of Article 370 of Jammu and Kashmir, the hosting of the G20, etc. By using these political strategies, they have put hyper-nationalistic elements in the minds of people in India. It demanded people stand with the "US." If we are against the government, they have come to the conclusion that we are anti-national. Another kind of fundamentalism is associated with the Islamic religion. Their aim is to create a Muslim world. In order to achieve this goal, they used terrorist activities in different parts of the country.

7. Conclusion

The current interpretation of Indian nationalism is distinct. These days, it's a political tool to quell criticism; everyone who speaks out against the government is instantly labeled as anti-national. The main definition of nationalism is love and pride for our own country. The sense of nationalism could stem from common experiences, customs, and challenges. There is always a connection between nationalism and the aspiration for autonomy, sovereignty, and self-determination. India's nationalism faces numerous obstacles; it was established during the British era and continues to this day. As such, it is the responsibility of the populace to defend its nationalistic beliefs and ideals in the face of these difficulties.

Notes and References

1. Dincsachin, Sakir and Melis Arslan. "Development of Nationalism in India", Journal of Social Sciences, Vol 3 (2), October 2013: 242-245.
2. https://www. adda247. com/upsc-exam/rise-of-nationalism-inmovement-india
https://www. met. edu. /knowledge-at-met/nationalism-issues-and-challenges

3. Joshi, Pooja. "Nationalism issues and Challenges".
4. Longley, Robert. "What is nationalism? Definitions and Examples", https://thoyghtco. com/natioanlism-defenitions-4158265
5. Nirola, Basant. A sense of nationalism in Today's India". Youth Ki Awaaz 08 May. 2018.
6. Purinton, Malcolm F. "Origin and impact of nationalism", https://www.khanacademy. org/humanities/world-history-project-ap/
7. Roy, A. C. International Relations since 1919. Kolkata, World Press Private Ltd, 1965.
8. Sharma, Ashish and Samarth Mishra. Indian Nationalism and its Challenges in the Right Wing Era of Politics, Journal of Mass Communication & Journalism, Vol. 11(7): 2021: pp. 1-3.
9. Smith, Antony, D (2nd Ed.) Nationalism Theory, Ideology, History. Cambridge, polity press, 2010.
10. Tuli, Rajiv. "The Conflicting Claims of Nationalism" Opinion 30th July 2022.

Part - III

Scientific Spirit and Objective Reality

Chapter - 15

Science and Nationalism: Discursive shift in political discourses in India

— Dr Prashant Kumar Kain

1. Introduction

The World War II is considered to be one of the biggest manmade disasters in human history. This event not only killed millions of human beings but also had profound impact on the natural ecology. This was for the first time that nuclear bomb was used against the humanity destroying present and the damaging the forthcoming generations. It is difficult to imagine the social cost of this human tragedy where people lost everything they had, the family, friends, relations and so on. The bomb did not discriminate between Man and Women, aged and children, rich and poor, Japanese or Korean. Everyone turned into instant vapour because the temperature on the ground reached 7000 degree Celsius. Destruction could be imagined by the fact that the melting point of iron is only about 1500 degree Celsius. People did even get fractions of a second to realise what has happened to them. The memories of that tragedy are very much preserved in the form of widely known phenomenon called 'nuclear shadow'.

The Hiroshima and Nagasaki event proved the immense power of science and how destructive it can become if it is misused by and for sectarian interests. This is well experiences by people who died and survived the concentration camps in Europe. One of the survivors of this human tragedy shared his anguish and advice to the teachers. He writes, "I am a survivor of a concentration camp. My eyes saw what no person should witness: gas chambers built by learned engineers. Children poisoned by educated physicians. Infants killed by trained nurses. Women and babies shot by high school and college graduates. So, I am suspicious of education.

My request is this: Help your children become human. Your efforts must never produce learned monsters, skilled psychopaths or educated Eichmanns. Reading, writing, and arithmetic are important only if they serve to make our children more human" (Mitchell, 1980: 14).

Above incidents from history clearly demystify the neutrality of science. Science can be used as a weapon of mass destruction if it gets into wrong hands. The sectarian interests can go to any extent to use science for self glory and self fulfillment at the cost of others. The false notion of superiority, self pride and arrogance are well imbedded in the notion of nationalism. These are not a natural state of mind for human beings. It is a cultivated belief that is based on the notions of superiority and exclusiveness of one's given self. It requires constant promotion though consistent propaganda. Science and scientific inventions have made it easier today. The advances in information technology resulted in transfer of information with greater speed and volumes. This means that propaganda and myths can travel faster and with immense volumes, crossing the physical and cultural boundaries of nations. Human beings are becoming the repository and depository of 'information'. There is a mechanical production and reproduction of information on social media platforms. There is a mad race to quickly consume, react and forward everything that we feel appealing and suit to our interests.

Lately, there has been a narcissistic trend of jingoism in South Asian countries particularly in India. These trends are very much visible on social media platforms, chat forums and news debates. There are regular doses of conspiracy theories, sinister propaganda, character assassinations, loud prime time debates, attack and defence of identities, selective narratives of past, interpretation and reinterpretations of historical events etc. The 'information' sharing platforms are fast becoming ideological battle grounds between groups, nations and communities. There is a mad rush among companies to seek our attention in their viewership war. In this war, morality and ethics are secondary to revenue. Potter says, 'The strongest influence on the construction of news is its commercial nature. News organisations are businesses that compete with each other for audiences and advertisers' (Potter, 2001: 88). The information is being consumed at mass levels which are shaping the very discourses of public opinions. The social media today is not merely a information sharing platform but also a domain of false news and propaganda. State and the ruling classes are using this as an opportunity to promote its own interests.

What is the meaning of these changes for the society? What is the relationship between science and society? Who is controlling science and who is setting the agenda of scientific discourse today? Are the ruling elites using science to promote their ideological and political interests? Is the science and technology being used to promote nationalism lately? Are the information sharing platforms involved in influencing the public opinions and democracy? These are some of the important questions that need critical reflections and introspection today. It is important to go into history to understand the philosophy of science and its appropriation by certain groups to fulfill their sectarian agendas.

II. Science and Nationalism: Conflicting Philosophy

Nationalism is a highly debated concept in social science more so cultural nationalism. It is largely because of its claims of representing social as a singular whole. It has been criticized for its narrow and exclusive nature on account of region, leadership, religion, language, identity, history and so on. As a political ideology it creates certain kind of contradictions. On the one hand, it creates unity among the subjects on the other hand it differentiates them with others. In other words, it creates binaries at the same time opposing binaries. It is equally important not to confuse nationalism with patriotism. Patriotism promotes love and loyalty towards one's country while nationalism promotes hostility with 'others'. One of the most significant definitions and difference was articulated by French presidents Charles de Gaulle. He said "patriotism is when love of your own people comes first: nationalism, when hate for people other than your own comes first" (Garry, 1969:29). Quite clearly, Nationalism as an ideology is always constructed in opposition of 'someone or something' rather than in relation to self.

The relationship between science and nationalism is complicated. These complications arise largely due to the contradictory interests they both serve. In order to understand this complexity, one has to see the relationship between science and modernity and culture and nationalism. History is an important site where these relationships were built and concretized. Western enlightenment thus becomes an important reference point to understand this. Critical Rationalism was the product of western enlightenment that emerged in the medieval Europe. It emerged as a response against the orthodoxy and narrow worldview of the universe imposed by the dominant aristocracy and priestly class. Hamilton says, 'It combines the application of reason to social, political and economic issues with a concern with progress, emancipation and improvement and is consequently critical of the status quo' (Hamilton, 1992: 20). Enlightenment driven modern knowledge was imbedded on certain moral and ethical concerns. It was viewed as an effective tool to understand and transform human societies.

The rationality driven modern science is an objective inquiry of this world that is based on facts and evidences. Science and scientific inquiries are based on the assumption that there is a fundamental unity of the world as everything is made of same matter and substances. It lays down strict processes and procedures to arrive at any conclusion. Science therefore not only transcends the time and space barriers but also sees human beings as an inseparable whole. Similarly, Modernity is always equated with modern way of life and thinking. It is based on rational, logical and progressive evolution. Consequently it is perceived as opponent of traditions and traditional ways of thinking. Science and modernity are always held to be anti-traditions or opposed to traditions for certain historical reasons. According to Pathak, 'modernity as a distinctive form of civilisation originated in the west. It began to emerge in the west from about the fifteenth century. But it was essentially the European enlightenment in the eighteenth century that gave a specific meaning to it' (Pathak, 2015: 21).

The European roots of enlightenment, development of science in west and colonialism made the very concept of 'modernity' problematic and contestable. Firstly, Modernity is always equated and associated with west. Secondly, it is seen as products of colonial discourse introduced to show inferiority of the colonialised subjects. Thirdly, modernity is always presumed to be incompatible with local traditions and values. Modernity is often seen as a challenge because of the above and overlapping factors. This makes modernity as a challengeable concept especially by those who are the beneficiaries of traditions and traditional social order. They have projected modernity as an ideology which is alien and threat to the indigenous cultural practices and traditions. The brute colonial rule of the past has helped that projection both convenient and smooth. These dominant interests project an 'imaginary' unity of subjects to divert attention from self introspection and self evaluations. Postmodernism is often used as a shield to justify those interests in the name of differences or traditions itself are projected as modernity.

Nationalism is often a response or manifestation of those defensive interests. Nationalism is a political ideology holds that the nation and state should be congruent. According to Emile Durkheim, Culture is the collective and shared representation of something. By the term 'representations' he meant the 'cultural beliefs, moral values, symbols and ideas shared by any human group. Such cultural components serve as a way of representing the world meaningfully to members of a particular cultural group' (Bocock, 1992: 238). Culture is always held to be sacred because it represents a shared collective meaning. Similarly, Nationalism is an ideology that is based on these shared, exclusive and collective interests. This collective identity is always based on certain common parameters like shared territory, history, cultural beliefs, languages and so on. Nationalism thus plays dual functions; one is inclusive and other is exclusive. In the former case it binds people together under an often 'imaginary' identity while in the latter case it separates them from others using the same identities. As a political ideology it forces people to submit themselves to those collective interests. It leaves no space and scope for self critique and self determination of people.

Science and nationalism project mutually opposite view of social reality. Science advocates free and fair enquiry of the world while nationalism promotes submission to the established beliefs. Despite these antagonistic tendencies, the growth of modern science and nationalism is simultaneous and parallel in history. The idea of nation and its political expression couldn't have been possible without mass production and spread of 'knowledge'. Benedict Anderson in his important work imagined communities (1983) showed how the mass production and circulation of knowledge played an important role in the spread of nationalist ideas horizontally (Anderson, 2006: 37). Science has been used as an ideological tool to promote the interests of dominants in the society. In other words, science both directly and indirectly promoted nationalism and vice versa. Those in power can easily use science to promote their interests. For example, in Nazi Germany, scientists were pressured to conduct research that supported the Nazi ideology of racial superiority. Scientists actively used their scientific knowledge and collaborated with the power elites to create favourable results supporting their ideology (Weindling, 2015: 21).

III. Inventing Demon: The Indian Way

There is a certain kind of historisation when we think of Indian nationalism. We tend to think that nationalism as an event was over with the departure of the British in 1947. This is largely because Indian nationalism has largely been imagined in relation to the British rule. It was a colonial product borrowed from British and European model for self governance. Rag says, 'Indian nationalism emerged out of contested visions involving a whole context of strands, conflicts, combinations and permutations among many imaginations which evolved over time' (Rag, 1995: 69). These contested visions and conflicts are largely located within the fragmented social which were brought under an exclusive and imaginary identity which could not be found at the grass root levels.

Indian nationalism copied itself on European model of similarities which were not to be found in India due to inherent diversity of its history and cultural practices. However, nationalists ignored those diversities in favour of a singular, exclusive and pervasive whole. The nationalists in pursuit of their class interests created its own parallel, contradictory and self justifying version of modernity drawing heavily from pre-colonial history. Accordingly to Aloysius, 'the colonial period of Indian history is not merely a period of shame and servitude but also a period during which, in its own peculiar way, India stepped into modernity…it is a period of great social and political upheaval in which we shall seek the emergence or non-emergence of a new national community' (Aloysius, 1997: 21). The national community could not emerge more concretely due to the hegemonic interests in the primordial social relations in India. Attack on these primordial interests by the British led to the invention of the ideal nation.

The colonial roots of Indian nationalism and its elite leadership make it a highly debated concept for certain reasons. Firstly, the colonial impact was not uniform on all sections of the society. Secondly, India stepped into modernity during this period by due to secularisation and universalisation of education and work. Thirdly, the investment in science by colonial powers was seen as a strategy to exploit natural resources for its own gains rather than natives. Modernity and science were seen by elite native with suspicion or as a strategy to colonialise the nation mentally and psychologically. Even though, they realised the power of science and modernity but they were not ready to accept it at the cost of their culture and traditions. Bankim Chandra Chatterjee, a staunch nationalist observed even before the founding of India National Congress, "nation with historical reminiscences of its past glory tries to retain its glory, and if this be lost, it tries to regain it" (Deshpande, 2011: 1313).

The nationalist discourse in India has passed though different phases and stages. Even though there has been significant changes over the years but its inner core has remained unchanged. This core is represented by the core social interests. Historically, Indian nationalism was invented to preserve those core interests. These interests are very much present even today. It did not simply fade away after the departure of British from India.

The changing times have also brought significant changes in nature and form. There are new meanings, definition and alignments formed over a period of time. New distinctions have been introduced of modern and traditional, friends and foes, collaborators and resistors, nationalist and anti-nationalists and so on. The nationalist discourse which was already narrow is further becoming complex, aggressive and exclusive with its own twists and turns.

The struggle during the colonial phase was to get independence from colonial rule. However, the debates today are to decontaminate or decolonize the society of those 'colonial' effects. There are numerous enemies found within the society. These new enemies are western philosophy, English education, Macaulay education system, civil society groups, secularism, modernity, English speaking classes etc. today's state sees them as a challenge to the state and the society equally. It does not want a dialogue rather believes in forceful impositions. It has conveniently found enemies in everyone whoever raises questions and asks for state accountability. Some of them are farmers, socialists, journalists, Muslims, Christian missionaries, feminists, rights aware dalits, conscious adivasis, resistive workers, vast chunk of backward classes etc. Contrarily, Indian state is firmly and apologetically stands with the corporate in pursuit of achieving the lost status of 'vishwaguru' (world teacher or path shower). The private capital and corporate are not seen as a challenge rather a collaborator to achieve that dream.

The corporate are selling what can be sold more conveniently. Brute nationalism and cultural pride are the new commodities sold today in the name of swadeshi. Babas (Indian godmen) are becoming the new representive and guardian of culture and religion. They are the news maker and model of swadeshi capitalism today. These self pro-claimed are being projected as a savior of India from west controlled multi-nationals corporations and exploitive global capitalism. Contrastingly, in this changing atmosphere, the educated and intellectual are seen with suspicion and with a sense of hostility. They are mocked today for being rootless and ignorant of glorious Indian past and culture. Mass media is a collaborator of generating such narratives. The difference between the news and propaganda is blurred and shrunken. State is a big source of advertisements and revenues of print and electronic media. Many news channels controlled by the corporate houses have become a mouth piece of the governments. Today, news is not reported rather created in the four walls of the newsroom with mutually calculated interests. This is a big threat to democracy as companies manipulate public opinion therefore creating threat to the very idea of democracy.

IV. Discursive Shifts in Knowledge Production in India

There have been significant shifts in the perceptions, purpose and philosophy of knowledge in India. In political discourses, there is a certain push for 'indigenous', 'local', 'self reliance', 'decolonise'. This discourse is built on the assumptions that there is something which is alien, foreign and enslaving element in the Indian education and cultural landscape. Indian society has to be freed from those alien and foreign influences and create parallel, alternative and culturally relevant discourses and solutions. These shifts manifests itself in diverse areas and mean moving from universal to local, west to east, modern to traditional, empirical to historical, individual to community, rights to duties, knowledge to skills, and English to vernacular languages with Sanskrit and Hindi retaining special place. There are consciousness efforts to shift attention from former to latter and gradually establishing the superiority of latter over former. The implications of these shifts are vast and long lasting given the diverse and heterogeneous nature of Indian society.

These drastic changes and shifts bring certain kind of contradictions and confusions in the society. On the one hand, it belittles the progress that India has achieved over the years following these existing norms on the other hand ruling it reduces masses as object of experiments by the ruling elites according to will and fancies. It has already created certain kind of restlessness within the federal structures. Many states are already resisting this ideological exclusivity in the name of language, history, religion, terminologies and so on. They are already coming up with their own alternative and parallel ideas. The very idea of history and culture are undergoing drastic changes. Firstly, there is a push to dilute the boundaries between physics and metaphysics, knowledge and ideology and empirical and historical. Secondly, replace the former with latter as superior over a period of time. There are clear indication of cultural appropriation of the science, modernity, past and present in pursuit of ideologically defined future. Vania says, 'Fringe groups that harp on unrealistically fantastic achievements of the past constitute the most aggressive challenge to contemporary science. Men and women, trained in skeptical rationalist approach to studying nature in all its aspects, are unwilling to accept any claims of past glory without critically evaluated evidence and are proving to be the strongest challenge to these groups who wish to glorify our past beyond logic and reason' (Vahia, 2015: 2145). There are attempts to reorient our imagination.

The new and aggressive variant of nationalism today is using diverse means and platforms to push for its agenda of revivalism of Indian past and scientific achievements. It is interesting to note that the modern inventions that owe its roots and philosophy to the west and enlightenment period are not seen as threat. These are rather put into better use for functional necessities. The nationalist discourse is not rejecting science either because of the undisputable nature of science and its discourses. Instead, science itself is claimed to be an indigenous and historical tradition in India much before the western discovery of it. Propagandas are circulating on social media platforms and internet that shows the superiority of indigenous knowledge over the west while simultaneously claiming the scientific achievement of the west inspired at local history and religious texts. The examples which are often cited are the prevalence indigenous healing practices in Ayurveda, cosmetic surgery, charaksahita, arthashastra, khagolshastra, naksatra-vidya, vaastushaastra, and so on. Interestingly, it is history which is used as a site of carrying those evidences of scientific achievements. Contrastingly; the same has been questioned and critiqued for being sectarian, discriminatory and unrepresentive of Indian social reality.

One of the important sites where these narratives are being pushed through is public educational and research institutions. This is not the first time now the last time that it happening. Ruling classes always wish their narrative or version of reality represented in the syllabus. Nair says, 'most Asian nationalisms are not merely invented traditions but have primordial roots, and textbooks are seen as instruments for carrying and transmitting these ancient ethnic and cultural consciousness (Nair, 2010: 30). Today, Public educational institutions are fast becoming ideological grounds where these selective narratives are pushed through. There is an aggressive push for agenda though co-curricular and extracurricular activities within the institutions. There are huge structural changes taking places in its functioning and priorities of the universities. Certain kinds of courses, selective languages and syllabus are being promoted. Controversies have generated in the past when certain books, chapters and sections were removed from various central universities syllabus. Public health and medical profession is also undergoing drastic changes in their courses, syllabus and functioning. some universities have already started courses on 'bhoot vidya' or 'science of paranormal' that is being taught to doctors holding Bachelor of Ayurvedic Medicine and Surgery (BAMS) and Bachelor of Medicine and Bachelor of Surgery (MBBS) degree holders. It is not merely happening with the universities but also becoming a part of state culture to show adherence to their cultural norms.

It is not only the teaching and syllabus that are being revised and reframe to suit the particular ideological interests but research and research priorities are also being affected by these ideological and discursive shifts. Sometimes back, The Uttarakhand government allocated 25 crores ($37 million) Indian rupees to search for mythical medicinal herb called sanjeevnibooti (Abraham, 2016). The justification for this research was that it was mentioned in one of the mythological texts. The euphoria of nationalism is reaching to a new height with the passage of days. Religious dogmas and superstitions are being seen as a sign of cultural conformity and nationalist identity. People felt so nostalgic and overwhelmed to see ISRO scientists visiting Tirupati temple to seek divine blessing for Chandrayaan 2 or defence minister visiting France and putting lemon and chilies as remedy to avoid bad omen.

Modernity brings certain modern dilemma, contradictions and adjustments to us. In certain contexts, traditions itself are projected as modernity to avoid those adjustments. This was particularly witnessed during the Covid-19 phase. Cow dung and urine were promoted as effective cure against the virus on social media and chant platforms. "There is no concrete scientific evidence that cow dung or urine work to boost immunity against COVID-19, it is based entirely on belief," said Dr JA Jayalal, national president at the Indian Medical Association. Such belies get some legitimacy when it is propagated by ruling parties and state bodies. The head of a BJP's West Bengal unit, Dilip Ghosh claimed that milk produced by Indian cows contains traces of gold due to which it's slightly yellowish in colour. The Cow Commission of India or Rashtriya Kamdhenu Aayog (RKA), a Body under ministry of animal husbandry and fisheries, in its 54 page documents revealed that diseases like psoriasis, skin disorders, eczema, arthritis, inflammation and leprosy, among others, can be treated by consuming 'Panchgavya' products — cow milk and its derivatives as well as cow urine and dung. Such beliefs go against the science and scientific body of knowledge. According to national center for biotechnology information, 'there is no concrete scientific background behind the use of cow dung or urine to boost immunity against COVID-19. But significant health risks are associated with smearing or consuming these products.

Other diseases can spread from the animal to humans through this process' (Daria & Islam, 2021).

The saviors of country's dharma, rasta and samaj are people with dubious credibility. The Hindu godmen with significant followers are being hailed as savior of the dharma and nation. Historically, it is no surprise that many of the politicians submit themselves to these godmen to get legitimacy among the masses and vice versa. This is a mutual relationship with mutual gains. Godmen are the new savior of dharma and rastra and they play an important role in shaping public opinion about a party, politicians or ideology. Anybody who questions are either public mocked and humiliated or worst they are killed. Many of the people who raised voices against magic, superstition and psedu-science have been killed in the past. Journalist Gauri Lankesh, physician and social activist Narendra Dabholkar, politician Govind Pansare and academic M. M. Kalburgi are some of them. The debate has taken a new turn today, those who raise question to the state or talk about rationality and justice, they are labeled as leftist, agent of west and worse anti-national.

V. Conclusion

The Indian nationalism was exclusivist from its inception is becoming more exclusive today. Earlier, It pretended to represent the interests of all at least in theory. Today it is not even pretending, rather aggressively and unapologetically pushing for exclusive religious ideology, symbols, celebrations etc. The obsession and nostalgia about the past is continued and has taken a new form today with more aggression and intolerance. The use and display of weapons in religious celebrations, glorification of certain historical icons and aggressively changing names of places are becoming new normal today. The rise has seen people developing defensive attitudes towards religion, culture and history. This has resulted into people submitting themselves to cult figures, political leaders, parties and ideology. The science driven modernity which promised a just, fair and rational enquiry of the world has now being seen as being alien and threat. The ideas like justice and freedom are duped as sectarian, divisive and propaganda of the west. The rise of nationalism has also brought with it the certain kind of selectivity, reinterpretation and appropriation of past events and empirical issues. The knowledge which was assumed to play a decisive and level playing role in the society is being used as propaganda. The lines of propaganda and knowledge are fast becoming blurred today.

There is a significant shrinkage of the idea of science, occupation, freedom and justice today. The information technology has connected human being together virtually but separated them physically from each other. We are controlled by our devices, and these devices are controlled by big capitalists. These are controlling our imaginations, tastes, thinking and actions. In this technology driven world, the information sharing platforms are redefining the relationships between individuals, groups and nations today. Technology is hailed as a solution to address our "modern" problems. However, modern itself is going through transition. Indian state is not seeing technology with hostility rather a tool to reach out to masses and propagate its ruling ideas. This connection with the masses is made possible with cheap internet, information technology devices and other entertainment sources. Big Multinational companies, corporate houses, influential godmen are the collaborators and facilitator of this dream. They stand firmly with the government to achieve its ideological goals. This is very much visible with the government's aggressive push for digitalisation and digital integration of the nation. Interestingly, this digital integration is being promoted without having the digital equity at first place.

Notes and References

Aloysius, G. (1997). Nationalism without a Nation in India. New Delhi: Oxford University Press.

Anderson, B. (2006). Imagined Communities: Reflections on the Origin and Spread of Nationalism. London: Verso.

Bocock, R. (1992). The Cultural Formations of Modern Society. In Hall, S. & Gieben, B. (Eds.), Formations of Modernity (pp. 229-274). Cambridge: The Open University.

Deshpande, A. & Despande, A. (2011). Colonial Modernity and Historical Imagination in India. Proceedings of the Indian History Congress, 2011, Vol. 72, PART-II (2011), pp. 1311-132.

Garry, R. (1969). Quite End to Grandeur. In Life. Vol. 66, No. 18, pp. 26-31.

Hamilton, P. (1992). The Enlightenment and the Birth of Social Science. In Hall, S. & Gieben, B. (Eds.), Formations of Modernity (pp. 17-70). Cambridge: The Open University.

Mitchell, J. (1980). Children of the Holocaust. The English Journal, Vol. 69, No. 7, pp. 14-18.

Nair, D. (2010). Textbook Conflicts in South Asia: Politics of Memory and National Identity. Journal Of Educational Media, Memory & Society, Autumn 2010, Vol. 2, No. 2, Special Issue: Contextualizing School Textbook Revision (AUTUMN 2010), pp. 29-45.

Pathak, A. ((2015). Indian Modernity. Delhi: Aakar Books.

Potter, W. J. (2001). Media Literacy. (2nd Edition). Sage Publications: California.

Rag, P. (1995). Indian Nationalism 1885-1905: An Overview. Social Scientist, Vol. 23, No. 4/6 (Apr.-Jun., 1995), pp. 69-97.

Vania, M. (2015). Evaluating the claims of ancient Indian achievements in science. current science association, Vol. 108, No. 12 (25 June 2015), pp. 2145-2148.

Weindling, P. (2015). Victims and Survivors of Nazi Human Experiments. London: Bloomsbury.

Web links

Abraham, b. (2016, July 29). Uttarakhand Government Allocates Rs 25 Crore to Search for Mythical Medicinal Herb-Sanjeevani Booti. Indiatimes. Accesed on 25/10/2023, retrieved from: https://www. indiatimes. com/news/india/uttarakhand-government-allocates-rs-25-crore-to-search-for-mythical-medicinal-herb-sanjeevani-booti-259122. html

Trend desks (2019, Nov. 5). BJP leader claims Indian cow's milk contains gold, sparks laugh riot on social media. Indianexpress. Accessed on 30/10/2023, retrieved from: https://indianexpress. com/article/trending/trending-in-india/dilip-ghosh-bjp-leader-says-desi-cow-milk-contains-gold-starts-laughing-riot-online-6104086/

Indo Asian news service. (2019, Dec. 24). 'Bhoot Vidya' a legitimate course at BHU now. Hindustantimes. Accessed on 22/09/2023, retrieved from: https://www. hindustantimes. com/education/bhoot-vidya-a-legitimate-course-at-bhu-now/story-GgMSSJ0KwYRiQiMjwUE6AJ. html

Web desk (2021, Jan. 21). Cow urine a rare gift for mankind; enhances longevity, cures diseases: Govt body's reference document. National herald. Accessed on 25/09/2023, retrieved from: https://www. nationalheraldindia. com/india/cow-urine-a-rare-gift-for-mankind-enhances-longevity-cures-diseases-govt-bodys-reference-document

Reuters (2021, May 11). Doctors face uphill battle as cow dung rises as COVID-19 cure. Dailysabah. Accessed on 20/10/2023, retrieved from: https://www. dailysabah. com/life/health/doctors-face-uphill-battle-as-cow-dung-rises-as-covid-19-cure

Dhingra, S. (2022, May 08). The Politics of Ayurveda. Outlookindia. Accessed on 23/10/2023, retrieved from: https://www. outlookindia. com/national/the-politics-of-ayurveda-news-195533

Daria, S & Islam, M. R. (2021, May 26). The use of cow dung and urine to cure COVID-19 in India: A public health concern. The International Journal of Health Planning and Management. Accessed on 27/11/2023, retrieved from: https://www. ncbi. nlm. nih. gov/pmc/articles/PMC8239506/

Chapter - 16

Science and Indian Nationalism

— Gitashri Kalindi

1. Introduction

Nationalism is a modern ideology that tries to explain the individual's devotion to the nation state by neglecting other interests. It has taken many different shapes in various geographies, cultures, histories, and political systems. Even in a particular location, nationalism has transformed from one form to another throughout history. The core of nationalism is nation. Science recognised as science by scientists or by historians or sociologists of science – 'science' is always both more and less than 'science', in that its semiotic range and connotative potential surpasses the narrow set of practices it describes. The relationship of science to nationalism is a counter-intuitive one, science after all has tended in an age of confidence in progress to denote internationalism and universalism. And even nationalist movements have sought to mobilise science precisely for reasons of internationalism, universalism and progress. For a national movement in search of a state, or a nationalism in possession of a state. The Nation-State has been seen as an indispensable player in scientific politics and in the politics of science. The physicist Meghnad Saha, a man who worked and studied in Calcutta, in London and in Germany, and in Allahabad, was among the first politically active scientists who objected to the conflation of science with technology as required by the instrumental needs of the state. He defended a pure and disinterested science unfettered by the demands of capitalism and perhaps idealistically so, because no really existing socialism has succeeded in unfettering science either. Science as self-strengthening is something that is evoked by many nationalist movements, including many nationalist movements that proclaim themselves to be 'backward' and seek to overcome this backwardness either through the practice of science. As such an attempt is made in this paper to ascertain the quantum of scientific achievements and advancements in terms of promoting the feeling of nationalism in India. Hence the paper try to address (i) the dynamics of scientific temper in promoting the nationalist feelings, (ii) to take stock of the contributions of Indian scientists and (iii) to draw a scientific calculus in measuring and carrying forward the feelings of nationalism among the common people.

2. Science and Technology in the Global Context

The fate of the state remains the central puzzle for IR scholars in the context of continuous technological innovation and the progress of scientiûc expertise. However, the study of technologies and large technical systems, as with many other issue areas, suffers from the "territorial trap": because this common IR mindset foregrounds relations among unitary (territorial) states instead of contextualizing states within different and interlinked local, regional and transnational processes and forms of organisation (Agnew, 1994), technology is merely added to a pregured theoretical puzzle. But innovation economists and sociologists generally doubt the merits of a dichotomist approach that locates technologies and technological changes in a vague conceptual region of tensions between sovereign nation states and global forces. Studies of European integration, for instance, emphasize the complex interplay of states, spaces and transnational technological systems. Similarly argue that National Aeronautics and Space Administration (NASA) is typical for large techno scientic undertakings in that it needs to be situated in "transnational or global frameworks, in recognition of the interdependence and interconnectivity of the modern state". It is hardly surprising, that critical reactions within innovation studies, with regard to the analytical treatment of states and technology, run in parallel to respective IR debates:

> Nations and states are important in ways techno-nationalism does not capture, and the international and global dimension is crucial in ways which techno-globalism is ignorant. In any case, politics, multinational rms, empire and race were also crucial factors in shaping the use of technology which cut across the national and global divide in complex and changing ways. The nation, the state, and the global, are central to the history of twentieth century technology, but not in the ways the relations are usually understood. We need to rethink not only nation-technology, but technology-state relations, and the place of technology at a global level too.[1]

3. Science and Technology in the Indian Context

In the developing countries, science and technology plays an important part in bringing about social and economic transformation in our country, especially in rural areas. In the case of development of the rural areas, utilisation, protection and enhancement of natural, physical and human resources is essential to make long term improvements in the rural living conditions. The significance of science and technology is recognized, it also makes provision of jobs and income opportunities for the rural people while maintaining and protecting the environment of the rural areas. There has been an increasing interest in rural development, the main reason being, systematic effort is necessary to create better living conditions within the rural areas where the vast majority of the populations of the developing countries reside. After India achieved its independence in 1947, during the first three decades, there was extremely less economic growth within the country only at about three percent, but there was an increase in the infrastructural facilities for science and technology. In later decades and particularly during the commencement of the twenty-first century, there have been developments, improvements and introduction of innovative scientific techniques within the country. Science and technology has not experienced the improvements as compared to the business and the industrial sectors. The systems of science and technology are experiencing crisis situations and setbacks, public sector science and technology systems are facing major predicaments. Income generation within the country through the science and technology services have led to greater prosperity for the educated middle class people, in most cases, in the area of information technology.

In India, most of the development has taken place through science and technological factors; technical factors have a major role to play particularly in the development of rural areas. Within the rural areas, there have been various sectors such as the agriculture, small-scale industries, houses, dwellings, buildings, medical facilities, education system, offices and so forth. For the purpose of developing these sectors, it is vital that significance of science and technology should be realised. It is only through science and technology that major improvements can be made. There was development of science departments in the central government; these included the departments of science and technology, biotechnology, non-conventional energy sources, ocean development, scientific and industrial research and space. All these sectors got wider development and achievements just because of the earlier contributions made by the scientific communities in India. Hence a peep back to such gains and achievements would serve the primary objective of this paper.

4. Indian Scientists and their Contributions

Jagdish Chandra Bose (1858-1937). Dr Jagadish Chandra Bose is famous for the invention of the Crescograph that can record even the millionth part of a millimeter of plant growth and orbital movement. Dr Bose proved, by virtue of the Crescograph, that plants have a circulatory system. The Crescograph has also proved the fact that the upward movement of sap in plants is the doing of living cells. He was also the inventor of wireless coherer which was later modified by Marconi as the radio. Really his contributions not only boosted the next generation scientists but, it also cemented the feeling of India in more vibrant and colourful heights.

C. V. Raman (1888-1970). C. V. Raman was not only a great scientist but also believed in social development. In 1930, he won the Nobel Prize for Physics becoming the first Asian to do so. He is associated with the concept of Raman's Effect, which says that when a light passes through a transparent substance, it scatters. Raman studied the concept of broken light and observed that "there were two spectral lines of very low strength (strength) parallel to the incident monochromatic light." This proved that any broken light was not monochromatic in nature even though the incident light was monochromatic. When scientists were confused whether the form of light was like waves or like particles, the Raman Effect proved that light is made up of particles known as photons.

Meghnad Saha (1893-1956). Meghnad Saha was a renowned Indian astrophysicist who developed the ionisation theory, explaining stellar spectra' origin. Meghnad Saha rose from humble beginnings in a small village to become one of the world's most renowned scientists of his time. In 1917, the University College of Science in Kolkata appointed Meghnad Saha as a professor. He taught quantum physics there. He presided over the Indian Science Congress in 1934. Meghnad Saha was also the chairman of the calendar reform committee established by the Government of India. In 1947, he founded the Institute of Nuclear Physics, later renamed the "Saha Institute of Nuclear Physics." Saha also used a device to determine the weight and pressure of solar rays.

Dr Homi Jahangir Bhabha, (1909-1966). He was an Indian nuclear physicist, founding director, and professor of physics at the Tata Institute of Fundamental Research (TIFR). He studied nuclear physics at Cambridge, where he published groundbreaking papers on cosmic rays and electron-positron scattering, a phenomenon now called Bhabha scattering. Colloquially known as "Father of Indian nuclear programme". Bhabha was also the founding director of the Atomic Energy Establishment, Trombay (AEET) which is now named the Bhabha Atomic Research Centre in his honour. TIFR and AEET were the cornerstone of the Indian development of nuclear weapons which Bhabha also supervised as director. Homi Bhabha was awarded the Adams Prize (1942) and Padma Bhushan (1954). He was also nominated for the Nobel Prize for Physics in 1951 and 1953–1956.

Dr Vikram Ambalal Sarabhai (1919 – 1971). He was an Indian physicist and astronomer who initiated space research and helped develop nuclear power in India. He was the key person behind the launch of India's first satellite 'Aryabhatta'. His studies of cosmic rays have made it evident that cosmic rays are a flow of energy particles with its source in outer space. He was honoured with Padma Bhushan in 1966 and the Padma Vibhushan (posthumously) in 1972. He is internationally regarded as the Father of the Indian Space Program. Under his supervision, the Thumba Equatorial Rocket Launching Station (TERLS) was set up. He wanted to take education to villages through satellite communication.

Dr. A. P. J Abdul Kalam (1931-2015). He was an Indian aerospace scientist and statesman who served as the eleventh President of India from 2002 to 2007. He was born and raised in Rameswaram, Tamil Nadu and studied physics and aerospace engineering. He was known as the 'Missile Man of India' for his work in the development of ballistic missile technology. From 1992 to 1999, Kalam was the Chief Scientific Adviser to the Prime Minister and the Secretary of the DRDO. Between the 1970s and 1990s, Kalam made an effort to develop the Polar Satellite Launch Vehicle (PSLV) and SLV-III projects, both of which proved to be successful. In the 1970s he also directed two projects which developed the ballistic missiles from the technology of the SLV programme. Kalam was the Chief Project Coordinator during the Pokhran II tests. He also played a pivotal organisational, technical, and political role in India's Pokhran-II nuclear tests in 1998, the first since the original nuclear test by India in 1974.

5. Science and Technology as a Catalyst Promoting Indian Nationalism

India has a rich heritage of science and technology. The dependence on nature could be overcome by developments in science. In ancient India, religion and science worked in close proximity. Ancient Indians made considerable scientific progress in the fields of science and technology. Their contribution in astronomy, mathematics, medicine, metallurgy, chemistry have made an impact on modern scientists. During the medieval period Indians came in contact with Arabic scientific knowledge.. During the medieval period (eleventh to eighteenth century) science and technology in India developed along two lines: one concerned with the already charted course of earlier traditions and the other with the new influences which came up as a result of Islamic and European influence. Turkish rulers and Mughals introduced gunpowder. Astronomical observatories were set up at Ujjain, Varanasi, Mathura, Jaipur and Delhi. In modem India scientific development has been duly recognised by the government and is being implemented through the Five Year Plan. Nuclear energy is being used for peaceful purposes as well.. In India the government has consistently tried to use modern science and technology for industrial development. Two government organisations, Council for Scientific and Industrial Research (CSIR) and Defence Research and Development Organisation (DRDO) cover between them a wide range of science and technology research for civil and defence purposes. As a result many branches of knowledge got indigenous development both in the theoretical and practical ways. This took place in the case of both natural sciences and social science.

6. Science and Technology and its Impact on Other Domains

Science is a systematic approach to understanding the natural world through observation, experimentation, and analysis. It seeks to uncover the underlying principles governing various phenomena. Technology, on the other hand, focuses on the application of scientific knowledge to create practical solutions and innovations. It involves developing tools, processes, and systems that improve human life in diverse fields such as healthcare, transportation, communication, and more.

(a) Physical Science

Physical sciences encompass disciplines such as chemistry, physics, and geology, which study the fundamental particles of the natural world. Chemistry analyzes the composition and behaviour of matter, finding applications in fields like pharmaceuticals and materials science. Physics investigates the principles governing matter, energy, and motion, driving innovations in areas such as electronics and renewable energy.

(b) Chemistry and its Application

Chemistry, a fundamental domain of science, encompasses the study of matter, its properties, and the changes it undergoes. Its applications are vast and impact various industries. For instance, in the pharmaceutical field, chemists develop new drugs and study their interactions with the human body. Environmental chemists analyze pollutants and develop methods for remediation.

In materials science, chemistry enables the creation of new materials with enhanced properties for industries like electronics and construction. Additionally, chemical processes are utilised for food production, energy generation, and even forensic investigations. Understanding the applications of chemistry paves the way for innovative solutions to real-world problems.

(c) Physics and its Application

Physics, a fundamental domain of science, finds extensive applications in various fields. Its practical applications include:Electronics: Physics principles enable the development of electronic devices like transistors, diodes, and integrated circuits. Energy: Understanding physics helps in harnessing renewable energy sources such as solar panels and wind turbines. Transportation: Physics concepts guide the design and functionality of vehicles, from aerodynamics for airplanes to propulsion systems in rockets. Medical Imaging: Technologies like X-rays, magnetic resonance imaging (MRI), and ultrasound rely on physics principles for diagnostic imaging. Material Science: Physics provides insights into the behaviour, properties, and manipulation of materials, contributing to advancements in manufacturing and engineering. These examples highlight the tangible impact of physics in shaping our everyday lives, technology, and scientific advancements.

(d) Geology and Earth Sciences

Geology and Earth Sciences examine the physical structure, composition, and processes of the Earth. It encompasses a range of sub-disciplines, including the study of rocks, minerals, landforms, and natural resources. Understanding these domains of science is vital for several practical applications. For example, geologists assess geological hazards such as earthquakes, landslides, and volcanic eruptions, helping communities plan and prepare for such events. They also investigate the Earth's history through fossils and sedimentary layers, shedding light on past climate conditions and evolutionary patterns.

In addition, geology plays a crucial role in the exploration and extraction of natural resources like oil, gas, minerals, and water. By studying geological formations, scientists determine the most suitable sites for resource extraction, ensuring efficient and sustainable practices.

(e) Biological Sciences

Biological sciences encompass the study of living organisms and their interactions with the environment. It includes various fields such as biology, genetics, and biochemist. Understanding biological sciences is vital for advancements in medicine, agriculture, and environmental conservation. Insights from biological sciences have led to breakthroughs in areas like genetic engineering and biotechnology. Practical examples include the development of new pharmaceutical drugs and genetically modified crops to enhance food production. Biological sciences also contribute to our understanding of diseases and their prevention. It plays a crucial role in the exploration of ecosystems and conservation of endangered species.

(f) Biology and Biotechnology

Biology and Biotechnology encompass the study and manipulation of living organisms for various applications. In this domain of science, researchers explore topics such as genetic engineering, molecular biology, and microbiology to develop new medicines, agricultural advancements, and environmental solutions. For instance, biotechnologists have created genetically modified crops that are resistant to pests, reducing the need for harmful pesticides.

Additionally, advancements in biotechnology have led to the production of biofuels as a more sustainable alternative to fossil fuels. By harnessing the power of biological systems, biology and biotechnology offer innovative solutions to address real-world challenges.

(g) Genetic Engineering and Biochemistry

Genetic engineering and biochemistry are prominent domains of science that have revolutionised various industries and fields. Through genetic engineering, scientists manipulate the DNA of living organisms to enhance desirable traits or create new ones. This has applications in agriculture, medicine, and environmental conservation.

For example, genetically modified crops are designed to be resistant to pests or have increased nutritional value. Biochemistry, on the other hand, studies the chemical processes occurring within living organisms. It helps in understanding diseases at a molecular level and developing drugs to target specific biochemical pathways. Researchers use biochemistry to unlock the potential of enzymes for industrial applications such as biofuel production or waste remediation. These domains contribute to advancements in medicine, sustainable agriculture, and industrial processes.

(h) Pharmaceutical Sciences

Pharmaceutical Sciences, a prominent domain of science, focuses on the discovery, development, and evaluation of medications and drugs. It plays a significant role in improving human health by advancing our understanding of diseases and developing effective treatments. This field encompasses various disciplines such as pharmacology, pharmaceutics, and medicinal chemistry. For instance, pharmaceutical scientists study the interaction between drugs and the human body to ensure safe and efficacious therapies. They also contribute to the development of novel drug delivery systems for targeted treatments.

(i) Engineering and Technology

Under the domain of science, Engineering and Technology are prominent fields that drive innovation and practical applications. Engineering involves the application of scientific knowledge to design, build, and improve various structures, systems, and processes. It encompasses diverse disciplines like electrical, civil, and computer engineering. Technological advancements in this domain have led to innovations like renewable energy systems, smart cities, and artificial intelligence. For example, engineers have developed efficient solar panels to harness clean energy and improved transportation systems with autonomous vehicles. The combination of science and engineering has the potential to solve complex challenges and shape the future of society.

(j) Electrical and Electronics Engineering

Electrical and Electronics Engineering is a significant domain of science that encompasses the study, design, and application of electrical systems and electronic devices. Here's a concise look at this field: It involves the exploration of electricity and how it can be harnessed to power various devices and systems. Electrical and Electronics Engineering plays a crucial role in the development of renewable energy sources like solar panels and wind turbines. This field is instrumental in the design and optimisation of telecommunications systems, such as mobile networks and satellite communication. It is an essential component in the creation of advanced electronic devices like smartphones, computers, and home appliances. Electrical and Electronics Engineering contributes to the development of automation and control systems for industries, improving efficiency and safety. By continuously advancing this domain, scientists and engineers can drive innovation and shape the future of technology.

(k) Civil and Environmental Engineering

Civil and environmental engineering is a vital domain of science that focuses on infrastructure development and ecological preservation. Civil engineers design and construct buildings, bridges, and transportation systems, while environmental engineers devise strategies to tackle pollution and promote sustainable practices. Through their expertise, they contribute to the betterment of societies and the protection of the environment. For example, civil and environmental engineers play a crucial role in designing and implementing wastewater treatment plants to ensure clean water for communities, as well as developing sustainable construction techniques to reduce resource consumption. Their work directly impacts the quality of life and the health of ecosystems.

(l) Information Technology and Computer Science

Computer science and information technology have revolutionised every aspect of modern life. From smartphones to artificial intelligence, these domains of science play a significant role in shaping our world. Computer science involves the study of algorithms, programming, and the design of software systems. Information technology focuses on the practical application and management of computer systems. Together, they drive innovation in areas such as data analysis, cyber security, and software development. For example, advancements in computer science have led to the development of self-driving cars and voice recognition technology. Information technology enables businesses to streamline operations through cloud computing and data analytics. The continuous progress in these domains enhances our lives and creates new opportunities for the future.

(m) Social Science

Social sciences encompass various fields that study human behaviour, societies, and their interactions. Anthropology and sociology explore cultural practices and social structures, providing insights into diverse communities and societal dynamics. Political science and international relations analyze political systems, diplomatic relations, and global governance. Psychology and cognitive sciences unravel the intricacies of the human mind and behaviour.

These disciplines help us understand societal challenges, influence policy-making, and shape effective strategies for social development. For instance, sociological research aids in devising inclusive public policies, while psychology contributes to designing interventions for mental health. The knowledge gained from social sciences enhances our understanding of human society and enables informed decision-making.

(n) Anthropology and Sociology

Anthropology and sociology are two distinct yet interconnected domains within the social sciences. Anthropology focuses on understanding human cultures, societies, and evolution through ethnographic research and fieldwork. Sociology, on the other hand, examines social behaviour, institutions, and structures, aiming to uncover patterns and analyze societal dynamics. These disciplines provide invaluable insights into human behaviour, social interactions, and cultural norms. By studying anthropology and sociology, researchers gain a better understanding of diverse societies and how they function. This knowledge can be utilised in various practical ways, such as designing inclusive policies, addressing social issues, and promoting cross-cultural understanding. For instance, insights from anthropology can help in developing effective strategies for cross-cultural communication and conflict resolution. Sociological research can guide policymakers in shaping social programmes and initiatives to address inequality and social injustice.

(o) Political Science and International Relations

Political Science and International Relations, as domains of science, study the complexities of political systems and the interactions between nations. They provide insights into the functioning of governments, policy-making processes, and global affairs. By understanding political science and international relations, individuals can comprehend the dynamics of power, diplomacy, and conflicts. This knowledge can be applied to various real-life scenarios, such as analyzing geopolitical trends, predicting global partnerships, and formulating effective foreign policies. For example, understanding international relations can help policymakers navigate complex negotiations, anticipate the impact of economic sanctions, or predict the consequences of diplomatic actions.

(p) Psychology and Cognitive Sciences

Psychology and Cognitive Sciences delve into the intricate workings of the human mind and behaviour. These domains study psychological processes, emotions, learning, memory, and decision-making. Understanding these aspects has practical applications in various fields. For example, in marketing, knowledge of cognitive biases helps create persuasive advertising campaigns. In education, understanding how memory works can inform effective learning strategies. Moreover, psychology plays a vital role in improving mental health treatment and developing therapies. By examining human cognition and behaviour, these sciences provide valuable insights that can enhance our understanding of ourselves and lead to practical advancements in multiple industries.

It has been repeatedly proved elsewhere that the advancement in science and technology bears the torch of modernisation and development. The renaissance and reformation witnessed to the European societies is a grand indication that their social advances were further from the same spring of scientific progress and development. In the case of India, given the background of its plurality and social challenges, a development like the European ones were not possible. But the indegenous scientists of the nation strived hard to keep Indias head high among the comity of nation by way of their great achievements. In this regard a calculus of science and technology and Nationalism would serve the purpose of its proper measurement.

8. The Nationalism Calculus

This is a hypothetical calculus. However, the assumption are based on real facts. This calculus is detailed on the assumption that the feelings of people in terms of their notion about the nation makes an incremental advancement in tune to the greater achivements made by its scientists over a period of time. If the feelings of nationalism indicates the level of water in a jar, every pebble put in to the jar is supposed to increase the water level on a proportionate way. Here the pebbles indictes the invetions and discoveries which is historically put in to the jar of Indian nation whereby its water level [the feelings of nationalism] goes up by periodically upwards. The response of the General public in this process is purely natural and organic in nature. In every sequence of such achievements people feel proud of being an Indian and this feeling is a natural sentiments and mood reflected by the citizens without any prejudices. As such this paper, due to time limitations do not go deep in to the statistical data for such a scientific calculus, rather would like to recommend it for the future researchers, which would be a fertile domain for asserting the pure form of nationalism deriving out of such scientific advancements. Interestingly the rationale of such a calculus will systematically measure the level of advancement of scientific achievements passing through social developments and finally culminating in the nationalist feelings.

9. Conclusion

The discussion makes it clear that from very old times to the present, various scientific advancements were made by the respective scientists in India, which more rapidly helped the Indian society to move forward to the further advanced levels of social life. Science, in this respect acted as a catalyst for social change and progress. As a result, the socio-economic profile of the nation changed rapidly. Life style of the people from 1830 to 1990 to 2005 witnessed to a revolutionary shift. Even under the British periods our scientists did their great service. In this regard the role played by Bose, C. V. Raman, Homi Jahangir Bhaba, and Vikram Sarabhai etc were unique and not comparable any of their counterparts anywhere in the world. Along with the same stream line, the contribution of APJ Abdul Kalam is also worth mentioning. These scientists did their great service to the nation by making its nationalities proud of being an Indian where by the very idea of science itself got popularised. In fact the feeling of Indianness is commonly spread and taken over to new heights by the achievements the nation made in its leap towards the scientific advancements on a incremental rhythm which is in proportionate to the ratio of such inventions and discoveries.

Equally, the contribution made by the these scientists did corresponding changes and development for the life style of the average Indians. In fact, it helped the general society indirectly to conceive the spirit of scientific temper including the notion of Nation, Nationalism and Nationality. Actually, these Scientific achievements made Nationalisma more vibrant and dynamic. Such feeling of nationalism also made people proud as a result of which every citizen is elevated to a higher level of thinking both in the national as well as international contexts. In fact, this paper proposes to work out a nexus or calculous in between the scientific advancements and the level of nationalist feelings the common man is supposed to be witnessed to. In recent times, during the landing of Chandrayan-1 both the media as well as the general public took it as an occasion of festivity and the common man celebrated the news of its landing with sweets and gestures of dances in public. This was the context when people forget about their narrow divisions of religion, caste and regions. The people as a whole took it to their heart and chanted the songs of nationalism. Thus, Indian nationalism, a longing for the nation by its citizens without any other narrow considerations, is a dialectical and natural development, contributed equally by the great Indian scientists of all times.

Notes and References

Rag, P. (1995). Indian Nationalism 1885-1905: An Overview Social Scientist, Vol. 23, No. 4/6(Apr-Jun, 1995), pp. 69-67.

Singh, V & U. C. (2011). "Satellite based Identification of archaeological monuments sites of Gwalior, MP, India". Vol. 4, No. 1. ISSN:0974-6846. Indian Journal of Science and Technology.

Dincsahin, S & Arslan, M(2013). Clit/Vol. VI Sayi/Number 2 Ekim/October 2013 SosyalBilimlerDeegisi/Journal of Social Sciences.

Vania, M. (2015). Evaluating the claims of ancient Indian achievements in science. Current science association, Vol. 108, No. 12(25 June 2015), pp. 2145-2148.

Thakur, H & Sahu, Deepika (2016). "Biological Effects of Electromagnetic Waves:Case Studies and Safety Standards". Vol. 9(47), ISSN:0974-5645. Indian Journal of Science and Technology.

Shalley, M & Sahin, I. (Eds.). (2022). "Studies on Education, Science, and Technology 2021." ISBN:978-1-952092-28-2. ISTES Organisation.

Webliography

https://analyticsindiamag. com/all-the-tech-innoation-that-shaped-india-in-2022/

https://calenda. org/science, technology and Nationalism in India.

Part - IV

Art, Culture and Literary Expressions

Chapter - 17

Hindi Literature and Nationalism: The Discourse of Nationalism in Prem Chand's Literature

— Dr Reetambhara Pandey

1. Introduction

Literature is the creative expression of human society. In its broadest sense, any creation by humans in any language is considered literature. This includes not only creative literature but also works in art, society, science, politics, etc. In this context, literature is often seen as a reflection of society. In colonial societies, the concept of the nation emerged through interactions with foreign rule. In India, this urge for nationhood and national consciousness is most powerfully expressed in the literature of Premchand. As a storyteller, essayist, novelist, editor, thinker, and freedom fighter, Premchand's literature serves as a comprehensive discourse on the ideas of the "nation" of his time i.e. under the conditions of coloniality.

2. Premchand's Literature and Indian Nationalism

This paper attempts to understand how Premchand, through his literature, critically engages with various contemporary and contradictory notions of colonialism and the nation. He not only dialogues with these ideas but also harshly criticizes the idea of narrow-minded, communal national concepts. His novels and stories often reflect the clash between Gandhian integrative ideas and the Marxist progressive people's nationalism, revealing at times an overly romantic Gandhian vision of society. During a time when narrow reactionary communal forms of nationalism were emerging in India, Premchand called nationalism the "scourge of our society." This paper examines how Premchand's literature portrays the concept of "progressive people's nationalism" and critiques the elitist concept of the nation, which supported feudal and classist values. His novels "Godan" and "Sevasadan" and numerous stories exemplify this literary expression.

3. Nationalism and Social Reform

Premchand aimed to move the Indian national concept away from elitist abstractions and root it in the significant social components—disadvantaged castes, women, Dalits, tribes, workers, and farmers. In this way, he rejects the elite driven abstract discourse of nationalism on one hand and, on the other, through his novels and world famous stories provides a realistic portrayal of the various strata of society and their struggles. He envisions a progressive society and nation, revealing his commitment through his literature. In contemporary times, with deepening of capitalism and its anti-people and anti-women tendencies masked by communal nationalism, Premchand's literature shines like a torch for the progressive national concept and ideologies of progressive resistance.

4. Premchand's Transitional Vision

The era represented by Premchand was marked by multiple ideological and cultural processes, contestations and instabilities. On one side were the British colonial rule with their idea of colonial-imperial nation-state and on the other the emerging national consciousness for independence, marked by regional aspirations and linguistic-cultural renaissance, alongside traditional and communal resurgence. In contrast to these two, there was a trend towards secular, multicultural nationalism and revolutionary people's nationalism focused on inter-culturality, more inclined towards inter-nationalism. Premchand's trajectory of complete literary works document this multidimensional liberation struggle of a composite Indian identity.

5. Language and Nationalism

The discourse on nationalism in Premchand cannot begin without discussing his views on language. Until 1915, Premchand wrote primarily in Urdu under the pseudonym Nawab Rai. This was partly because most educated writings at the time were in Urdu, but also a critique of the Sanskrit-oriented Hindi promoted by revivalists and conservatives rigid traditionalists. Later, he adopted a form of Hindi that incorporated the emotions and expressions of common life, blending local dialects and colloquialisms. In a 1930 essay in the magazine "Zamana," Premchand wrote:

"If we could investigate how many Hindus speak Urdu and how many Muslims speak Urdu, I believe the numbers would not differ much. It is another matter if Hazrat Niaz does not consider the Urdu spoken by Hindus to be Urdu and vice versa. Urdu is neither the exclusive property of Muslims of India nor of Hindus."

6. Cultural Unity and National Identity

Premchand opposed the narrow, revivalist tendencies and emphasized the cultural unity in the everyday lives of Hindus and Muslims. In 1931, he described in his essay "Culture" how the linguistic and cultural practices in regions like Awadh or Bundelkhand did not differentiate between Hindus and Muslims. In another essay, Premchand criticized the limited perspective of the educated elite on the language dispute:

"The dispute between Hindi and Urdu is confined to a small educated section. Muslims in other regions do not worship Urdu or oppose Hindi. They use the language of the region they live in. We need to correct our mistaken history."

7. Literary Representation of Liberation

The diverse and vast body of Premchand's literary work, including stories, novels, and essays, position him as a leading contemporary writer. His work is not only vast and diverse but deeply sensitive to the varieties of experiences of the common people. His literary expressions highlight the multidimensional aspirations for liberation among various social strata in Indian deity. Premchand's vision of nationalism does not indulge in a nostalgic glorification of a mythical golden age. Instead, he criticizes revivalist and regressive notions of freedom. In a 1930 letter reviewing Jaishankar Prasad's novel "Kankal," Premchand expressed his vision of nationalism:

"First, let me congratulate you on 'Kankal'! I read it from beginning to end and was enchanted. My old complaint against you is completely gone. I once criticized your book 'Samudra Gupta' for digging up the past. I faced much backlash for that. But the pen that can present contemporary issues so attractively to the public, moving hearts, should not be concerned with old grievances. The past has its place, but we need to create a new world from scratch."

8. Conclusion

Prem Chand's literature, addressing issues like women's liberation, class exploitation, poverty and colonial oppression, stands as a unique document advocating the liberation of various exploited groups in India. By placing the question of "human liberation" at the center of the discourse on groups in India. By placing the question of "human liberation" at the center of the discourse on nationalism, Premchand's work provides a direction towards a people-centric view. He wrote: "A nation is a mental construct. When this tendency becomes strong, it fosters a sense of brotherhood among the residents of a region. Ancient India was a nation in this sense, having a unified culture." However, he immediately stood against the historical inequalities of patriarchy, caste, and class: "The first condition of nationalism is to uproot caste hierarchy, discrimination, and religious hypocrisy."

In the "Jagaran" magazine on November 27, 1933, he stated:

> "Nationalism is the scourge of the present age, much like communalism was the scourge of the medieval age. The result is the same for both. Communalism sought to establish complete peace and happiness within its circle, but it had no qualms about exploiting the world outside. Nationalism, too, aims to create a utopia within its limited area, considering the outside world its enemy. Until this ends, global peace is impossible. Enlightened minds are advocating for internationalism, but a world chained by nationalism dismisses them as dreamers or fools."

Prem Chand was aware of the double-edged use of nationalism. He warned how the elite in Indian society would use nationalism for the exploitation of various stratagem of people and against the liberation of the masses. His novel "Godan" exposes the nature of the colonial feudal-Brahminical-patriarchal-capitalist nexus and also identifies the revolutionary potential of the rising working classes.

In the "Jagaran" magazine on November 6, 1933, he wrote: "Everywhere, capitalists are racing ahead. They don't care if the farmers' crops fail. Like the fable where a man cuts the branch he is sitting on, this community is cutting the neck of the farmer, whose sweat waters their fields."

As this quote shows, Premchand's progressive socialist view was alert to the economic reasons behind political thoughts and institutions. He saw religion and nationalism's political narrowness behind political thoughts and institutions. He saw religion and nationalism's political narrowness in the emerging capitalist system as tools for exploiting the lower classes, particularly working class proletariat. In concluding we may say that Premchand's literature shines as a torch for society, illuminating the path toward a progressive and inclusive national consciousness, while being scathingly critical of ideas of ethno-communal nationalism as regressive and anti-people

Notes and References

Premchand's unobtainable literature, Kamal Kishore Goenka, 1988, pp. 25–26.

Miscellaneous incidents, 2, Amritrai, 1980, pp. 333–34.

Ibid., p. 331.

Ibid., p. 332.

Chapter - 18

Cultural and National Consciousness in Hindi poetry; The changing narratives

— Dr Asha S Nair

Introduction

It is supposed that Nation is based on geographical, political and cultural units. These units like caste, religion, culture, language, history etc are important in the process of building up any nation. Community of people living on a certain territory and bound by the thread of its own civilisation, culture, tradition, customs, and way of life is and can be called a nation. In such a situation, it is easy to have a feeling of love and respect for the nation and obviously a spirit to maintain it. Literature throws light into time and history. While going through the pages of Hindi literature, we come to know that our literature is compact, full of emotions and full of its aura. The development of literature from ancient times to modern times and from there to post-modern and technological era is amazing and thrilling. In ancient times the seeds of cultural and national consciousness which were sown in the hearts of the people, started flourishing in the time of Bhakti period. People kept flowing in the cultural and spiritual flow and the Bhakti movement started spreading all over India. The lamp lit by Kabir, Soor and Tulsi and its flame is still burning in literature and in public mind without being extinguished. Poets like Maithilisharan Gupta, Makhanlal Chaturvedi, Dinakar, Pant, Nirala, Subhadra Kumari Chauhan etc. tried to maintain it through their writings.

The feeling of national and cultural consciousness has been there in Hindi literature since ancient times. The poets of ancient times, with their creative power, infused national and ethnic consciousness into people's lives. This was the aim and objective of the literature of that time. The literature of the Bhakti period spread devotion. The relationship between soul and God, the relationship between devotee and God, which has been expressed, also has echoes of nationalism in it. Keeping in tune with the luxurious expression of Ritikaal, the voice of nationalism became vocal through the poetic voices of Bhushan, Senapati etc. The modern period was born in the lap of national consciousness. Along with national consciousness, cultural stream was also threaded in the literature from ancient to modern times. The poets of modern times nourished and strengthened it with their vigorous voice.

The philosophical and cultural thoughts and customs reflected in the literary trends of the Middle ages were not free from the shadow of feudalism. Coming out of its grip is not as easy as we think. Kabir continued to fight against the ostentation, hypocrisy, fanaticism, casteism, conventions, superstition etc. in the name of religion. Not only Kabir, Nathpanthi saints also tried to bring changes in the society. He kept raising his voice to remove feudalistic luxuries from the lifestyle of the society. Kabir's mysticism and monotheism indicate complete devotion to God without religious rituals. They have gone far beyond righteousness. The literature of the Bhakti period actually became an expression of the conflicts and inconsistencies of social reality. For Kabir, Hari, Ram, Govind, Rahim are the symbols of the supreme element. Hari and Rahim are two names of the same God. According to Kabir, after hearing these two names one should not have any kind of confusion. Kabir was in favour of religious unity and he kept reminding it throughout his life.

'हरि रहीमा ऐक है, नाम धराया दोई।
कहे कबीर दोनाम सूनि, भरम परोमत कोई।।'1

According to their belief, where there is kindness there is religion, where there is greed there is sin, where there is anger there is destruction and where there is forgiveness, there God resides. By blindly following religion, selfishness and ego are pulling man towards degradation.

'जहाँ दया तहा धर्म है, जहाँ लोभ वहां पाप।
जहाँ क्रोध तहा काल है, जहाँ क्षमा वहां आप।।'2

Kabir has explained about Nirguna Parabrahma that, just as there is a pupil inside the eye, similarly God resides within us. Foolish people do not know this and keep searching for God outside in all the places of pilgrimage.

'ज्यों नैनन में पुतली, त्यों मालिक घर माँहि।
मूरख लोग न जानिए, बाहर ढूँढत जाहिं।।'3

No one has challenged the social system as Kabir has done in protesting against the malpractices and atrocities prevalent in the society. Kabir is definitely a guide for modern writers. He opened a new path by integrating knowledge, yoga and devotion. There is a feeling of equality in the devotion of Kabir which is appropriate for every person. Kabir was a social reformer of his era, who was full of progressiveness. Kabir tried to give good advice to the people, so that they can walk on the right path and improve themselves. The cultural and national consciousness prevalent in his works is relevant in the context of present life.

Like Kabir, Tulsidas's literary works were also filled with cultural and national consciousness. The fame of 'Ramcharitmanas' spreads across the country. Tulsi was an ardent devotee of Ram. He liked nothing else except the love of Ram. By incorporating all the high ideals of human life, he made Ram a Maryada Purushottam.

'राम प्रेम बिनु दूबरो राम प्रेम हीं पीन।
रघुबर कबहुँक करहुगे तुलसि हिज्यों जलमीन।।'4

Through Ramcharitmanas, Tulsi has depicted the emotional picture of the ideals. They will always continue to pave the way for human society. He has pictured Sagun-Nirgun Bhakti, Shaiva-Vaishnav bhakti which has been expressed in a very effective manner with the aim of bringing coordination among sects etc. He has been skilled in describing various forms of human nature vividly. It teaches a culture and a set of ethics which is publicly accepted. Tulsi has sown the seeds of social and political values in the hearts of people through Ramcharitmanas.

When Gandhiji made his debut in the freedom struggle, there were discussions about Swarajya. Their vision of independence was based on Ramrajya based on self-confidence. The source of self-confidence and determination will be found in Ramcharitmanas. But despite having faith in Sita's power and strength, Ram's sacrifice of personal love was for the country. Ram considered the interest of the nation more than his personal happiness, joy and peace. Cultural values and true nationalism can be found in Ramcharitmanas.

The specialty of tradition in Tulsi's works and our cultural dignity has broad dimensions. On the one hand, Tulsi's literature gives insight into the complexities of life, while on the other hand it also preserve and protect humanity. Tulsi is seen in Ramcharitmanas making a successful attempt to bind a disorganised society into the fabric of human relations. The relevance of Manas is appropriate in the cultural and national perspective of our nation.

'तुलसी ममता रामसों समता सब संसार।
राग न रोष न दोष दुख दास भए भवपार।।'5

Soordas, Meera, Raskhan of the Krishna Bhakti branch established themselves as carriers of spiritual consciousness by describing the various pastimes of Krishna. He led the society towards good deeds and devotion.

'सूर-संगती रहें साधू की अनुदिन, भव-दुःख दूरी नसावत।
सूरदास संगती करी तिनकी, जेहरी सुरती कहावत।।'6

Ritikaal was representing lust and passion. Poets like Bhushan, Vrind, Matiram came forward raising the voice of national consciousness. Bhushan's feeling of love and devotion towards the nation amused the people.

इंद्र जिम जंभ पर बाड़व ज्यौं अंभ पर
रावन सदंभ पर रघुकुलराज है।
पौन बारिबाह पर संभु रतिनाह पर
ज्यौं सहस्रबाहु पर राम द्विजराज है।7

The modern period of Hindi literature is filled with national consciousness. The contemporary political and social environment had become blurred due to dependence. Writers cannot keep themselves far from the contemporary circumstances. It is easy for society and life to have an impact on literature. The wave of freedom struggle was running across the country and echoes of patriotism were heard in literature. From the beginning of the freedom movement till the attainment of independence, there was a flood of poems filled with national consciousness. Waves of nationalism were rising not only in poetry but also in the hearts of the people. Bhartendu Harishchandra made the society aware of the real condition of India by writing 'Bharat durdasha'.

अँगरेज राज सुख साज सजे सब भारी।
पै धन बिदेश चलि जात इहै अति ख्वारी,
ताहू पै महँगी काल रोग विस्तारी।
दिन-दिन दूनो दुःख ईस देत हा हारी,
सबके ऊपर टिक्कस की आफत आई।
हा! हा! भारत दुर्दशा न देखी जाई,8

Maithili Sharan Gupta was the first person to write nationalistic songs in the Dwivedi era. His poetry collection 'Bharat Bharati' became the inspiring force of many youth. It also became the reason for the participation of the youth of India in the freedom movement. They faced the oppressive rule of a foreign power and also endured the tortures of prison. Poets wrote poems which praise India's past and call upon the people of the country to wake up.

यह पुण्यभूमि प्रसिद्ध है इसके निवासी 'आर्य' हैं,
विद्या, कला-कौशल सभी के जो प्रथम आचार्य हैं।
सन्तान उनकी आज यद्यपि हम अधोगति में पड़े।
पर चिह्न उनकी उच्चता के आज भी कुछ हैं खड़े।।'9

In the Chhayavadera, along with activities like nature depiction, description of beauty, humanisation, poems of national awakening were also composed. Some untoward incidents had taken place in the country (suppression of the Rowlatt Act and Jallianwala Bagh massacre) as a result of which Mahatma Gandhi called for non-cooperation movement. In the pitiable condition of the country, the Chhayavadi poets could not stop themselves from writing in favour of the country. Many inspirational poems started being born from the pen of many awakened poets like Prasad, Nirala, Pant, Dinkar, Balkrishna Sharma 'Naveen', Subhadra Kumari Chauhan, Makhanlal Chaturvedi, Bachchan etc. Love for the country and the indomitable desire to gain independence were expressed in the poems of that time. Makhanlal Chaturvedi's poem 'Amar Rashtra' calls for going on the path of sacrifice.

सूली का पथ ही सीखा हूँ,
सुविधा सदा बचाता आया,
मैं बलि-पथ का अंगारा हूँ,
जीवन-ज्वाल जलाता आया'10

In the context of national consciousness, we cannot ignore the sentiments expressed in the poems of Subhadrakumari Chauhan. National consciousness is reflected in every word of her poems.

परिमल-हीन पराग दाग-सा बना पड़ा है।
हा! यह प्यारा बाग खून से सना पड़ा है।
आओ, प्रिय ऋतुराज! किंतु धीरे से आना।
यह है शोक-स्थान यहाँ मत शोर मचाना।।'11

Jaishankar Prasad's literary works are imbued with national consciousness. The amount of patriotism reflected in his plays is rare anywhere else. They are proud of India's past. He liked to look at mythological elements in the context of modern life, remembering the old glory of India.

'हिमाद्रि तुंग शृंग से प्रबुद्ध शुद्ध भारती
स्वयं प्रभा समुज्ज्वला स्वतंत्रता पुकारती।'
अमर्त्य वीर पुत्र हो, दृढ़-प्रतिज्ञ सोच लो
प्रशस्त पुण्य पंथ है, बढ़े चलो,बढ़े चलो'12

He is a unique revolutionary and dynamic poet. His poetry is as effective as his brilliance. Nirala opposed the superstitions, malpractices and religious traditions of that time. He has been a progressive poet, and continued to support it throughout his life.

बार-बार उर की वीणा में कर निष्ठुर झंकार
उठा तू भैरव निर्जर राग,
बहा उसी स्वर में सदियों का दारुण हाहाकार
संचरित कर नूतन अनुराग।'13

Ramdhari Singh Dinkar is a poet who treats love and nationalism equally. Dinkar's poetic style is enhanced by his reaction against the slavery of foreign powers and the atrocities and exploitation of the British. His patriotism is humanitarian.

'शैल-श्रृंग चढ़ समय-सिन्धु के आर-पार तुम हेर रहे,
किन्तु, ज्ञात क्या तुम्हें भूमि का कौन दनुज पथ घेर रहे?'14

Harivanshrai Bachchan's poetic journey has passed through many stages which also include patriotism and national consciousness. Elements of nationalism are visible in many of his poems. It is fair to say that like other poets of his time, his creations of social consciousness is relevant today.

एक उदासी में डूबी हैं
तृण-तरुवर-पल्लव-लतिकाएँ;
आंधी के पहले देखा है
कभी प्रकृति का निश्चल चेहरा?

इस निश्चलता के अंदर से
ही भीषण तूफान उठेगा।

मुझको है विश्वास किसी दिन
घायल हिंदुस्तान उठेगा।'15

Sumitranandan Pant is a painter of nature, a humanist, conscious of the environment of the society and the nation, and was influenced by Mahatmas like Gandhiji, Aurobindo. Along with time his poems take on a serious form. It is appropriate to recognize the poetic dignity of Pant, a subtle poet and user of pictorial language. The poet is loyal to Gandhiji.

'गत संस्कृतियों का आदर्शों का था नियत पराभव,
वर्ग व्यक्ति की आत्मा पर थे सौध धाम, जिनके स्थित;
तोड़ युगों के स्वर्णपाश अबमुक्त हो रहा मानव,
जनमानवता की भव संस्कृति आज होरही निर्मित।'16

Conclusion

Culture cannot be kept separate from nation and nationality. The rules of life, systems, values, conduct and thoughts etc. that are passed on from generation to generation come under cultural heritage. The essential elements for a nation are cultural and national consciousness, which is a collective feeling due to which the nation moves forward. As the circumstances of the nation change, literature also changes accordingly. The circumstances due to which the public became aware in the Middle Ages and the society was made aware by the poets of the Bhakti period, those reasons started changing with the passage of time. In the Ritikal period, along with the traditional compositions, heroic compositions also started being created. The upliftment of the society is not possible only through ritikalin poetry. Therefore, along with Shringarbhare poetry, other poetry also started being created. The feeling of patriotism and patriotism was awakened in the minds of people in the nineteenth century. Pride on the glory of the ancient, disappointment and anger on the plight of the present, message of awakening, demand of sacrifice for the country, longing for freedom, infusion of strength and vigour etc. were reflected in literature.

In the present era, national consciousness or cultural consciousness has changed according to the vibration of the society. Before attaining independence, the people were troubled by the disillusionment, resulting disappointment, frustration, depression etc. But after attaining independence, due to the shattering of dreams, the people were pushed back to their previous situation. Disappointment and anger started getting reflected in literature. What is meant to say is that according to the change of era and environment, there will be a difference in the literary creation and its impact on the public and it continues to increase like this.

Notes and References

1. Kabir's couplets, hindisahityadarpan. in
2. Kabir's couplets, hindisahityadarpan. in
3. Kabir's couplets, https : odiakey. com
4. Tulsidas, kavitakosh. org
5. Tulsidas, kavitakosh. org
6. Surdas, kavitakosh _ org
7. Bhushan, hindikavita _ com
8. Bharatendu, hindi _ kavita _ com
9. Maithili Sharan Gupta, hindi _ kavita _ com
10. Makhanlal Chaturvedi, Amar Rashtra, Kavitakosh. org
11. Subhadra Kumari Chauhan, Spring in Jallianwala Bagh, kavitakosh. org
12. Jaishankar Prasad, kavitakosh. org
13. Suryakant Tripathi Nirala, Udbodhan, Kavitakosh. org
14. Ramdhari Singh Dinkar, Hunkar, Kavitakosh. org
15. Harivansh Rai Bachchan, Ghayal Hindustan, kavitakosh org
16. Sumitranandan Pant, to Mahatmaji, kavitakosh _

Chapter - 19

Rabidranath Tagore's Concept on Nationalism; A critical reflection on the majoritarian nationalism in India and Beyond

— **Sushama Archana Topno**

1. Introduction

At a time when Nationalism works as a catalyst in building the blocks of political process in India, a peep back to the historical backdrop and cultural backyards seems imperative. Being an European concept, Nationalism took the imagination of the Indian elites and English educated middle class who used it as a weapon against the British Imperialism. As such, many social reformers, thinkers and writers began to articulate on the theme of nationalism. However, when it comes in the context of writers like Tagore, he reflected the universal values and national cultural legacies in interpreting the concept. Being a writer and poet taking positions closer to nature and humanity, he transcends his nationalism and takes a cosmopolitan vision on the same. Thus, he relies fully on the ancient Indian culture of sanadhana Dharma and the notion of 'Vasudhaivakudumbakam', means the world is one family.[1] Thus, Tagore cuts across the national boundaries and takes an eternal journey in defining the notions of nationalism. At the same time he was fully aware of the historical developments leading to different nationalist and cultural claims made by the distinct societies all over the world. His book on 'Nationalism in India'[2] is a testimony to his stand on cosmopolitan and universalist appeal on sublime Nationalism. As such his conceptualisation and understanding of nationalism is worth revisiting. From the very outset, the author takes a position that Tagor's perception and narratives on nationalism is in tune with the ancient ethos and values of Indian culture and the same do questions the narrow connotations of majoritarian nationalism propagated and carved out by the right wing forces of India. While taking such a position, author takes a historical and analytical approaches to bring home the said concepts in to more candid reality and the same is made by relying on the works of Tagore, his own characters and the reflections of other scholars on the positions of Tagore on nationalism.

2. Definitional Positions

When the national political process in most of the regions takes as a right-wing turn in several countries around the world, the idea of nationalism is being hotly debated and new narratives are in making. From the traditional understanding of nationalism as being bounded by ideas like culture and territory, the discourse now needs to shift to more complex ideas and reflections of nationalism. Nationalism that is dependent on the identification and demonisation of an "other", be it another country or another community, is obviously divisive and helps to foment a culture of violence.[3] Many scholars who have tried to define the term subject to the liberal and democratic underpinnings of the term. Benedict Anderson for instance defines nationalism [Imagined communities, 2019] as a bond between people that comes to exist when the members of a nation recognise themselves and their compatriots to be part of a nation.[4] Earnest Geller believed that a nation is formed "if and when the members of a category firmly recognise certain mutual rights and duties to each other in virtue of their shared membership."[5] Today, this membership is exclusive to the majority, while minorities are being excluded from this recognition of commonality. This peculiar developments add new lease of controversy to the very term nationalism in the present times. This controversy is not confined to India alone but it spills over to many other societies.

> Its nothing but fact that the Indian nationalism grew in the wake of our struggle for independence against the British Raj. The tone of that sort of nationalism was naturally emancipatory since it would be the rhetoric upon which the Republic of India would be founded. Interestingly many scholars have looked in to the Tagors concept of nationalism and tried to interpret to the context of modern time. Now, when the rhetoric of nationalism has taken a turn in an exclusionary direction. If we look back into our own history, there have been those who have provided us with alternative narratives that warn against an aggressive and narrow understanding of nationalism. Such caution can be found in the works of Rabindranath Tagore. Tagore conceptualises that the term

nationalism was derived from the term nation-state which was nothing but the embodiment of Western ideas of capitalism and mechanisation. He believed that these ideal were intrinsically against the Indian tradition of self-autonomy, pluralism and religious tolerance which one would find in what he termed as the samaj. As his Nandy explains further on this when he says that: Tagore's understanding of nationalism that is, its genuine European version that took its final shape in the nineteenth century as an inseparable adjunct of the modern nation state and the idea of nationality is explicit in a number of essays and letters. In effect argues that the idea of nationalism is intrinsically non-Indian or anti-Indian, an offence against Indian civilisation and its principles of religious and cultural plurality.[6]

Ghare Baire is a story of how nationalism dismantles community life and releases the demon of ethnoreligious violence. Similarly, Char Adhyay is an early, perhaps the first exploration of the roots of industrialised, assembly line violence as a specialisation of the modern times. Mohinder Singh also contributed to this narrative, stating:Tagore's critique of modern civilisation finds clearest expression in his reflections on the concepts of nation and nationalism.[7] Tagore defines nation as the political and economic union of a people and this union is the one that a whole population assumes when organised for a mechanical purpose. Commerce and science are used by nationalisms instrumentally to attain their ever-expanding power goals.

Tagore traced all the deep flaws of modern Western 'political civilisation' back to the nexus of the political and the commercial in the apparatus of the modern state. In contrast, the defining feature of the Indian, as also of the Chinese, was for him the communities' self regulation of their own affairs. In fact, if his essays on nationalism and on the theme of samaj (community) if read together, a clear distinction emerges in his works between the nature of the political in case of the nation state and the pre-national political formations. Amartya Sen has argued that "it would be wrong to see nationalism as either an unmitigated evil or universal virtue. It can be both, boon and curse-depending on the circumstances two sides of the same coin."

Nationalism, in the present era, is a complex myriad phenomenon whose positive impact cannot be only emphasized without addressing its negative impact or the vice versa. There are endless debates and discussions regarding its different roles (positive or negative) in different contexts. While Eric Hobsbawm shows how 'invented customs and traditions' play an important role in the formation of national consciousness and John Breuilly emphasizes the importance of political institutions and geo-politics in shaping and maintaining the foundation of nation and nationalism, Benedict Anderson argues that nation should be considered as an 'imagined community' which is perceived and conceived in a shared imagination through a 'common rint language.' As it suggests, Anderson is more interested in the positive power of nationalism of uniting people of a particular geo-political territory than its tendency of provoking conflict with other nations or within its own boundaries. The intricacies underlying different views on nationalism shed light on the essence of Tagore's nationalism that offers philosophical ideas to resolve the issues related to the binary role of nationalism.

However, Partha Chaterjee, [on Andersons][8] raises considerable objection to the rationale raised by Anderson when he says;'I am not sure that the distinction between bound and unbound seriality, despite its appearance of mathematical precision, is the appropriate way to describe the differences in political modalities that Anderson wants to demarcate. It is not clear why the "unbound" serialities of the nationalist imagination cannot, under specific conditions produce finite and countable classes.'

Explaining unbound seriality, Anderson says it is that which "makes the United Nations a normal, wholly unparadoxical institution". But surely, at any given time, the United Nations can have only a finite number of members. And that is because, with its explicitly laid-down procedures and criteria of membership, the imagining of nationhood has been reduced to the institutional grid of governmentality. Here Chatterjees logic is that imagined community can be a reality on certain specific situations. Just like nation and the unseen faces, the United Nations Organisation is also formed by peoples on an imaginary notion and space.

3. Transends from nationalism to Universalism

Tagore's encompassing definition of patriotism is a solution to distortions of the term which was primarily the work of Hindu nationalists of the time. His definition is embedded with values of cooperation and coexistence that transcends boundaries and is meant for humanity at large. This is comprehensively reflected in his work entitled Gora which Tanika Sarkar in her article brings out:

> The novel was written a 100 years ago. Many of the critical questions that it had asked at that time remain unresolved and contentious matters even today; caste, faith, freedom of country and of individual self-

> determination, socially forbidden love and patriotic love. It reproduces and then thoroughly problematises certain arguments of Hindu nationalism: first elaborated by late nineteenth century revivalists and then, in a different way, powerfully developed in Bankim Chandra Chattopadhyaya's novel Anandamath, written three decades before Gora. In a contrapuntal mode, Gora then offers a radically new way of being an Indian patriot.[9]

Equally, the characters of Tagore within its fold talk about the social and political confusions prevailing over the time, and it is not that its arguments are weak. If we analyse two of Tagore's famous novels, The Home and the World (1916) and Four Chapters (1934), which are set against the backdrop of political upheavals, for the purpose of examining this point. The protagonists from both the novels—represented by Nikhil, Bimala, Sandip (from The Home and the World) and Indranath, Ela, and Atin (from Four Chapters)—embody the happenings that took place during their subjugation by the British colonisers, amidst the Indian freedom struggle. The main focus in both the novels is on the discourse encompassing cultural, political, social, and economic issues which reflect the mindset of the people during those times. The novels clearly depict the British colonisation of India, the bold rejection of subjugation by the protagonists, and the reasons for doing so. Thus, the need for self-identity and recognition was beginning to take root in the heart and soul of the people of India at that time. Tagore's initiative to instil self-worth into a colonised people is portrayed through his novels (Ebenezer, 2005).[10]

But, surely, Tagore cannot be assessed fully by a single discourse, let alone by postcolonialism. His works, when keenly examined, transcend postcolonial thinking. Michael Collins in his 2011 book, Empire, Nationalism and the Postcolonial World: Rabindranath Tagore's Writings on History, Politics and Society, argues that postcolonial historiography has not accorded Tagore the intellectual standing he deserves. His book strives to explain, on the one hand, why "Tagore has been consistently misunderstood, misrepresented, sometimes ignored, and in many respects diminished as a writer and thinker" (Collins, 2011: 1). On the other hand, it attempts to locate more precisely Tagore's importance for historians, political scientists, and theorists of modernity, postmodernity, and postcolonialism alike.

It does so by laying out Tagore's "distinctively universalist philosophy," presented as a critique of certain aspects of modernity, and as an alternative to both empire and nation. On the other hand, Collins (2011) claims that "Tagore can help us better understand some of the failures of postcolonial theory."

4. Anti-colonial postures

It goes without saying that in contemporary times, particularly in the aftermath of globalism, internationalism and transnationalism, Rabindranath Tagore's idea of nationalism, though propounded and expressed more than a century back is extremely pertinent to critically examine the construction of individual and collective identity, the operation of global trading and the relationships among the countries across the world. There is much difference between the time he was pronouncing his ideas of nationalism and the contemporary time which is marked by the high technological and digital development that seems to 'deconstruct' the demarcations among the cross cultural communities. The world has turned into a "global village" by the means of technological and digital development. Tagore too, at that point of time, proclaimed that "the world is becoming one country through scientific faculty."

But the question that seems to arise is that 'is this the world structure Tagore had envisioned?' It seems that Tagore's critique of the extremism of anti-colonial nationalism and his vision of 'internationalism' which were misunderstood and criticized during his lifetime, not only challenge colonialism but also neo-colonialism-a phenomenon that arose in the aftermath of decolonisation. It appears apparent that the visible branches of colonialism have been cut down but a critical investigation will show that its seeds are still active and are sprouting new brunches, invisible in nature, which are spreading across the world. Tagore rightly sought to find the trunk (the root being the result of the scarcity of natural resources) of Western nationalism by looking at it as a product of the Enlightenment Era-indicative of early industrialisation and capitalism.

The Western nations, dominated by capitalist ideologies, in order to improve their infrastructure and prove their superiority, started colonizing different parts of world. This way, Western nationalism gave birth to the rise of colonialism and the sustenance of colonialism eventually gave birth to the rise of anti-colonial struggle and resistance which, in turn, espoused 'West-influenced' different approaches of nationalism in the [post]colonial countries. In order to resist colonialism, while most of the political and nationalist thinkers were interested in tearing off the branches of "colonialism". Tagore was of the opinion of uprooting the seeds of greed, envy, hatred and violence which foster all sorts of evils like parochialism, colonialism, cultural hegemony and communal disharmony.[11]

5. Position against narrow sense of Nationalism

Tagore was aware of the dangers of a nationalism that was rooted in the Western concept of a nation state. He had observed European forms of nationalism and concluded that the West had turned chauvinistic. In Europe, nationalism was a sentiment that was being promoted in order for a nation to become more powerful, especially commercially. Tagore's brand of nationalism sought to caution against this. His thoughts on nationalism developed from his inquiry on what it meant to be human. It was rooted not in the power that commerce could bring to Western political civilisations but in human agency and its traditions that emphasized tolerance that Indian civilisations used to be characterised by. As Rudolph C Heredia, pointed out ;'Tagore's idea of India was distinctly syncretic. He imagined a civilisation 'embedded in the tolerance encoded in various traditional ways of life in a highly diverse plural society', welcoming all peoples and cultures'.[12]

On the other hand, Tagore's notion of nationalism, is now comparable to 'humanitarian internationalism', seems to transcend the boundaries of imperialist nationalism and anti-colonial nationalism both of which demanded means of violence and hatred. Fanon in The Wretched of the Earth has argued that "decolonisation is always a violent event." If, for Fanon, subjectivity can be recovered and liberation can be acquired by the use of violence which seems, however, necessary at many points; for Tagore, the culture of violence only leads to the loss of self-worth, and moral degradation. Tagore did not support the mode of resistance, undertaken by nationalist extremists, which, he thought, was an adoption from Western nationalism. Furthermore, Tagore, unlike Gandhi and Fanon [both of them differ extensively] who were directly associated with politics and wanted political result, was a poet and philosopher who had faith in the essence of humanity and wanted philosophical and moral development of human hearts. He was against anything that he thought as a threat to humanity, even to a single person.

Thus, it emphasises that Tagor's concept of nationalism challenges the ideals of utilitarianism and promotes humanism. His vision of the world is immensely idealistic but not impossible to achieve. It calls for a 'humanitarian enterprise' to uproot all the seeds of hatred and violence from the discourses of nation and nationalism. The day it is achieved, the shackles of parochialism shall shatter and a "heaven of freedom" shall emerge.[13]

6. Critique of Twentieth Century Nationalism

Tagore saw Japan as a symbol of hope as well as caution. Japan being an Asian nation had reinvented itself to become a force to reckon with. It became an example for other Asian nations and broke the myth that only Western nations were capable of modernisation. However, Tagore also expressed a note of caution saying that the method by which Japan achieved this transformation was similar to that of other Western nations that followed a form of aggressive nationalism which he believed was corrosive and characteristic of nationalism in the twentieth century. Amartya Sen in his article wrote: 'Rabindranath Tagore appreciated and praised the importance of the Japanese experience in economic and social development as something that gave hope and some basis of self-confidence to countries outside the West.'[14]

Sen goes onto talk about how Tagore was also cautious by the imperialistic tendencies of Japanese nationalism. It fact that in 1916, Tagore went on to criticise sharply the emergence of aggressive nationalism in Japan and its new role as an imperialist. Tagore's worries and concerns were already specific in 1916, the subsequent events, particularly the Japanese treatment of China, shocked him deeply. At the same time Sen take a position that nationalism is both a boon and a curse.[15]

In fact Tagore made extensive enquiry on Nationalism by his very many ways. He discovered the real India. It was the nation where both, the Tagore estates and deprived and oppressed subjects, were located. His efforts to uplift the masses have been chronicled elsewhere and I would not like to expand on that. The way Tagore perceived the state of the nation is amply clear from two telling statements from the same article, in which he juxtaposes the 'imagined' and the 'real' country.

Rabindranath Tagore in his study at Shantiniketan, West Bengal made it very specific;

> "To imagine that Mother India is sitting on a peak of the Himalayas and strumming a melancholic tune on her Veena, is to hallucinate. But (instead), the Mother India in our village, sitting on the porch of her hut by the mud-full and weedy pond, and vacantly looking at her empty cupboard. On her lap is her malaria-struck son with a spleen. This deserves our keen attention. One distant greeting is enough for the (one) Bharat Mata that is watering the troughs of the Shami trees in the hermitages of Vyasa, Vishwamitra and Vashishta. But the (other) Bharat Mata in tattered clothes, who is hungry or half-fed, is cooking away in others' kitchens, so

that she can send her son to an English school. All this to acquire for him the insufferable life of an office clerk. This deserves much more than a mere greeting."

This portrayal of a suffering woman in both the instances is doubly significant, as women in this region once occupied the lowest of the low positions in households and the society. This form of nationalism is characterised by 'inclusiveness,' at a time when the society was deeply marked by the absence of it. Tagore did not care about which religion a person belonged to. It did not matter to him whether they were Hindus or Muslims. The communal divide had caused him much agitation. Often, his writings criticized Hindus for their high-handed social insensitivity. His vision covered both horizontal and vertical dimensions, as he focused more on the underclasses, irrespective of their communal identity. His poem 'Bharat-tirtha' and the song 'Jana-gana-mana' bear witness to this truth.

Looking from the inside of the national boundary, this was Tagore's idea of a nation. It was not just a geographical entity, a map or a beautiful, bountiful and natural expanse. A nation was to be fundamentally honored as a space full of people. Tagore's outlook was not selfishly limited to his own class, but moved beyond and below his social status. Tagore's perspective included those for whom liberation or independence did not mean having good jobs, but entailed surviving with dignity, on equal terms with others. This Tagore embarked on his own 'journey' of nationalism. He was committed to changing the lives of his subjects, a campaign which was later dubbed as 'reconstructive nationalism' by historians of the national movement. A mere two-word term such as this cannot give us any idea of the love and passion that was behind his works and pronouncements.[16]

Tagore's 'nationalism' has to be also defined by moving beyond the national map. He kept himself abreast of the happenings outside his country. Some of his poems in Naibedya (1901) alert us about imperialism that was tearing Africa asunder during the Second Boer War (1899-1902), which he felt would lead to greater world catastrophe. This was perhaps the juncture at which he discovered the limitations of nationalism and the potential dangers of its excesses.

7. Sublime nationalism with secular and humanistic appeal

We can also derive clues on Tagore's understanding of nationalism through his understanding of cultural unity. Unlike many nineteenth century thinkers like Ram Mohan Roy, Swami Vivekananda and Sri Aurobindo who rooted Indian cultural unity in canonical texts, Tagore believed that religious texts could be central to classical indian culture but not to Indian unity which had to be rooted in temporal ideas. Ashis Nandy brings this out eloquently when he says:

> Unlike many others in his and our times, Tagore believes that the canonical texts of India – the Vedas, the Upanishads and the Gita might be at the centre of India's classical culture but they do not constitute the heart of Indian unity or provide the basis of it. Here he differs radically from the likes of Ram Mohan Roy, Swami Vivekananda, Sri Aurobindo, and an array of eminent nineteenth century thinkers who believed that the canonical texts of Hinduism defined the basis of Indianness. Indian unity, Tagore insists, is built on the thoughts and the practices of the medieval mystics, poets and religious and spiritual figures. In such a country, importing the Western concept of nationalism was like Switzerland trying to build a navy.[17]

Here it is again evident that Tagore's perception of nationalism has mainly relied on ancient Indian philosophy, where the world was accepted as a single nest. In this way, Tagore was striving to dissociate himself from the general belief of nationalism and trying to associate it with ideas such as peace, harmony and welfare. He argues further that if anyway India decides to contribute the world; it should be only in the form of humanity.

While talking on Humanity he takes the specific position that humanity world over does not require a narrow but broad sense of nationalism. Therefore, it should be formulated through various means of life. Tagore's idea of humanism goes beyond any boundaries or barriers and seeks at large a common place where humanity comes before any other kind of identity. He adds further that the saints such as Nanak, Kabir, Chaitanya ignited the flame of humanism in Indian minds. But unfortunately, it was faded over time with an aggressive rise of racism and caste-based disintegration of our society. The ideas like purity and impurity of race have massacred millions over centuries. Even two World Wars and other racial conflicts were provoked based on the false notions of superiority. Nothing as such has really existed in this world where men and women can be straightway divided and disintegrated. Therefore, his belief: 'Only those peoples have survived and achieved civilisation who have this spirit of co-operation strong in them' receives a cardinal significance. At large, human beings all over the world should be glanced only through the mirror of co-operation and humanity. Thus, Tagore talks of an inclusive approach to nationalism.

This Tagore implied that apart from political freedom, the freedom of mind is more important. The Euro-centric notions of freedom have forced us to consider political freedom as an ultimate destination in the journey of the freedom movement in our country. Blind faith in Europe will instead increase our greed for possession. Hence, we should give up this narrowness and be more comprehensive in our inward and outward expressions that extend freedom of mind. Ultimately, this freedom of mind finds harmony with the human soul and at large human life. He also believed that there is only one history, i.e. history of man and other histories are mere chapters in the larger one.

8. Conclusion

Thus, Tagore was very much convinced of his understanding of the prevailing society, nation, nationalism and even trans-national and sublime common nationalism of the humanity. His notions on Nations with spiritual integration, love, and sympathy for others may find a permanent place in any age. He also believed that Indian nationalism or nationalism of any kind is nothing but a mixture of integrated ideals of humanity and human welfare. It should be a tenable progression that outsets within. As such Tagore underpins the imperatives of sublime nationalism rooted in love, compassion and harmony. In fact, he not only had talked and written on the imperatives of having a universal mode of humanism but he also did the same through the immense characters he gave birth to in his literary life. Ironically, today when we witness to narrow and short spaces and canvasses of nationalism, it's a paradox that Tagor's characters and Tagore himself smiles at us. When we feel proud of our past and boast of our rich civilisation and culture where do we accommodate this great writers vision on nationalism. This is the question being repeated and reminded by the various characters of this great writer of all times in India.

Unfortunately, in contemporary times, majoritarian and religious nationalism try to take a mainstream position in India. The right-wing political parties claim to have their legacy of nationalism from the past cultural background of the nation. When Tagore represents the soul of Indian culture and civilisation, his criticism on the narrow and selfish end of nationalism should be an eye opener to the apostles of the right wing parties and their narratives on nationalism.

Notes

1. It's a Sanscrit phrase found in Maha Upanishad, which implies that every individual is primary and stands for the welfare of all members in the collective family of the world.
2. Tagore, nationalism in India, Fingerprint Publishing, 2015, New Delhi.
3. EPW, What kind of Nationalism do we need Today? Exploring Tagore on Nationalism, [epw. in/engage/article on 18/01/2024]
4. Benedict Anderson, Imagined Communities, Rawat Publications, New Delhi 2019 [re print] Anderson takes the position that in a nation though people donot see face to face do believe that they are a nation and this ties is bound by the feeling of nationalism.
5. EPW n. 3; Also for a detailed discussion see Earnest Geller, Nation as and Nationalism, Cornell University Press, 1983.
6. See for further reading, Ashis Nandy, Illegitimacy of Nationalism, New Delhi; Oxford University Press, 1994.
7. Mohinder Singh, 'Tagore on Modernity, Nationalism and the surplus in Man' EPW, Vol. 52, Issue. No. 19, May13, 2017.
8. Partha Chatterjee, Grounds of Comparison; Around the work of Benedict Anderson. Diactrics, Vol. 29, No. 4, John Hopkins University Press, 1999.
9. Tanika Sarkar, 'Rabindranath's Gora and the intractable problem of Indian Nationalism.' EPW, Vol. 44, Issue. No. 30, 25 July, 2009.
10. Swapnajeet Das, Beyond Nationalism; Rabindranath Tagore's Concept of Nationalism in the Colonial Era and the Postcolonial Era, International Journal for Multidisciplinary Research (IJFMR), Volume 5, Issue 5, September-October 2023.
11. For a detailed idea of his positon on India and Tagore see; Rudolf C. Heredia, Recocilling Difference; Beyond Collective Violence in India, Speaking Tiger, New Delhi, 2021.
12. Swapnajeet Das. n. 10.
13. Amartya Sen, Is Nationalism a Boon or a Curse?, EPW, Vol. 43, No. 7, Feb. 16-22. 2008, pp. 39-44.
14. Also see Tagore on Nationalism; In conversation with Prof. Ahis Nandi, Interview by Gopala Krishnan, Published on 07 December 2017 in Saha pedia. org. tagore visited on 19/ 01/2024.
15. Rabindranath Tagore's Theology of Work I Pradip Kumar Datta, 2017.
16. The Daily Star, 18, Jan 2024.
16. Rabindranath Tagore and the Democracy of Our Time I Asok Sen, 2017.
17. Tagore, Rabindranath. Gora. Penguin Books India, 2009.

References

Tagore, Rabindranath. Nationalism. Penguin Random House India, 2017.

Tagore, Rabindranath. The Home and the World. Penguin Classics, 2005.

"The Ballad Of East And West" Poetry. com. STANDS4 LLC, 2023.

https://www. poetry. com/poem/33360/the-ballad-of-east-and-west>.
"Where The Mind Is Without Fear" Poetry. com. STANDS4 LLC, 2023. Web.
https://www. poetry. com/poem/29628/where-the-mind-is-without-fear
Xidias, Jason. Benedict Anderson's Imagined Communities. The Macat Library, 2017
The Daily Star, May 9, 2022.

Notes on Contributors

EDITOR

R. Sreekanatan Nair is the Academic Director, JKM Group of Educational Institutions, Salboni, Jharkhand. He is specialised in International relations, India's foreign policy and Human Rights. He is the author of **Dynamics of a Diplomacy; Delayed; India and Isarael**. He was the editor in Chief of a research quarterly-**Human Rights Global Focus.** He was in NSS College services in Kerala and retired as Asso-Professor & HOD, Department of Political Science, VTMNSS, College, Dhanuvachapuram, Tvm, Kerala. He has been a visiting professor in the Kelinya University Srilanka. Besides, right now he is Chairing an NGO-**Safe Foundation.** He can be contacted – **drsreekantan2022@gmail.com**

CO-EDITORS

Shashikant Pandey is Asso. Professor, Dept of Political Science, Agra College, Agra. Formerly, he was HOD in the Department of Political Science, Narain Pg College, Shikohabad. Earlier he had served as the Regional Editor of a research quarterly; **Human Rights Global Focus**. Besides, he is a consulting editor, Political commentator and analyst at **Jan chowk Media**, New Delhi and associates with all progressive Democratic movements of the nation. He can be contacted - **skpasia@yahoo.com**

Dr. Moushumi Mahato is the HOD, Department of Education, JKM College, Salboni, Jharkhand. She has authored a good number of articles in the specific area of Teacher Education and class room learning. She can be contacted -**moushumimahato@rediffmail.com**

Contributors

Yagati Chinna Rao is the Professor and Chair Person at Center for the Study of Social Exclusion and Inclusive Policy, School of Social Science, JNU, New Delhi. His areas of specialisations are **Dalit Histories and Politics**, **Discrimination and Exclusion**, **History of Education** and **Affirmative Action.** Among a good number of books he published on the same areas, the notable editions are-**Dividing Dalits, Writing Dalit History, Other Essays, Labour, Diaspora and Marginality, Exclusion and Discrimination, Dalit Intellectuals and Social Exclusion Matters.** He can be contacted- **ycrao@mail. jnu. ac. in**

Dr Nadeeka Damayanthi Mahamadachchi is a Senior Lecturer in the Department of Political Science, University of Kelaniya, Sri Lanka. She gained her Bachelor of Arts degree in Political Science (Honours) from the University of Peradeniya, her Master of Philosophy in Political Science from Peradeniya University, and her Master of Public Policy and Governance from North South University in Bangladesh. She has completed her Post-Graduate Diploma (Economic Development) at Colombo University, Sri Lanka. She also worked as a Research Officer at the Hector Kobbekaduwa Agrarian Research and Training Institute, in Sri Lanka prior to joining the University of Kelaniya. She has written a good number of papers including books, research reports, and articles. She can be contacted– **komaleenadeekadamayanthimahamadachchi<maha0135@flinders. edu. au>**

Dr Hamid Rasool is an Assistant Professor in the Dept of Political Science and International Relations, Gautham Budha University, Greater Noida. He is specialised in Multiculturalism and security problems in Central Asia, on which he took his PhD from JNU, New Delhi. He has numerous articles and research papers published in reputed journals. Besides, he has participated in various International seminars and Conferences, particularly in central Asian countries. He can be contacted- **Hamid53_isg@jnu. ac. in**

Dr Raju Ojha is an Assistant Professor of Education Department at Jmshedpur Co-poperative College, Jamshedpur. He attended many national seminars and conferences and has contributed extensively many research papers and articles. He can be contacted-**rajuojha1979@gmail.com**

Dr Ashita. R is a freelance researcher with specialisation in Terrorism and International relations. She has authored many articles on the subject matter of her specialisation. She can be contacted-**ashitharaveendran86@gmail.com**

Bir Abhimanyu Kumar is Associate Professor, Department of Elementary Education National Council of Educational Research and Training (NCERT), Sri Aurobindo Marg, New Delhi-110016. He can be contacted-**Abhimanyu. Ncert@gmail.com**

Rajiv Kumar is Post-Doctoral Fellow, Department of Studies in Science Technology and Innovation Policy, School of Social Sciences, Central University of Gujarat, and Dr Ambedkar International Centre Ministry of Social Justice and Empowerment, Government of India, 15-Janpath, New Delhi, He can be contacted-**rajivkumarcug@hotmail.com**

Dr Veeragoni Shirisha, is Assistant Professor, Centre for the Study of Social Exclusion and Inclusive Policy, School of Social Sciences, JNU, New Delhi. She is specialised in Social exclusion, Globalisation and She has a good number of scholarly articles in many reputed journals and publications to her credit. She can be contacted-**veeragoni@mail. jnu. ac. in**

Prity Kumari is a Research Scholar in Developmental Studies, IGNO. She did her Post Graduation in JNU, New Delhi. She can be contacted-**Pritysingh2404@gmail.com**

Shivangi Singh is a PhD candidate in the Center for the study of Social Exclusion and Inclusive Policy, JNU, New Delhi. She can be contacted – **shivangisingh2010@gmail.com**

Mohan Lal Meena is a PhD scholar, Center for the study of social exclusion and inclusive policy, JNU New Delhi, He can be contacted-**mmmohan 5167 @ gmail.com**

Vikas Patel is the Doctoral Fellow, Center for the Study of social exclusion and inclusive policy, Jawahar Lal Nehru University, New Delhi. He had done his Masters in Political science from JNU, New Delhi. He can be contacted -**upsainianvikas2949@gmail.com**

Dr Vinay Chandra Pathak is an Assistant Professor of Education, Jamshedpur, Jharkhand. He is active in several national; seminars and Conferences and contributed many papers in reputed journals. He can be contacted – **vinaychandrapathak@gmail.com**

Dr Deo Krishna Choudhary in an Assistant Professor in the faculty of Education at Baharagora College, Jharkhand. He has contributed scholarly articles in the area of his specialisation. He can be contacted-**deokrishna2012@gmail.com**

Dr Khushwant Kaur is Assistant Professor in the Faculty of Education at Jamshedpur Cooperative College. She has contributed extensively on the area of her specialisation both in the national and international Journals. Besides she is a poetess and contributed poems in English. She also serves as an Editorial Board Member of an International refereed journal-DAS LITERARISCH. She can be contacted-**kaurkhushwant@gmail.com**

Dr Prashant Kumar Kain is Assistant Professor in The Department of Social Exclusion studies at EFL University, Hyderabad. He took his PhD Social Medicine and Community Health from JNU, New Delhi. His areas of specialisations are leather Indusrey, Labour Issues, cultural history and Social Movements. Besides he has contributed extensively on accredited journals and chapters in many edited volumes pertaining to his areas if specialisation and interest. He can be contacted-**prashant.kain@efluniversity. ac. in**

Gitashri Kalindi is the Asst. Professor in the Jamini Kant B. Ed. College, Salboni Ghatsila, Jharkhand. She is specialised in Educational Administration and Management. She can be contacted - **gitashrikalindi@gmail.com**

Dr Reetambhara Pandey is Asso. Professor in Hindi, at Smt BD Jain College Agra, Agra. She has participated in numerous National and International Seminars. She has also contributed many articles and research papers in books and accredited journals. She can be contacted - **drritupandey89@gmail.com**

Dr Asha. S. Nair was the Former Head of the Department of Hindi, N. S. S College for Women, Trivandrum-695040. Kerala. She has contributed many scholarly articles in the Hindi poetry and literature. She can be contacted-**drashasnair@gmail.com**

Sushama Archana Topno is Assistant Professor in Education, Jamini Kalyani Mahato College of Management, Science and Commerce, Salboni, Jharkhand. She is pursuing her PhD in Netaji Subhash University, Tata Nagar. She can be contacted-**archana. topno. 2020@gmail.com**

Index

B

D

E

I

J

M

N

O

P

Q

R

S

U

V